Brian W. Grant, PhD

A Theology for Pastoral Psychotherapy
God's Play in Sacred Spaces

Pre-publication
REVIEWS,
COMMENTARIES,
EVALUATIONS . . .

"**B**rian Grant's *A Theology for Pastoral Psychotherapy* is a brilliant integration of psychology and theology. Rather than applying theology to psychotherapy, he sees the action of God in the therapeutic process, transforming the consulting room into sacred space. His achievement will be valuable to all theologians and pastoral counselors and should be read by all students of the discipline."

Harville Hendrix, PhD
Author, *Getting the Love You Want: A Guide for Couples*

"**B**rian Grant's book is a compassionate and sophisticated synthesis of theology and psychoanalysis. His wise, warm grasp binds a community of healers with the personal qualities, responsibilities, and burdens of the pastoral psychotherapist. His capacity to bridge from eco-systems to inner maturation of the pastoral therapist is a unique and inspiring gift.

This book celebrates the personhood of the pastoral psychotherapist, locates the therapist in the context in which he or she lives and works, and offers inspiration for the often thankless role of healing that the therapist pursues. This generative work combines knowledge and wisdom, compassion and understanding. It is at once sophisticated and simple. I recommend it to the beginner, to the teacher, and to all who practice the fine art of pastoral psychotherapy."

David E. Scharff, MD
Co-Director, International Institute of Object Relations Therapy

More pre-publication
REVIEWS, COMMENTARIES, EVALUATIONS . . .

"**B**rian Grant's *A Theology for Pastoral Psychotherapy* not only brilliantly provides a theological underpinning for pastoral psychotherapy, but also reflects Dr. Grant's profound *integration*—an identifying characteristic of pastoral counseling—of his seasoned clinical experience, impressive understanding of psychoanalytic (intersubjective school) and family systems theories, theology (process and feminist) and biblical studies, and his rootedness in his faith community. Dr. Grant's theological position is clearly reasoned, heartfelt, feisty, and it invites serious response.

I hope that this text will not only become essential for training pastoral psychotherapists, but will be used in the ongoing formation of seasoned pastoral counselors. In working with the text, I believe that it will inspire pastoral psychotherapists whose theology or therapeutic system might differ from Dr. Grant's in their own integrative process.

This complex—but accessible—book deserves a wide audience! It addresses the layperson's question, What is 'pastoral' about pastoral psychotherapy? However, it also speaks to the professional—psychoanalytic colleagues might also appreciate Dr. Grant's theological insights about their work."

Margaret Kornfeld, DMin
President,
American Association
of Pastoral Counselors;
Author,
Cultivating Wholeness:
A Guide to Care and Counseling
in Faith Communities

"**W**hat a compelling literary work! Brian Grant has truly gripped this reviewer and compelled me to plumb its depths. Author and reader join together in 'play in sacred places'—in the thinking of some of the great masters of 'object relations' psychoanalytic thought (Wilfred Bion, for example)—and in the truths uncovered by some of the most respected theologians of the last century.

Dr. Grant develops a theme, and works it like a musical fugue: we hear again and again the notes of tension between the individual and the community. He continues offering harmonic perspectives of God at work in human community, the creation of 'self' via the community of 'others.' Through 'sabbathing,' therapist and client hallow the sacred space of play. Both grow—each affecting the other in a fundamental Winnicottian transitional way of being. The therapist bears the Spirit in this unfolding mystery of container and contained which we have come to call 'psychotherapy.'

I recommend this book with a zeal. It is long overdue! I prefer to think of its use as a textbook for preparing pastoral counselors and psychotherapists. For Christian counselors, Grant's book offers substantial theoretical and practical material. And, in the hands of those who support the profession as ministers, teachers, laity, yes—and clients, it is a gift!"

Walton E. Ehrhardt, EdD
Faculty, International Institute
of Object Relations Therapy;
Chair, IIORT (New Orleans Satellite),
Louisiana

A Theology for Pastoral Psychotherapy
God's Play in Sacred Spaces

A Theology for Pastoral Psychotherapy
God's Play in Sacred Spaces

Brian W. Grant, PhD

Routledge
Taylor & Francis Group

LONDON AND NEW YORK

First published 2001 by

The Haworth Pastoral Press®, an imprint of The Haworth Press, Inc.

Published 2013 by Routledge
711 Third Avenue, New York, NY 10017, USA
2 Park Square, Milton Park, Abingdon, Oxon OX14 4RN

Routledge is an imprint of the Taylor & Francis Group, an informa business

ISBN 978-1-315-80924-3 (eISBN)

Cover design by Marylouise E. Doyle.

Library of Congress Cataloging-in-Publication Data

Grant, Brian W., 1939-
    A theology for pastoral psychotherapy : God's play in sacred spaces / Brian W. Grant.
        p. cm.
    Includes bibliographical references and index.
    ISBN 0-7890-1200-6 (alk. paper)—ISBN 0-7890-1201-4 (pbk. :   )
    1. Psychotherapy—Religious aspects—Christianity. 2. Pastoral counseling. 3. Pastoral psychology.
I. Title.

BV4012.2 .G73 2001
253.5'2—dc21

                                                                    00-069716

*To the discipline of pastoral counseling,
in the various forms it will inevitably take.*

ABOUT THE AUTHOR

Brian Grant, PhD, is Professor of Pastoral Counseling and Marriage and Family Therapy at Christian Theological Seminary in Indianapolis, Indiana. He trained in the Religion and Personality Program at the University of Chicago, where he received his doctorate in 1971. Dr. Grant has been associated with Christian Theological Seminary ever since. He was named Lois and Dale Bright Professor of Christian Ministries in 1999.

Dr. Grant is a Diplomate in the American Association of Pastoral Counselors, and served as the Association Chairperson for Centers and Training (now Institutional Membership) from 1975 to 1980 and for Membership (now Certification) from 1993 to 1997. He is also a Clinical Member and Approved Supervisor of the American Association for Marriage and Family Therapy and a licensed psychologist in the state of Indiana.

Dr. Grant has published four previous volumes: *Schizophrenia: A Source of Social Insight; From Sin to Wholeness; Reclaiming the Dream;* and *The Social Structure of Christian Families.* His papers have appeared in *Voices,* the *Journal of Pastoral Care,* the *Journal for Supervision and Training in Ministry,* and *Encounter.* He loves thoroughbred horseracing, the Chautauqua Institution, and time spent in his garden and the concert hall.

CONTENTS

Acknowledgments

This work owes much to many. No one has given more to it than my wife, the Reverend Claudia Ewing Grant, herself a pastoral counselor. She has read every word several times, contributed stylistic, substantive, and mechanical suggestions, rooted around in libraries, and put up with her husband's preoccupation with this volume through her own convalescence from a serious injury. I want to be as publicly grateful as is possible.

Unique contributions were also made by the faculty and administrative leadership of the International Institute of Object Relations Therapy, earlier of the Washington School of Psychiatry. Particular thanks go to David and Jill Scharff, Kent Ravenscroft, Christopher Bollas, and colleagues and friends from the Object Relations Theory and Therapy Training Program. Louis Reed and Walt Ehrhardt deserve special thanks for helping me find this enormously fertile place. It took the psychoanalytic theory I had loved from a distance for decades and brought it to life at close range. Its participants stand as the immediate donors of a stream of historical transmission, and I am in debt to every part of the flow.

The faculty and administration of Christian Theological Seminary gave a great deal. Their sabbatical support made the time for the writing available. The faculty Writers' Group has provided much encouragement and technical assistance, often providing the courage to keep at an exciting but daunting task. They have made the work better. Marti Steussy, Ron Allen, Dan Moseley, Newell Williams, and Felicity Kelcourse have been central contributors. A special thanks goes to my friend and dean, Clark Williamson, who has participated in the discovery of most of the truths that follow, and to my longtime collaborators and fellow learners, David Marshall and Bernie Lyon.

Generations of clients, supervisees, and students have shaped this document on every page. They have changed me, taught me, and moved me, and we have together celebrated the gifts I have been given by all these others. Through this work I hope we can give to a broader circle than we touch in the flesh. Thanks for putting up with my continuing need to learn and for joining me in this broader community of discourse.

Introduction

Pastoral psychotherapy is the calling of a growing number of religiously committed clinicians around the world. There are over 3,000 members of the American Association of Pastoral Counselors. More than 1,000 students are presently enrolled in graduate programs in pastoral counseling. Thousands more call themselves Christian counselors, along with a large number of secularly trained but theologically committed psychiatrists, psychologists, social workers, and marriage and family therapists.

They share a belief that the psychotherapy they perform is a ministry, performed on behalf of God and/or their religious community. They believe God to be an ally, an active agent in the process of formation and re-formation of persons. They experience moments of surpassing holiness in their therapeutic encounters. They believe those moments disclose knowledge about how God works and who God is that is not directly available to nonclinicians, knowledge they are called to make more widely available. They believe that their knowledge and experience of God, through the work of their religious communities, provides them resources as clinicians, informs their selection of theories and interventions, establishes goals for their work and that of their clients, and provides criteria by which that work should be evaluated.

They inherit a wide literature. They are informed by a century of psychoanalytic writing, three quarters of a century of behaviorism, half a century of humanistic psychology, and slivers of insight over time from a hundred theoretical perspectives. They are enriched by the spiritual traditions of 3,000 years of Jewish and Christian scriptures (plus those of many different faiths), twenty centuries of Christian and other theologies, and an immersion in the daily life of church and synagogue. They are students of the modern social sciences and their ethical applications, and are informed by sociology, economics, political theory, and their counterparts in liberation theology and social ethics.

However, within the pastoral counseling movement itself the literature has been thin, and necessarily aimed at tasks too broad to decisively inform clinicians. Pastoral counselors have taken the overall theological corpus and demonstrated that it mandates and informs counseling competence, particularly through the work of Seward Hiltner, John Patton, Charles Gerkin, Carroll Wise, Wayne Oates, Lowell Colston, and Paul Johnson. More recently, pastoral counselors have demonstrated how theological concepts illumine and justify the standard events and moves in the therapeutic hour, especially in the writings of Don Browning, Chris Schlauch, Merle Jordan, and Jim Ashbrook. Others have demonstrated how the claims of justice and the knowledge derived from psychotherapy join to provide guidelines for pastoral care more broadly, with significant contributions being offered by Larry Graham, Jim Poling, and Jim Leehan. They have introduced significant insights about the impact of feminist thought on pastoral process through the writings of Valerie de Marinis and Ann Belford Ulanov.

Though they have dealt with questions of how pastoral psychotherapy is ministry, they have rarely addressed my central questions: "What is God doing in pastoral psychotherapy? How does it relate to the rest of God's creative and redemptive activity? What is at stake for God in pastoral psychotherapy?" Those are the primary foci for this book.

Almost all Christian pastoral psychotherapists understand their task as ministry in either the narrowly professional sense or, more broadly, as the witness and service of the Christian community. They see it as representative of the church. This book explores why the church should want such representation. What is it about this activity that is faithful to the church's mission? By what warrant can people who claim the formal title "minister" or understand themselves as unofficially offering ministry devote their time to this task? This book addresses those questions.

Further, if the people of Israel and the Christian church are called into being by God and act as God's agents on earth, legitimate ministries must directly advance God's objectives for life on this planet. I argue that pastoral psychotherapy is one of the methods God uses to intensify and focus the lives of individuals and communities in a historical epoch subject to unique stressors, stressors that brought psychotherapy into existence and selected it as a remedy of choice for the ills of this age. I argue that psychotherapy is consistent with and an extension of God's other activities in bringing fully equipped and faithfully functioning persons into being, so that they are available to form, sustain, and lead redemptive communities, desperately needed everywhere. I argue that particular distortions of human community in our own time thwart God's hope for us, and that pastoral psychotherapy is one of God's ways of restoring God's own hope. I affirm that the principalities and powers, the systemic sources of evil including but not limited to economic and political oppression, the links between capitalism and militarism, racism, sexism, and the structured worldwide oppression of women and children, have a central role in corroding these hopes; and that even an individually focused pastoral psychotherapy is relevant and indispensable in countering those evils.

I do so from a base that is unmistakably white, male, Protestant Christian, Midwestern, middle class, straight, and urban. This base grows from and is limited by my fate as the older brother of a sister, the grandson of powerful women and less remarkable men, the son of an economically frustrated Depression-era father (himself a younger brother of powerful sisters) and an uneducated but feisty only child mother. I expect many but not all the truths in this book (if any) to be the same as differently fated persons engaging the same questions might discover, but I know that there are areas, perhaps very broad, where persons from different contexts will find my answers erroneous or irrelevant. I trust that representatives of other communities will engage these questions from those perspectives, perhaps pointing out the error of my ways, and that the resulting dialogue will enrich us all.

THE BASIS IN FAITH

The Christian faith on which my clinical work and theology is based takes its outline from a constantly changing and loosely boundaried canon-within-the-canon of Christian and Hebrew scripture, the naming of which may help the reader identify this viewpoint within the broader range of Christian options.

When I have the opportunity to present only one fragment of scripture to illustrate my Christian experience, I typically choose I John 1:1-4.

> That which was from the beginning, which we have heard, which we have seen with our eyes, which we have looked upon and touched with our hands, concerning the word of life—the life was made manifest, and we saw it, and testify to it, and proclaim to you the eternal life which was with the Father and was made manifest to us—that which we have seen and heard we proclaim also to you, so that you may have fellowship with us; and our fellowship is with the Father and with his Son Jesus Christ. And we are writing this that our joy may be complete.

The passage witnesses to redemptive events that happened to a person, events for which he is profoundly grateful, which have changed his life and linked him to a community that shares both his memory and the experience of being joyously changed. He acts now in hopes that others will hear and choose to share that fellowship, which he feels as holy, of God, and rooted in a direct personal encounter with the sacred. The transmission of the knowledge he has been given amplifies his joy, and mine.

Many affirmations grow from this passage. Change in human experience comes from concrete, discrete meetings of self with other and with God. When such change has taken shape in us, it cries out to be shared. It creates new communities and transforms those that had existed. Things are never the same again. The gift of life is magnified, but cannot be fully savored until the saving experience is passed along.

All of us are graced. The word of life has come to us through our parents, our neighborhoods, our churches, our therapies, our training, our marriages. God is in all of that. We teach, we train, we do therapy, and we write in hopes that the centering, energizing, hope-producing impact we have experienced will move through those we encounter, and this gift which was never ours to hold will bear fruit and joy in ever-widening and overlapping circles of lives.

A second normative scripture from my canon-within-the-canon is Matthew 25:31-46, the "least of these" passage. It identifies the universal human tendency to be most kind to those who can benefit us, and reminds us forcefully that the lowest and most alien human person has a sacred claim on the best we have. It flatly proclaims that the Holy One comes to us in the guise of the outsider, the one with nothing, and that pouring ourselves into that encounter ushers us into a joyous community that we could not have predicted from the apparent beauty or power of the supplicant. It reveals that all our attempts to select those worthy of our efforts make us vulnerable to judgment at the hands of those excluded, who will not be powerless forever. It invites us to the joy of seeing the elevation of the one scorned, of participating in that elevation ourselves. It alerts us, as do many other passages, to God's preferential option for the poor.

A companion passage, Luke 19:10, has Jesus saying, "For the Son of Man came to seek and to save the lost." He identifies Jesus with the active attempt to intervene in the lives of those heading in hopeless directions, and clearly states that there are people whose lives will be destroyed or will destroy themselves in the absence of active intervention. The call of the Christian in general and of the pastoral counselor in particular is to extend Jesus' ministry through engagement with such persons and communities. The Luke passage appears to encourage the development of skill at seeking and saving (noting that throughout the Gospels, Jesus consistently places credit for the saving with God, though He does His share of seeking). It is a powerful assertion that Jesus did not consider it an option for Him to acquiesce in the self-destruction of others, in their lostness, but that He and a faithful people of God must seek positions from which to make a decisive difference in the lives of those who are being destroyed.

The context for this call, both to Jesus and to ourselves, is established in a pair of Hebrew Testament passages, Deuteronomy 26:5 and Hosea 11. In the first, a liturgical recitation of the history of Israel, the Deuteronomist exhorts his reader to respond to God: "A wandering Aramean was my father; and he went down into Egypt and sojourned there, few in number; and there he became a nation, great, mighty, and populous."

The passage continues for paragraphs, in which Israel's affliction, betrayals, and liberation are recounted, and duties are laid upon the people for the honoring of God. The second, Hosea 11, has God speaking through the prophet: "When Israel was a child, I loved him, and out of Egypt I called my son." It recounts the tender nurturance of God and the stubborn willfulness of Israel (and of us all), wailing "How can I give you up, O Ephraim! How can I hand you over, O Israel?"

In both of these passages, faith is the response of an individual and a community to the persistent, steadfast love of God, a love that has called a community into being and sustained it in spite of its own waywardness, and has gifted it with wisdom and leadership, law and judgment, through the centuries and into the present. They speak of a God who works patiently through history, who expects, fights against, grieves, and punishes betrayal, and who does not give up in the face of the apparent disinterest of the beloved. The writers accord sanctity to the processes of nurturance, to the development of families and nations over centuries, to loyalty to traditions passed down through a people's memory. They invite those who would represent God and God's people to honor the effort to sustain communities, to remember histories, and to expect a life that is rich and full to be lived in regular, active dialogue with those histories and traditions. Pastoral counselors are called to be such persons and to help call such persons into being.

Another scriptural anchor for my thought is expressed in parallel traditions in Deuteronomy, first appearing in 11:26ff, with the fuller expression laid out in Deut. 30:15-20. In both these passages, God, through Moses, sets before the people a drastic pair of opposites: "Behold, I set before you this day a blessing and a curse," and, in the second narrative, "I have set before you this day life and good, death and evil . . . therefore choose life, that you and your descendants may live, loving the Lord your God. . . ."

In the basic sense of Torah, Moses proclaims here that there are habits and commitments that generate life, and ways to live that produce death. He names the alternatives and calls his people to deal responsibly with them and their consequences. Though the passage is phrased in the language of obedience, it can be read in the discourse of practical wisdom. Certain actions have certain consequences. It is life giving to love the created world and its Creator, to discern what actions flow from a realistic assessment of that world, and to name those actions as having a moral claim on us—for the sake of our own harmony with life and our ability to remain a part of it. The therapist's role is to help create moments in which the alternatives become clear, when the individual, family, or couple sees that the pursuit of a given course will lead to destruction, and that another carries the promise of life. Moses set out these alternatives shortly before the Israelites crossed the Jordan, and Moses himself died in Moab. He was not demanding obedience to himself; he was predicting the consequences of behavior he knew he would be in no position to control, punish, or reward. Such is the pastoral psychotherapist's role—to show the direction in which life can be found, and to abstain from a claim of authority to enforce compliance.

The final piece of the canon-within-the-canon is the Voice from the throne of Revelations 21:5: "Behold, I make all things new." It is the constant witness of both Christian and Jewish faith that even the most hideous of circumstance can be overcome, the most grievous of sin forgiven, the greatest degradation reversed. The pastoral therapist is called to recognize the magnitude of the obstacles and wounds that people bring, and to hope realistically with them that the identification and faithful choice of life giving ones will carry them beyond what they believed was possible.

This book rests on the foundation of a faith that first calls on us all to be joyful stewards of the gifts we have been given, and to complete the integration of those gifts in our own lives by offering them to the lives of others. It calls us to acknowledge that we received far more than we earned from parents, faith community, culture, teachers, therapists, and God, and that the opportunity to share what we have received is the opportunity to broaden the community that embodies our joy. The sharing is beyond obligation but, as a gift, opens us to treasures we cannot have known existed in persons and communities otherwise alien to us. This faith calls us to be responsive to enduring threads of historical existence, to families, to cultures, and to the ways a people receives the leading of God and follows it to their own uniqueness and to the way God cares for them as they do it, and lures them to maximize the intensity and relatedness of their lives. It instructs us that there are life choices that bring our truths to their fullest realization, and ways that doom life to destruction. It relies on the ability of persons, with the help of God, to respond faithfully to alternatives once seen, and to move into God's ever-opening all-newness with the enthusiasm and hope of one who sees the world with new eyes and finds new paths toward communion with others and with God.

THE PLAN OF THE BOOK

The book begins with the consideration of God and the world. Since I propose that pastoral psychotherapy is a work of God, it is necessary to define the terms. What is God like? What is the nature of the world? How are they related? What does it mean to say that God does something, when the something is also a human activity? God will be described as that force, personal yet beyond personhood, that strives to lure lives of increasing intensity and contrast into being in the midst of a radically pluralistic universe. I argue that the holiness of existence is enhanced when communities and individuals that have seen themselves as committed to one another's destruction, or are indifferent to one another, discover the always existing possibilities of mutual enhancement while retaining separate identities. It is argued that grace is always discerned in relationship, through a good not our own, and that the possibility of such grace is central to the goodness of creation.

The world is described as a setting that spawns new community after new community and brings those communities into both productive, expansive life and dangerous but inevitable and often creative competition. Expansion, creativity, and competition are explored as sources of the stress that has generated the appetite for and possibility of psychotherapy. The work of Meland, Loomer, Tracy, McFague, Ashbrook, and Graham will be important to sketching this God and this world.

This context being set, the argument moves to the work of communities at doing the work of the world and the play of God. God's play is the development of ecosystems with increasing harmony, contrast, and intensity, in which individuals also continue to hold intensifying contrasts within themselves. For selves to do so requires their communities to be increasingly varied, flexible, and resource rich. Communities redeem. God uses them to do so. The relationship of individuals and communities will be explored, with the intent of showing that these two forms are competitive only when the structures of an ecosystem are flawed. If our theologies pit the interests of the two against each other, they encourage us to lose faith in the human experiment. As Wilfred Bion has taught us, the exceptional individual functions on behalf of the group, is needed by the group, and cannot function without the group.[1] Yet many of our systems suffer from what Larry Graham calls contextual impairment, structured to compromise commitment to either self or community.[2]

Institutions mediate between the individual and the broader society, carrying functions on behalf of the society in the same ways that exceptional people function on behalf of their groups. The faith community carries a function for God on behalf of the world, and for the world on behalf of God. As such it authorizes, limits, supports, and challenges the pastoral psychotherapist, who functions on its behalf in service of the world and participates in God's play by enhancing the ability of human-including ecosystems to hold and balance the bewildering array of stressors that bear upon them.

A crucial part of God's play in growing increasingly complex and intense ecosystems is the creation of larger and larger human selves, as Bernard Loomer has put it.[3] Such selves require an intimate, loyal, dialogical tie to the communities that spawn them and which they serve; which ties are often, perhaps always, most explicit and effective when mediated through powerful one-to-one relationships with persons who represent the community and its culture. They are particularly present through parents, spouses, teachers, pastors, political leaders, therapists, and intimate friends, who have the capacity to allow us to experience what Donald Winnicott termed "being alone in the presence of another"—the ability to invest wholly in our experience of ourselves while in the company of someone who wills us to do precisely that.[4] It is in those moments that what Christopher Bollas terms our own unique idiom, which articulates the particular form to which we most powerfully respond, can come fully to flower—both for ourselves and for the groups that constitute us.[5] Because we select singular human and divine others for that intimacy, there is inevitable competition to be chosen; and because we seek groups where the likelihood of finding it seems greatest, we cluster with persons who appear to share a belief about what it is and where it can be found.

Hence, some are excluded, and how to graciously respond to those who are excluded from such primary intimacy is a huge human problem. But to pretend we can live without such exclusions is a lie, and to attempt it would sacrifice those situations most hopeful for human growth as selves and societies. The attempt to create and preserve such groupings (families, churches, nations, castes) is a major arena for the development and exercise of human power, in both its redemptive and its hideously destructive forms. The pastoral psychotherapist often plays a key role in helping individuals develop the capacity to join, contribute to, lead, and transform such ambiguously redemptive/excluding/destructive human systems.

It is obvious that the same groupings which are the prime bearers of meaning and hope for some are the very structures of oppression that dominate and crush the lives of others. They can readily become the principalities and powers with which God contends. At both individual and cosmic levels, habitual ways of doing things, methods of preserving and enhancing what persons or society see as indispensable to hope, regularly harden into patterns that exclude some (persons, communities, or parts of self) from opportunity, expression, participation, dignity, and the very means of life. This is evil, sin, psychopathology, oppression. It is why the analysis of any group or individual's affairs needs to include the question "Who loses?" or "What isn't expressed?" Because of the intimate connection of individual development and community participation, whole societies grow up believing "It is I who am to lose" and fail to develop the capacity to resist oppression. We have taught women and African-Americans to do that for centuries. They, and those dependent upon them, are the populations most systematically blocked from full participation in the goods of the world. Overt and covert violence in the forms of rape, sexual abuse of children, economic discrimination, and ghettoization institutionalize the status. Rageful reactions against those realities are among the most familiar forms of the wages of sin.

Many of the solutions to these evils are political, but not all are. Angry, envious retaliation only reverses the direction of flow of evil. God's goal is not to replace one set of oppressors with another. This book explores the pastoral psychotherapist's role in removing the need to be oppressed and to oppress, to incite envy and to be envious. The objective is not to change who owns what, but to change how we relate to the persons, ideas, and things in our communities, families, and psyches. That is the work of God, and involves a critical reappraisal of what the community sees as health and illness, and of its methods of approaching one and limiting the other. That appraisal is attempted here.

That being done, the discussion moves to the inner lives of selves, addressing how we become and remain human subjects. It draws on the work of Thomas Ogden, Bollas, Bion, Meland, Jackson, Tillich, Loomer, Ashbrook, and Tracy to explore how our personhood is woven from the creating, negating, confirming relations of consciousness and unconsciousness, left and right brains, language that simultaneously conceals and reveals. It explores our unending tendency to substitute knowing for living, and the antidotes to it in play, curiosity, and illusion. We discover a central role for the reciprocal relationship of reverie and projective identification, the unconscious process by which we lend our own indigestible experiences to others (especially parents, therapists, spouses, and God) for processing, sorting, and return; in the process creating mental space in which persons and ideas can be held in ways that poison neither the container nor the contained. This process depends on constant and repetitive decentering, displacing what we claim to know and be with what we now experience and are becoming, and requires perpetual openness to disruption if it is to achieve even a partial capacity for detachment. Sources of the random are indispensable, as are memories that destabilize and move us, as revelation does, toward those until now unimaginable structures that God is always bringing into existence. It is the faith that this never fully known but always experienced Other will transform us and keep us open to the movement of the universe that is the heart of Christian and all religious experience. Psychopathology, reinforced by rigid communal structures, constantly attempts to fixate our vision of self and cosmos on a reality that no longer exists. Pastoral psychotherapy is God's ally in loosing these bindings and opening us to the newness of creation.

The heart of the argument is the exploration, from a theological perspective, of what happens in the pastoral psychotherapy hour. In the earlier sections of the book I set the contexts—cosmic, communal, anthropological—that create the need and possibility for this work. Now the warp and woof of the process itself are considered. The creation of the space within which the therapy happens is crucial. It is sanctuary, sacred space, liminal space, the *axis mundi,* the center of the world. Tracy, Eliade, Nouwen, and Ashbrook help us grasp the awesome richness of this territory at the edge of cultures, where one can catch one's breath, let the therapist hold one's commitments to the external world, and explore what God is leading one to be.

Ground rules, standards that establish the safety and resources within the territory, are theologically and clinically necessary. The role of dreaming and rest, of what Bion terms "alpha function," of transference, and of Bollas's "genera" are explored.[6] All this occurs in an attitude Meland calls "wonder,"[7] an attempt to be governed by the rhythms of that Other who constantly moves through the process and each of its participants. Wonder serves the effort to create greater beauty of soul and to further the divine experiment, the play of God in creating human ecologies of greater intensity and contrast.

With the contexts established, we are brought to the sacred central moments when the lure of God pulls us through the silence at the heart of things, into an amazing proliferation of images, awarenesses, and possibilities. We recognize these moments in retrospect, when the client's words or behavior reveals that we both, on some decisive yesterday (or last moment), had been aligned with and part of the Other to such an extent that what formerly seemed impossible is now not only possible but in place. This is what Tillich describes as the confluence of miracle and ecstasy, what Meland calls the breaking of the self, what I affirm as revelation.[8] It is enabled in part by the therapist's faith, enabling her or him to be fully present with neither memory nor desire, thus open to whatever God and the client bring forth in each fertile moment. And it is fueled by God's constant activity, refusing to settle for the givenness of any past, always presenting new possibilities and requiring new decisions.

This brings us to consideration of the therapist's personhood and its role in the healing. Pastoral psychotherapists both are and are not ordinary people. They are commissioned, often ordained and endorsed, by faith communities, and held accountable by those communities. They are often licensed by the state. They are sinful human beings, at best an example of the ancient principle *ex opere operato*—affirming that the sacrament is efficacious regardless of the sin of its celebrant. Yet the therapist's character can obstruct or enhance the process, as both psychoanalysis and many other healing traditions tell us. Psychoanalytic abstinence, the mystic's preparation of the self for the encounter with the holy, and analysis that is part of a therapist's training have much to teach us. We must become the bearer of being one to the other, "little Christs" in Luther's sense,[9] and are thus incredibly privileged.

The privilege is visible in two aspects: the joy of seeing the other assuming full stature as a child of God, while knowing one's own exaltation by means of participating in that healing; and the invitation into segments of reality from which one is otherwise excluded by social position, education, status, race, citizenship, gender, or age.

The hermeneutics of suspicion has taught us that the most transformative, complete knowledge of any human state of affairs comes from those excluded from power and privilege, those who suffer and are stigmatized. Pastoral psychotherapists are called to hear the suffering, and as a consequence have access to a version of our shared reality often denied to others with our education, income, and respectability. That is a powerful, redemptive gift to us, of which we then become the stewards. Because we know these things, we are obliged to speak on behalf of that knowledge in the broader world. This book is a part of that speech.

But how shall we speak? Where is it important to name God, and where better to leave unspoken the source of our commitment and hope? This is a constant question for therapists and a crucial matter for theological reflection. Many secular clinical descriptions appear to present the work of God with reverence and gratitude but leave its author anonymous. Clearly there are situations in which naming would end the conversation, aborting the invitation to the experience of the Holy; and others in which claiming the Christian interpretation of events is necessary for the faith community's identity and the deepening of exchange with the secular world. The key to the difference lies in how the knowing is held and passed on—whether it serves hating, merger, or our actual experience of the human and divine other. But, as McFague reminds us, metaphors produce reality, and participation in myth making remains part of our responsibility and our hope.[10]

This returns us to the question of how pastoral psychotherapeutic healing is related to the community. How does the community inform the work, and the work inform the community? In what ways does the sinfully flawed nature of our structures compromise our freedom to be faithful, and how do we maximize that freedom while remaining humbly conscious of our participation in the sin? This requires us to look at the economics of psychotherapy, pastoral and otherwise, and at the cultural definition of pathology. Who do we help by shoring up the wounded of our society's war? To what extent can we prevent being co-opted by materialism, careerism, and all their siblings? What are the implications for our stance toward the political issues impinging on psychotherapy?

All these considerations force us to attend to questions of the holy commonwealth. What is a graced community? Shalom? The good life? How can faithfulness be combined with enjoying God's creation to the fullest extent? What are the particularly dangerous temptations that come with that attempt? It is argued that psychotherapy out-

comes, to be faithful, must
transgenerational ledger of just
ability, forgiveness, and reunion
tual causes of human pain. They
cover their (our) own self-righte
give them up again and again.

When we reach the conclusion,
possible way to understand both the
ute reality of pastoral psychotherap
Protestant Christianity, psychoanaly
thought, and feminism. It is hoped that
fiction, a stimulus to their own spiritual   consider their time in the consulting room as   central to faith
as is time in the sanctuary; and to consic   the path between the two
as one of unique gifts the church and world make to them in their vocation as pastoral psychotherapists.

PART I:
THE CONTEXT OF PASTORAL PSYCHOTHERAPY

Chapter 1

God and the World

Every starting point for theological writing is arbitrary, yet each has implications for the shape of the finished document. The starting point is always an illusion. It cannot avoid presupposing experiences and imagery that can only be detailed later in the book, and some that can never be detailed at all.

A pastoral psychotherapist's speech about God always carries the marks of the experience of the holy in the therapeutic hour, and the hope of making it intelligible to people who have never been there—at least in the same chair. The therapist-reader will recognize the divine support that he or she experiences with clients; the nontherapist reader may recognize that support as of the same form, having plausibly the same source, as redemptive events experienced in other arenas of life. Both readers will hopefully sense the fit of those experiences with saving events they find in scripture and with the character of the author of those events.

For me the affirmations begin with the concrete experience of healing, both my own partial liberation and others I have been privileged to share. I claim God as the source of those events, and identity God by characteristics of those events. I call on the Revelations passage cited in Chapter 1, "Behold, I make all things new," as God's central self-affirmation, and take the biblical accounts of the calling of prophets, the healing of demoniacs, the recruitment and growth of individual disciples and their community, and the conversion and commissioning of Paul as paradigms for God's participation in bringing human persons and communities to fruition.

THE MARKS OF HEALING

Such healing has discernible marks. It frees and focuses energy, moving beyond the alleviation of present distress to goals shared with a wider community. It produces a sharper focus and the ability to shift that focus from point to point within a context. It reduces total suffering, while increasing the sense that unavoidable suffering is meaningful, in the process often carrying the sufferer through a period of more intense pain than had been known before. It establishes ties with a community, typically a more inclusive community than the sufferer had known. It generates hope, understood as an affect and a stance rather than a conviction about specific outcomes. These are the signs of healing, hence of the activity of God.

They are consistent with the marks of divine activity described by many theologians, particularly those in the process theology tradition. Bernard Meland centers this activity in the language of redemption, arguing that "redemption is a renewal of creative good [his term for God] in our natures, accentuating the lure of the . . . image in our subjective life. . . ."[1] At another point he writes of grace, ". . . out of the creative ground and the redemptive life working simultaneously to impart to us a new freedom—a freedom to partake of the freedom of God."[2] Wieman writes of the encounter with God as the creative event, showing itself through an integration of new meanings with others previously held, expanding the richness in quality of the appreciable world, and deepening the community with those who have conveyed God's energy to the recipient.[3] Gordon Jackson talks of God's aim giving "each nascent occasion its best 'shot' for its richest possible attainment."[4] Sallie McFague takes healing as the ethical norm for her model of God as lover, arguing that it unites spiritual and physical reality, emphasizes the balance of the organism and the environment, and calls on awareness of both our resistance to evil and our identification with those who suffer.[5] Paul Tillich repeatedly pointed out the identification of God's activity and healing. He identifies the two closely in his 1946 lectures on the relation of religion and health: "When salvation has cosmic significance, healing is not only included in it, but salvation can be described as the art of 'cosmic healing.' "[6] Later he argued that "Salvation . . .is the ultimate aim of all divine activities . . ." and that "saving the person is healing him."[7]

One of the marks of God's activity is human healing. The healing is the expression of God's grace, the product of God's spirit, which is "always discerned in relationships," as Meland writes.[8] Furthermore, those relationships always carry the person toward community and are always expressive of existing community. Meland writes that "we live on the grace of one another. . . . The qualitative meaning of human living is as communal as the symphony."[9]

The intention of these authors and myself is not to claim that healing takes precedence over all marks of God's presence and action, but to show how all acts claimed as God's by the witnessing community (with the possible exception of creation) have a dimension of healing, as they can also have a dimension of redemption, liberation, revelation, purification, judgment, and so on. Creation is exempted only because the tradition has understood God to generate substance and energy out of nothing, and healing involves the transformation of a preexisting condition. It could be argued that since the emergence of sin, suffering, disease, and death, all God's acts are attempts to restore and complete creation; hence healing and other dimensions of God's action are part of the ongoing process of bringing the world into being, in accord with God's will. *Creatio ex nihilo* (creation out of nothing) has the effect of a divine first draft, with all God's subsequent acts, all at least partly healings, being analogous to sacred editing.

A WORLD FLAWED AND GOOD

God's saving, healing power moves through an infinite web of relational strands, conveying transformative energy serially to being after being. But God also operates in the macrocosm, before and beyond any given dyadic relationship, establishing the conditions that enable such relationship and give it its salvific power. Though the full range of God's nature and activity is beyond the scope of this or any book, there are affirmations about God's character that must be made to place the healing activity in context. We need a way to identify

God, to know that we are talking about a God who has many names and complicates our theologies by not answering clearly even when we choose the right one. We have Tillich's Ground of Being; Tracy's "power not our own," borrowed from Meland's "a good not our own"; Wieman's "creative event"; McFague's "mother, lover, friend"; and Jesus' "Abba." As McFague reminds us, all are fictions, all emphasize some aspects of what we believe about God and omit others, and all are at best inadequate and skewed.[10]

Yet believe we must. I contend here that God is the Source from which all being emerges and by which all being is set free. God is the lure for adventure, in the Whiteheadian sense,[11] the constant generator of new possibilities in every moment of existence, that which makes us and all beings take pleasure in increasing the intensity of harmony and contrast; and Who takes pleasure in the harmonies we create and share in our own lives. This God has generated a reality in which all beings are internally related to all other beings in every moment of time, so that Wordsworth's line "I am a part of all that I have met" is literally true.

It is true in a reality, a world, we hold as essentially good, though flawed, and which we understand God to affirm, though perpetually seeking to improve it. To call the creation good is to contend that new fulfillment is always possible, that God is always capable of and intent upon generating the possibility of greater contrast, harmony, and intensity, a new adventure building on the present reality; and that that is more important than the equally vivid reality that some creatures will not respond, will not be fulfilled, will be effectively walled off from life by the wounding of their own individual or corporate past. It is to contend that the world is worthy of love, and that loving it and seeking to cooperate with it will produce more gratifying and fruitful life than will hating it and seeking to obstruct its processes. It is to argue, with David Tracy, that there is a bond between how we ought to live and how things really are.[12] We are equipped for fulfillment, but not determined to it.

These resources move through an enormous variety of channels into the lives of selves. They are transmitted through genetic structures, conveying the achievements of eons of life. They are transmitted through geological and physical processes that precede and underlay life, necessary for its emergence and continuation. They are transmitted through human engineering, such as the canals of the Ganges basin or the highways, railroads, and bridges of the United States. They are transmitted through the sociological forms of a culture, such as the development of voluntary organizations in Western democracies or the tribal structures of ancient Eurasia. They are transmitted through intellectual achievements, such as the invention of calculus or the development of sonata form. And they are transmitted through the explicit and the more amorphous manifestations of religious traditions, such as the massive infusion of energy, focus, and identity that lifted the Hebrew people out of anonymity during and after the life of Moses; and the surge of hope, thought, creativity, and organization that the life of Jesus of Nazareth loosed into the Mediterranean and broader Western worlds.

These processes function at the level of conscious thought and teaching like the discourse of this essay; but far more inescapably, more constantly, and less refutably (because less explicit) at vague, diffuse, and unconscious levels, conveyed by the tonality and meter of music, the aroma of spices, the rhythm and sound of a language, and the symbolic structure of a culture's religion, poetry, advertising, architecture, social exchange, kinship system, and a myriad of other vehicles. This last body of resources is the stuff of which our selves are formed and flows to us through that combination of conscious and unconscious processes termed "causal efficacy" by process thought. It is taken in by what psychoanalysts call the internalizing of object relations and is what makes a conversation in the same language and on the same subject feel so different when the partner is a South Indian than when that person is from Alabama, Nicaragua, the Philippines, or French Canada. If my language structure was formed in the mold of Luther's Bible, it has a different feel than if those patterns grew out of the Book of Common Prayer, or the Koran, or the Mahabharata. The processes by which these incredibly complex influences constitute our selfhood are explored in detail in Chapter 4. For now it is sufficient to understand that God is one of the influences luring us to combine and integrate the meanings we bring to this instant with whatever other stimuli the instant provides, offering us optional methods and contents for the combinations, and binding us into the community with others who have made similar choices.

Hence God fuels enormous variability, enormous pluralism, by presenting each of us with new possibilities of integration, forever luring us into greater elaboration of the selves we are becoming. Much of the combining constitutes glorious adventure and creativity, as new syntheses emerge that hold contrasts of increasing intensity and energy in fruitful, exciting tension: as with the linking of Gandhi's ideas on nonviolent resistance with the Gospel tradition of the African-American church in the work and thought of Martin Luther King Jr.; or the blending of African, Caribbean, Native American, and European peoples together into an exciting if unsettled new ethnicity in Brazil.

But not all the opportunities for adventure are accepted, and not all of those attempted are successful. The application of the wisdom and hopefulness of liberation theology to the social structure of Nicaragua has not produced a stable and self-sustaining revolutionary process, though the attempt continues. Often the expansion of competing strands of human growth, meaning, and identity in the same territory produce hideous, intractable, pitiless conflict, as we see in Israel/Palestine, Bosnia, Sri Lanka, and on a less dramatic scale, many American inner cities. Will those conflicts eventually generate stable, new historical creations, such as the French people or the white segments of North American society, or will they continue to witness the triumph of force over persuasion, as in this century's struggles between Nazis and Jews, Turks and Armenians, Hutu and Tutsi? The fact that either outcome is plausible, and each eagerly sought by people who believe harm will be done if they fail, is a witness to the finitude of God and the ignorance of humanity. We do not always know which outcome is holy, and even when we think we know, we and God together cannot always bring it about.

THE CONDITION OF WESTERN SOCIETY

To arrive at a theological understanding of pastoral psychotherapy in this confusing pluralism, it will be helpful to conceptualize the current state of the society. The United States in the early twenty-first century inherits a history of relationship between cultures and families. My reading of that history suggests that as Euro-American people have come to believe in the possibility of increased prosperity, they have typically chosen to use that prosperity to produce more freedom and privacy for individuals and nuclear families.[13] The historical periods in most cultures and extended families when resources are most held in common are those in which economic necessity has forced increased efficiency. The difference expresses itself in the percentage of young adults permitted and endowed to marry and to live independently of their parents.[14] There is a strong correlation between periods when a high percentage of young adults have that opportunity, and the combination of technological innovation and prosperity.

History's most rapid increases in material prosperity, and in independence of traditional and familial authority, erupted in Europe and North America throughout the nineteenth and the first two-thirds of the twentieth century. They continue today in many countries of Asia and the so-called third world. These increases bring incredible expansion in the possibilities of individuals and massive upheavals in every aspect of life. To name just a few: patterns of acceptable moralities change (sex, care for parents, acceptability of economic striving); populations shift dramatically (rural to urban to suburban to exurban); life spans increase, creating essentially new life cycle patterns (the "empty nest" phase is now the longest epoch in the average American marriage); and old institutions lose their functions (small towns, passenger railroads, the factory, the print media, the church) and are replaced piecemeal by new patterns. New value investments that support a newly organized society are invented. The pace of change accelerates rapidly, and sources of human support and the comfort of stable structures become harder to find.

It is no accident that psychotherapy and its existentialist ancestors first appeared during this period. Much that psychotherapy provides replaces things no longer available in the culture at large: dependable meetings with interested, sympathetic persons; an arena in which to explore thoughts and feelings; a safe situation to try out new behavior; a setting that acknowledges the cost of stress, change, and loss; a plausible set of explanations for the bewildering experiences of modernity and postmodernity. Many of the things it provides were unnecessary in a setting where life was very similar from generation to generation, new behavior and values rarely had to be invented, and mass institutions provided satisfying guidance for the living of life.

Despite the glib title of a recent book, *We've Had a Hundred Years of Psychotherapy—and the World's Getting Worse,*[15] our decline (if any) is not evidence against psychotherapy as a method, but rather a marker of the magnitude of upheaval and distress for which psychotherapy has become a remedy of choice. For better and worse we have invented a societal pace that hurls many individuals to the outer edges of their ability to cope.[16] We have wrenched them out of stable community, familial, and institutional structures; presented them with the need to invent new roles and tasks; punished them severely when they failed; and offered them—even occasionally delivered to them—previously unthinkable privilege and comfort when they succeed. But because even the successes were in many ways unthinkable a generation earlier, there is little broad ideological and community support even for those who meet society's stated goals. We encourage our children to make as much money as they can, and raise searching questions and powerful condemnations about the salaries of corporate executives and professional basketball players. They get money, power, envy, isolation, and hatred. We shoot our wounded and demean the heroes we first created. No wonder we need so many healers.

One of the odd consequences of our pluralism and our pain is that nothing presented in a therapist's office, no matter how bizarre and damaging in its present context, has not served the growth and ennobling of human life at some time in some place. God has used wildly varying, even contradictory forms and processes to shape human beings and other creatures to their present stature. W. H. Auden once wrote that "no work of art is unjustly remembered,"[17] and the same could be argued of human behavioral patterns. It is not the identity and nature of the pattern itself that makes it sacred or profane, but the impact it has on its objects and surroundings. Processes that are holy if the energy and openness of individuals and systems are sufficient to embrace and contain the contrasts can produce an evil outcome if the selves and systems are not ready or equipped for the strain. "By their fruits you shall know them."

That awareness helps identify an exaggeration in much contemporary theological discussion. For instance, Sallie McFague, in her very helpful book *Models of God,* repeatedly refers to God as "destabilizing, inclusive, and non-hierarchical."[18] The adjectives are repeated often enough to have the quality of a litany, if not a mantra. For most of the world that reads theology—educated, Western, white, privileged—they are probably the right words. We need to be reminded that our present hierarchies and the attempt to perpetuate them more often frustrate God than bless the world. We need to be reminded that a stability that excludes broad segments of the population from respect and power needs to be upset, and that it often is God's will to upset it. But it would absolutize our present circumstances to say that that is what God is always doing. Reinhold Niebuhr had a crucial point when he said that the church must not simply choose justice over order, because disorder is injustice for everybody.[19] There are parts of the world today (and always) where order is desperately needed, and constant disorder obstructs the development of intensity, contrast, and harmony. One cannot see God as always on the side of destabilization while looking at the string of wars along the flanks of the former Soviet Union. Life there is being rendered trivial, difficult, and brief by the absence of order. Surely we would see the ordering work of the church in northern Europe in the fourth through ninth centuries as godly in many respects, just as we might view the destabilizing efforts of the contemporary women's movements as representing God's challenge to the hierarchies of contemporary North America.

THE TENSION OF INDIVIDUAL AND COMMUNITY

A similar theological difficulty infects much of the best theological and pastoral care literature, especially in authors most aware of systemic injustice. There are many cautions against identifying the object of God's love as individual. McFague is particularly critical of mysticism or any form of religious thought that emphasizes a one-to-one relation between the believer and God, growing out of her belief that anything so individualized supports hierarchies that become exclusive and oppressive. She emphasizes the relationship of love between God and the whole world, rather than between God and the individual believer. Larry Graham is similarly suspicious of pastoral care/counseling models based on what he calls the existential-anthropological model, for similar reasons. He opposes their ethical underpinnings in expressive individualism, which Bellah contends has subverted the institutions needed for a healthy society.[20] Graham objects to the model's prioritizing individuality over relationality, and its apparent belief that the locus of control is internal to the individual. He objects to the prioritization of private, intimate, one-to-one relationships over total-family and broader systemic health, arguing for the wisdom of family therapy and systems theory in ordering human communities.

Graham and McFague offer a useful corrective to the individualism of existentialism or the psychoanalysis of 1950, but appear to have dissolved the needed tension between individual and community phenomena. A more balanced concept can be found in dialectical approaches, including David Tracy's ongoing discourse between the route of manifestation and the route of proclamation,[21] or Jim Ashbrook's discussion of God as creator of both left and right brains.[22] Both authors maintain that God establishes and sustains tension between two (or more) always active, partial, and opposing movements. God is wholly identified neither with the stabilizing nor the destabilizing, but with the constant supplementing and completing of left brain with right brain, right with left; with proclamation supplementing manifestation, or manifestation completing proclamation, and, by inference, with community completing individual, and individual supplementing and challenging community. God has crafted us so that absolutizing either side of the dichotomy is destructive.

This is the wisdom of the Whiteheadian vision, identifying contrast as the core of beauty, the goal of adventure, the aim of God. "The teleology of the Universe is directed to the production of beauty," Whitehead writes.[23] It is not the maximization of any one variable that typifies God's triumph, but the elaboration of more and more sharply drawn contrasts of increasing intensity, which can be maintained in focused discreteness without the contrasting elements canceling each other out in blurring or triviality. "The perfection of beauty is defined as being the perfection of harmony," he writes, reasoning further that harmony requires strength, which "has two factors, namely, variety of detail with effective contrast." The argument leads to the recognition that adventure, the increased production of new forms of beauty, requires discordant feelings. "The social value of liberty lies in its production of discords," which then contribute to newer, more complex, more inclusive harmonic structures. Contrast is required to produce intensity of feeling, maximized in balanced complexity, tenderly lured into realization by God acting as poet of the world.[24]

Tracy points to a similar principle with his consistent emphasis on multivocity, the conviction that no single expression is adequate to represent the reality of any truth. The dissimilarities and negations are as necessary to locating the territory of God's action as the similarities and affirmations.[25] That is why only an analogical imagination is adequate to capture our experience of God, in Tracy's thinking, rather than an imagination that limits God to any singular set of univocal propositions.

When we consider God in this way, and consider how God thus conceived would relate to the world, the picture of a holy playfulness emerges. It is a play like that between lovers, whose exploration of one another in body and spirit is both profoundly appreciative and admiring, on one hand, and enormously growth-producing and fruitful, on the other. It is a play that moves from one side of the dialectic to the other, moving first closer, then farther, within a relatedness that sets the outside limit of the oscillations. It is a playfulness we recognize in the powerful harmlessness of a particular group of religious leaders, including the Dalai Lama, Desmond Tutu, Dom Helder Cámara, Mahatma Gandhi, and Mother Teresa. Not a playfulness that trivializes, but one that massively enjoys the beauty of the world while not taking itself seriously at all, simultaneously being a superb steward of itself as contributor to that world.

Such a God interacting playfully with such a world is all at once admiring, enjoying, luring, teasing, and stimulating into growth all that God loves. As we consider the primary objects of that love, the ecosystemic thought of family therapist Bradford Keeney will be useful in locating the focus of God's action. He invites our attention to the recursive relationships between different levels in any system, noting that similar phenomena exist on the level of organ systems, individual psyches, nuclear families, extended families, subcultures, galaxies, etc.[26] He notes that sustainable health depends on entire ecosystems, and examines how individuals' ways of combining into families and broader systems damage and/or heal all of them, and how the therapist's engagement can and should engage several recursive levels simultaneously.

A critical theological distinction concerns the biological scope of God's loving. There have been historical epochs in which theology saw God as primarily the champion of the human individual against his or her own sin. At other points God was seen as advocate and purifier of the human species vis-à-vis other species. Today we suspect that God may be as invested in the health of other species as in our own, and know for certain that if other species are destroyed, we are in grave jeopardy also. That obligates us to contend, as I do, that God's playful, loving, redemptive energy is directed to the health of ecosystems that include but are not limited to human beings. "God so loved the world." God's aim is to bring into being, to maintain and to enhance, ecosystems of ever-increasing beauty and adventure.

Unlike Graham and McFague, however, I contend that there are times, in fact a great many times, when the most powerful obstacle to the health of a given ecosystem is the stubbornly repetitive pattern of self-and-other destruction in the life of a particular person. Though typically that person is encouraged into those patterns by social forces and institutions that reward their continuation and punish their replacement, at some point in the individual's repentance, before or after political and cultural changes occur, those patterns can be effectively, deeply, and powerfully moved by that person's finding healing contact with the liberating power of God by means of work with an individual or marital therapist. That appears to be particularly true in an individualistic culture such as ours, which, for better or worse, claims to offer autonomy and privacy to everyone's psychic life.

If a culture believes, rightly or wrongly (and ours appears to), that each person has a right to the *private* exploration of individual psychic experience, that there is something utterly sacred about that process, healers will be given access to the deepest springs of motivation and awareness only in settings where third and fourth parties are not physically present. It may be that God understands that saving such a society will mean transforming a number of private relationships and individual psyches; unless God is to abolish it entirely, like pre-586 B.C. Jerusalem, Sodom, or the land of Noah. I believe that God, in this day and time, teases and lures us to maximum individual growth in the context of our families and communities, striving to bring us to the knowledge that their health is indispensable to our health, and that our health ultimately has meaning only as it contributes to the viability of the whole. That commitment to the common good must be individually chosen. God's pleasure grows as individuals and communities are in genuine conversation about how they enrich and impede one another's lives.

GOD AMONG THE INFLUENCES

This book understands God and pastoral psychotherapy to live and act in a world of incredible complexity and vitality, where multiple crisscrossing webs of energy and influence lure and coerce, block and inhibit, individuals and communities in relation to an infinity of possible choices.

It sees God as a very powerful but not all-powerful contender in that array of influences, ceaselessly and indestructibly moving to lure entities at all levels of complexity—from molecules to galaxies and beyond—into their fullest possible realization of harmony, contrast, and mutual disinhibition.

It sees God working in the face of active and inert opposition from decay, inertia, deliberate evil, ignorance, and insensitivity.

It sees God working through communities that have responded, some consistently and across centuries, most more haltingly and episodically, to the lure of their own possibility.

It hopes and believes that the church broadly, and the pastoral counseling movement more narrowly, are more often allies with God in that mutual enjoyment than they are mired in their own self-serving sinfulness, though it is acknowledged that the costs of their sins also are great. It believes that the psychoanalytic movement, and more recently the family therapy movement, have been witting and unwitting resources for pastoral psychotherapy as it seeks to participate in God's play and ecosystemic liberation. It believes that all human formation, growth, and healing grow out of our rootedness in community, and moves, in the next chapter, to explore the nature and power of those communities and of one in particular, the church.

Chapter 2

God's Play and Human Community

We are formed in, through, by, and for communities. Our lives are lived in concentric circles of systems, ranging from the huge collectivities of cultures across their entire history (such as north European and North American civilization from the fifth century to the present), through subcultural and time-bound groupings (such as Scotch-English North Americans in the twentieth century), to the completely local and contemporary realities of the persons within your and my particular households today.

We each belong to many such communities and are in active engagement with others. Some of these groupings are simply more and/or less inclusive—such as U.S. citizens and people from Kansas. Others are more clearly different and contrasting, such as U.S. citizens from Kansas who speak primarily English vis-à-vis U.S. citizens from Kansas who speak primarily Spanish. Then there are the many local communities that engage different aspects of our selves and our interests: members of specific congregations, employees of a given firm or institution, participants in groups of friends and extended families, etc.

COMMUNITIES JEWISH AND CHRISTIAN

Our most inclusive communities have enormous influence on the shape and structure of life, and largely prescribe the nature, function, and options of the smaller communities they include. How we perceive the world beyond infancy is guided by the language community into which we are born. The symbol structures of our culture's domi-

nant religions channel the emotional lives even of persons who claim
no faith, through their influence on the shape of public expression
and private valuations.[1] Our social class and national allegiances, our
racial identities, our anatomical status as males and females, and the
extent we claim the normative concerns of our gender, all these things
together establish the meanings of our lives and the process by which
we make new meanings. Each of these submeanings is prescribed by
the broader culture.

When we encounter the very rare individual—usually an orphaned
child raised by wild animals—who does not belong to this complex
of communities, our experience is of dealing with a being not quite
human, because such an individual lacks the language, the loyalties,
the skills, and the habits created and transmitted by human groups.
Group identity is so strong that it often creates immense human trage-
dies when members see the boundaries of humanness as identical
with their own community, excluding members of other races, religions, or nationalities. Our commitment to "our own kind of people"
can be so powerful that members of other groups can feel totally
alien, and their treatment can be subject to no social control.

This "group-formedness" is such a universal human reality that it
appears to be as much a part of God's will for us, as much a part of the
image of God, as is our physical form, our genderedness, our central
nervous system. Participation in and formation by communities is an
identifying mark of our species, and those communities are agents
God uses in our ongoing creation. They are the bearers of general revelation of what God is doing in the world and form the arena for very
specific manifestations of God's healing and revealing power. Christian faith has witnessed to God's having uniquely informed one man,
Jesus of Nazareth, to call a community into being. The thing we know
most surely about Him is that He recruited, trained, empowered, and
established the norms for the original cluster of followers, themselves
fully participating members of the earlier and continuing community
of Galilean Jewry. They carried into this new subcommunity the loyalties, theologies, ethics, and cultic life of the Judaism they knew,
seeking to intensify and purify it in the face of Roman occupation and
the frustration of Jewish hopes. It is one of the miracles and mysteries

of historic irony that this Jewish preacher to Jews fueled the overflow of Jewish thought and practice into the Gentile Mediterranean world, first offering liberation and redemption to that world, but subsequently bringing tragedy and oppression to the people from whom it came.

From the beginning, Christians have understood there to be an intimate connection between salvation and participation in community. "And the Lord added to their number day by day those who were being saved."[2] In the intensely family-governed culture of first-century Palestine, being born into the people of Israel established one's social location. One's fate rose or fell with one's biological tribe. In the first decades of the church, identity as a Christian was a part of being Jewish, as being a Presbyterian or Methodist is part of being Christian today. But as the community leaped across ethnic lines and radiated into Egypt, India, Asia Minor, Greece, and Italy, it struggled with the question of whether to require converts to first become Jews before they could be Christian. Just how much of the Torah could be made binding on Gentile converts? To what extent was it necessary, or possible, to honor the existing religious practices of a place in order to evangelize its people? Was Christianity to be a separate community? If it was, how did it resist being co-opted by Syriac, or Greek, or Latin culture, so that the new church was but a slightly edited copy of the community that preceded it on the same soil and with many of the same members?

When these questions intensified, as they did everywhere during the first century, they made it necessary (and therefore possible) to see the individual's link to God as different and separable from the link to family and ethnic community. It was clearly possible to not be part of the faith community into which you were born, or to be part of a family whose other members belonged to a different faith community than you did, or to be part of a faith community seen as the enemy of the political system under which you lived. Whereas in first-century Palestine (as in other traditional societies), being a Jew who followed Christ clearly included specific ways of being a carpenter, a father, a customer, and a student, as the Christian community included more and more people who were neither Jews nor Palestinians, it had to find ways of involving many persons whose definition of self was completely unrelated to Judaism. These were people who were also Syrians, Romans, and Persians, soldiers and tentmakers, former worshippers of Ahura Mazda and of Pan, who had parents, siblings, and spouses who saw Christian faith as everything from the salvation of the world to the destruction of all morality, economic progress, and political hope.

In that situation, to which our own is rapidly becoming similar, the single-mindedness with which persons were members of the Christian community was changing; and many who were intellectually and spiritually attracted to the content of Christianity had political, social, and economic reasons not to affiliate. Other community loyalties precluded it. Hence Ambrose of Milan, who became a major fourth-century theological voice, was governor of a Roman province, a position requiring public loyalty to the official cult of the city of Rome. His sister was already a Christian consecrated virgin, that century's equivalent of a nun. He was a regular Christian worshipper, but neither baptized nor ordained. When the bishopric was vacated, he was approached, agreed to become bishop, and was baptized a Christian and consecrated a bishop within eight days. His family loyalties pulled him toward the Christian community, his political and career interests away from it, and his formal action was delayed for years by the conflict. During this period of Western church expansion, many political figures were baptized on their deathbeds, having remained public devotees of the Roman gods while their careers demanded it.

This situation produced a series of theological questions with which we still wrestle. Can a person be a Christian and not part of the church? Does salvation depend upon baptism, upon receipt of communion, upon not being excommunicated? What is the role of individual conscience vis-à-vis the official voice of the church? Of the church versus the political role of the state? Many armies have marched, and many dissenters have burned in attempts to settle these issues. The questions themselves, and the violence with which their adherents (even today, in Northern Ireland, in the former Yugoslavia, in the Sudan) seek to answer them, show us the powerful tie between participation in a unified community and the heart of faith.

COMMUNITIES AND THEIR FAITHS

I, with many other Americans, am committed to pluralism and live with people who worship differently or hold different standards of personal morality. However, many of the world's peoples see our individualism about religion as quite odd; showing more indifference to faith than respect for individual decisions or equality of faiths before God. In many Moslem countries it is a capital offense to convert from Islam or to participate in the conversion of another.

In struggles between faith groups, the role of religious differences is inextricably entangled with issues of class, ethnicity, economic power, and political domination. Once religious commitments become dominant in a population, they become part of the public support for whatever choices that community makes, including some that appear quite alien to faith. In every wartime situation, communities argue about whether their faith mandates support for the military effort, even among faith groups that generally oppose war. As the church struggles to influence the texture and direction of culture, the political and economic structures of every society also seek to place their imprint on the church. Each succeeds to a certain extent.

When these questions first appeared to Christians, the survival of their community and the faith to which it witnessed were in doubt. The Roman Empire adopted it as the official religion while the Empire was shrinking, under assault from heretical Christian Germanic tribes (the Arian Goths were threatening to overrun Ambrose's Milan) or the non-Christian Norse, Saxons, and Franks. Missionaries would convert one new population only to see it, and often themselves, annihilated by the next wave of fierce invaders. No sooner was that wave of invasions and religious challenges stabilized than Islam was born, and the church was quickly wiped out or driven underground in most of west Asia and North Africa. Europe was threatened from the West by Moors in Spain and from the East by Turks in Asia Minor.

By the eighth century, the Muslim wave had spent its force in the West, and gradually a stable and increasingly Christian-identified culture took shape in Europe, subject to all the ambiguity of the alliance of religious faith and political power. It worked to change older notions of criminal law (reducing the fierce vengeance of the Salic law of the Germans, increasing the sanctions against murder and decreasing penalties for theft), to promote a sacramental view of marriage (moving away from a pattern of cousin and sibling marriages), and to bring local political leaders under the control of the sometimes unifying power of the Papacy. Though none of these outcomes proved unambiguously good, they and many that followed were direct consequences of the energy and organization that the church could lend to European culture at a time when all other stabilizing forces were in decline. The great cathedrals of Europe, Thomistic theology, the Protestant Reformation, the Renaissance, and even the development of modern science could be seen as direct consequences of these efforts. They represent a huge collective accomplishment, making possible the development of settled civilization supporting much larger populations, and undoubtedly bringing many millions into saving relationships with God.

I contend that God, acting particularly through the creative energies released via Jesus of Nazareth, had an active role in bringing this community and every community into being, and in perpetuating it over time. Through the divine lure presented to every occasion of existence, the call to more complex combinations of increasing clarity, contrast, and intensity has been and will be unceasing. The church and the civilization it helped form are the joint response of billions of persons over thousands of years to that call, though those responses are always partial, distorted, and compromised. In turn, no person is born on this continent (with the possible exception of those deeply insulated by Native American culture) and few in Europe, South America, or sub-Saharan Africa whose basic structures of conscious and unconscious life are not shaped by the responses their parents, families, and local communities make to the central themes of Christianity—whether acknowledged or not. Competing faiths certainly exist— capitalism, individualism, scientism—but none as widespread and pervasive, and all in some sense derivative from, or actively competitive with, the original Christian stem.

Within this enormous community, and in every local subcommunity as well, individuals knowingly and unknowingly take on roles prescribed by and on behalf of the whole. Erik Erikson taught that the group identity of any society prescribes, by the unconscious processes that flow through it and in response to the tasks and needs its environment requires, a set of individual ego identities among which individuals choose.[3] Those identities establish the central elements around which we construct personality and character. They have mutually reinforcing economic, political, social, and sexual components. For instance, in our society we have far more attorneys than wandering, socially revered and supported, celibate holy men *(sadhus)*, and in India that situation is precisely reversed. The shaping of individual character by societal need is tellingly described by Wilhelm Reich, writing that "character structure is the congealed sociological process of a given epoch."[4] Reich, the brilliant Marxist psychoanalyst, noted that his era was producing more obsessive-compulsive, heavily armored psyches because the factory system of industrial capitalism needed them to serve its political-economic purposes. We now see fewer heavily armored neurotics and more inadequately structured personalities, because our sociological processes have dismantled the institutional structures that produce strong psychic skeletons.

BION, THE SELF, AND THE GROUP

An even more immediately useful student of the unconscious links of individual and group is Wilfred Bion. He wrote that every group requires and seeks both evidence and experience of the raw, noumenal reality to which it is trying to respond,[5] whether that be God, in the case of religions, or engagement with the unconscious, in the case of psychoanalysis. The institutional life of groups, which they must have to survive, seeks to contain the unsettling effects of this direct encounter. The institution cannot produce it. That requires the genius, or, in Bion's language, "the mystic" (he also suggests "messiah" as an appropriate synonym). Because no group ever has enough mystics, it always has the problem of substituting for their direct experience of the Ultimate. To do that, it develops rules. But the rules and the impersonal process of communicating and enforcing them have a dual effect. They transmit the culture and belief of the community, but they also separate the recipients from the primary experience of ultimacy.

Bion wrote primarily to teach the psychoanalytic community about its own experience, and used his deep understanding of religion as a teaching tool.

> My object is to show that certain elements in the development of psychoanalysis are not new or peculiar to analysis, but have in fact a history that suggests . . . they transcend barriers of race, time, and discipline, and are inherent in the relationship of the mystic to the group. The Establishment cannot be dispensed with . . . because the institutionalized group . . . is as essential to the development of the individual, including the mystic, as he is to it. . . . The work group, under the religious vertex, must differentiate between man and god. Institutionalized religion must make man conscious of this gulf in himself. . . . One result of separation is no direct access of the individual to the god with whom he used formerly to be on familiar terms.[6]

When things are working well, individuals are aware of the distinction between themselves, their group (church), and God. But sometimes the separation fails and the group is not merely "seen to be *ideally* [italics mine] omnipotent and omniscient, but believed to be so in actuality."[7] The mystic is needed to reassert a direct experience of God, thus relieving both the drought of experience of the Divine, and the tendency to equate God and the group. Hence the group and the mystic have a very complex relationship: both need and fear the other, and try to contain the impact of the other on them, while being dependent on the other for their formation, their long-term survival, and their integrity.

Bion and others at the Tavistock Institute thoroughly established that individuals carry psychic functions for one another in small groups as well as major institutions. Groups mobilize members to carry their aggression, their sexual impulses, and their wish to merge or to withdraw. James Framo carried these basic object relations insights into the study of couples and families, and found spouses engaging in such function-sharing constantly.[8] Bion's students Carr and

Shapiro have pointed out how institutions within a society carry functions for the society as a whole. They identify that the church carries this society's conscious awareness of its dependence on the cosmos, of its need for a setting that denies the exhaustive utility of rationality, and provides a space for play and illusion.[9] God, through calling the church into being, created an institutional holding environment for the broader society, creating even for nonbelievers a setting in which life cycle events can be honored, affect can be neutralized, and experiences of ultimacy can be interpreted.

This interpenetration of God, the community, and the individual are further evident in the work of two parallel psychotherapeutic movements: the intersubjective movement within psychoanalysis and systems theory within marriage and family therapy. Both argue that our experience of ourselves is different depending on our interpersonal context. The intersubjectivists arrive at their understanding through a tradition descending from D. W. Winnicott's famous statement, "There's no such thing as a baby. There's only a baby and a mother."[10] In Ogden's discussion of Winnicott, he observes that the mother makes herself available to have her affective life transformed by the baby. To the extent she does so, she enables the baby to elicit experiences in her that enable the baby to deal with her or his own feelings. The mother's experience is felt, destroyed, and recreated in contact with the baby. The same thing happens, Ogden observes, between analyst and analysand,[11] and, by implication, between any persons who focus receptively on the experience of another. Like the transaction between the mystic, the group, and God, the cross-transmission of needs, experiences, and possibilities shifts our awareness without our being able to pinpoint the cause.

Family therapists, working in a somewhat less mysterious way, have long argued against what they (wrongly) believed to be psychoanalysis' insistence on the immutable interiority of persons. Salvador Minuchin speaks of the family as "the extracerebral sources of our minds."[12] He argues that if you change the structure in which a person functions, his or her experience and feelings will change. Other family therapists are even more intense on these subjects, relying on Gregory Bateson's contention that mind is a community phenomenon, constructed from the complex communications within a group, as much outside as inside the individual.[13]

For both family therapists and psychoanalytic intersubjectivists, theory and technique are based on the assumption that the state of the individual *always* reflects his or her immediate interpersonal environment. The self cannot avoid performing functions for the other, present and nonpresent; it carries feelings and commitments for the other; it informs and is shaped by the other. That is how God made us. God used our fellow (not only human) creatures to make us so. In broad patterns lived out by whole cultures over centuries, and in groups as limited in time and space as a nuclear family, separating individual and group functions is never fully possible, no matter how pragmatically convenient it would be.

COMMUNITY DISTORTION AND ITS PAIN

To be sure, it appears that God is more successful with some human ecosystems than others. Though one should assess eras and institutions with deep humility, it would appear that God is not having much success with contemporary North America, particularly among the Christian groups that appeared to be thriving fifty years ago. Church membership is down, giving is down, institutions are shrinking, knowledge of the tradition is narrowing, and church members are aging. Laity are deeply alienated from clergy, and cooperation at both denominational and ecumenical levels is difficult to get. The explosion of technology has largely been left for the evangelical churches to exploit and enjoy, and we remain tethered to the print medium in which this material appears.

The health of the broader society seems no better. Child abuse is up, the gap between the rich and the poor widens, willingness to address broad sociopolitical-economic problems is shunted to the fringes of political life, and racism and xenophobia seem poised to roll back the gains of the preceding three decades. The comparison with the Divine accomplishments among first-century Palestinians, or the Hebrews of the eighth through seventh centuries before that, of Reformation Strasbourg, or even eighteenth-century Philadelphia is not flattering to the present era. Though there are certainly successes one could attribute to God—the Assemblies of God, Bill Moyers on PBS, evangelism in southern Africa and Latin America—we suffer from a severe dose of what Larry Graham terms contextual impairment. This does not appear to be a high point for the glory of God in the life of our communities.

Graham describes contextual impairment as a situation in which there "is a fracture in one or more of the structures comprising the psychosystemic matrix." Overwhelming anxiety in an individual or corporate patient indicates its presence. It always discloses ruptured boundaries, disordered accountabilities, or a runaway system.[14] Robert Bellah and his associates have described the present malaise of our communities. They wrote that we live in a system dominated by large corporate entities, while remaining committed to language and values that are individualistic and isolating. In trying to create a world that serves the self, we "have instead made a world that dwarfs the self it was meant to serve."[15] We are left without a language to actually describe and manage the world we have created, so we distrust and withdraw from it. That withdrawal weakens the voluntary and other largely local centers of influence and connection, leaving their former power to the collectivities we increasingly distrust. In the ensuing public-private split, we have created what the Bellah team calls "lifestyle enclaves." They attempt to meet our need for community but are truncated in that they connect us only through one aspect of our lives, joining us almost exclusively to people similar in age, ethnicity, and economic level. Bellah further argues that privatized psychotherapy becomes an idealized relationship for many, enhancing the belief that the public world is unmanageable and that salvation must be sought in an individualized, dyadic, and insulated bond. Romantic love and the glorification of sexuality feed the same hunger, further adding to the experience of you-and-me-against-the-world.

So God has made us in and for community; our individual existence feels most fulfilled and is actually safest when part of community life; but we have lost the skill for creating communities of the kind we need and want. In the vacuum, we become adept at building the corporate wholes that satisfy (some of) us economically, but we distrust them and feel more controlled by them than in control of them. We move too frequently, separate into generational ghettoes, become increasingly committed to class loyalties and stratification, and weaken the ability of both government and church to represent the organic connection among all members of our society.

Religious community plays an ambiguous role in this picture. Christian faith first appeared with a passionate concern for widows and orphans, with what many now recognize as God's preferential option for the poor. The church has regularly spoken for the responsibilities that everyone has for and to everyone else, for restrictions on the freedom of the strong to exploit the weak. When the church ran society in theocratic New England, the system of land grants enabled at most an eight-to-one disparity between the holdings of richest and poorest. But as church life has changed with the development of independent congregations and weaker denominations, we have de-emphasized protecting the organic unity of the society in favor of "taking care of our own," and less is left to focus on people different from us. Even in Jewish life, with its long history of community responsibility and hospitality to the stranger, the affluence of parts of the community have made it difficult to maintain advocacy for the poor.

Despite the ambiguity of communities of faith, people unaffiliated with broader communities, particularly religious ones, are more vulnerable to predation, disease, and death. People in hospitals who are visited by members of their religious community are discharged earlier and at a higher level of health. People in every diagnostic category who find meaning in religious symbols have longer life expectancies and better quality of life.[16] There is something about the combination of supportive human contact and a shared structure of meaning that reduces anxiety, increases hope, makes practical assistance more available, and helps provide a rationale for the suffering that cannot be prevented. Students of religious phenomena as varied as William James, Anton Boisen, and Sudhir Kakar have reported dozens of instances in which persons suffering from apparently severe psychopathology have calmed, become more lucid, and taken on responsible roles of service upon joining religious communities, and experienced even greater transformations as they became leaders in those communities.[17] Community saves, or, more accurately, God uses community, and specifically religious community despite its imperfections, to effect our salvation.

So we have a quandary. We are called into being by a God who uses communities to form us, and who uses communities to pull us back together when we have torn ourselves apart; but we have lost confidence in the communities we know best. We often fear their attempt to control and exploit us, see them grow too large to feel familiar or too powerful to be responsive, and find their language and their values too far from those our individualism can trust. We seem to have lost the time and skill to generate lively, face-to-face, enriching clusters of persons who are mutually committed, share a sense of responsibility for the whole of life, involve more than one aspect of our being, and can compete with our individual comfort and convenience for our loyalty. In that quandary we generate floods of individual and corporate pain.

It is in that dilemma that we seek healing, and it is from that dilemma that God seeks to heal us. No means of healing that ignores our embeddedness in and need for community can ultimately succeed, yet any attempt that denies the importance or validity of the sufferers' deepest commitments, values, hopes, and fears will be ignored. What to do? If we are too individualistic, client improvement will be illusory, and may, as Bellah suggests, make the whole body sicker in the long run. If we are too visibly and exclusively committed to the religious community and its norms, we are likely to be dismissed as hopelessly old fashioned and irrelevant.

CHOICES WE MUST MAKE

Pastoral psychotherapists must make two explicit choices in these matters. They must decide (1) how explicit they will make their Christian and other community loyalties; and they must decide (2) the size of system at which they will direct their skills.

Both theological and pragmatic factors must be considered. From a pragmatic perspective, the psychoanalytic tradition has been eloquent and consistent about the therapist's anonymity. We have learned that the more the client knows about the uniqueness of the therapist, including that therapist's community loyalties, the more tools the client has to discount and defeat the therapy. The knowledge positions the client to discredit therapist positions linked to commitments different from the client's, and to overvalue interventions the client sees as expressing shared beliefs. So I do not tell one stridently Republican client about my left-of-Jesse Jackson politics, nor another that I was a student at Northwestern at the same time his wife was. Either disclosure would invite the client to believe our relationship was about something other than the healing we have contracted for. For some clients, knowing the precise nature of one's religious commitments functions in the same way, producing unanalyzable static in the relationship.

Theologically speaking, our primary fidelity is to God's healing play with human beings and the ecosystems they participate in. For those who think of themselves as missionaries to the strangers to God, that may mean choosing an anonymous office building, keeping the religious symbolism on our walls, desks, and persons at a minimum or nonexistent, and keeping our divinity degrees and ordination certificates in a drawer. Explicit identification as churchly might deny us access to the population we feel called to serve. That course carries its own dangers, and leaves those who choose it in need of other explicit connections with faith and community that might be less necessary for someone who practices in a church institution. If our ties are invisible to clients (one could question the extent of possible anonymity), they need to be more visible to others and to ourselves.

Other therapists are most committed to those with a history of religious involvement, but who currently feel betrayed or bored by the church. Pastoral psychotherapists often see themselves providing these unchurched quasibelievers a more intense experience of saving community than they find in congregations, but one they may recognize as stemming from the same Source they once found meaningful in religious community. These therapists will find it appropriate to work in recognizably Christian settings that identify them as church representatives but provide a religiously neutral microclimate, do not use much Christian language in their sessions, do not take offense at morally questionable behavior, and do not expect Christian affirmations from their clientele. This is my own situation. Yet others will see themselves as working for the intensification and purification of the acknowledged Christian community. They will typically work with members of their own institutions, use faith-based language consistently, rely explicitly on religious resources (scripture, prayer, liturgy), and expect a shared moral code prescribed by that community. Pastoral psychotherapists with all these identities are needed, as is their openness to learning from one another. Each will find it useful to reflect theologically on their choice.

Therapists must also decide whether to focus their work on individuals, couples, families, or institutions. Again, this is both a pragmatic and a theological decision. On the pragmatic side (which also has a theological component: we are obligated to be stewards of the resources we are given), we are all better at some things than others. I am a primarily kinesthetic person with a strong auditory (digital) subspecialty. I can be oblivious to visual data. This is a disadvantage in doing therapy in any configuration, but a much more severe one working with families and groups than with individuals and couples. I love words. I do a pretty good job of detecting their nuances, inflections, voice tones. They, and many other things, inform my gut, which slowly is reconfigured over a therapy hour by the interaction with the clients. This is highly useful with individuals, only slightly less so with couples, and downright confusing with six to eight other people in the room. It would be a poor use of resources, and not very good therapy, for me to specialize in working with large family systems, regardless of my fascination with family therapy theory. We all come with constitutional capacities to develop some skills more than others. We typically enjoy (and should enjoy) what we are good at. Good stewardship requires that we make realistic assessments of our gifts, and strengthen those that help us make significant contributions.

Many therapists cannot afford to be picky about what configurations to treat. Economics force them to accept the clients that come. Over time, our preferences and commitments aside, the market (the community) will decide what every therapist's specialty is, regardless of what he or she chooses. It will refer persons, couples, families, or whatever it has discerned the therapist is good at. Our commitments will influence how we structure that work and which persons are involved, but therapists who ignore the community's judgment about their skills will soon find themselves in another line of work.

Ecological considerations require attention to another question about the unit of treatment. As Keeney points out, "the so-called successful therapist or physician who sets out to completely exterminate human problems and disease will be acting out of step with ecology." Following the principle that exaggerating either side of a dichotomy automatically strengthens its opposite, unbalancing the total system, an "effort to minimize the variable 'pathology' and minimize the variable 'health' "[18] will produce an ecological re-balancing. As soon as we eradicate one disease, another appears. To further this thinking, if we intensify the therapeutic attention to one member of a system, making that person healthier and healthier, without somehow taking the other members into account, do we not make it necessary for them to become sicker to reestablish the balance? If they become sicker by a large enough degree, do they not contaminate the environment for the newly "healthier" one to such an extent that he or she is pulled back to the common level? It is possible that individual therapy that fails to engage broader systems temporarily makes the patient healthier, more intact, happier, at the expense of family members, who then reestablish the harmony of the universe by undermining the patient's health again so that community can be reintegrated. The work ultimately must have positive effects for the client's community commitments.

Therapists must regularly make theologically based judgments about the relationship of their work and the community, Christian and otherwise. Though this is neither a book on psychotherapy technique nor its ethics, I will indicate briefly the areas in which therapists must combine clinical and theological thinking about community realities:

1. How, in the assessment process, they signal their judgment about the importance of the formative communities in the client's life.

2. What their indications for intervention are—specifically, do they respond as quickly to offenses against the integrity of the client's communities as to more encapsulated, self-referential symptomatic acts.

3. Who they accept for treatment—how much money do they have to have? Do they give a financial or schedule break to leaders of religious or other communities?

4. How criteria for termination are established—is the quality of their clients' citizenship considered, their parenting, their investment in the healing of others?

5. How they relate to the conflicting demands for confidentiality, on the one hand, and community responsibility, on the other— duty to warn, abuse reporting, medical necessity, maintenance of family relationships, etc.

Each of these questions has a theological dimension directly connected to therapists' stance toward their community of faith, and that theology must be allowed into the dialogue about what constitutes good therapy.

OUR GIFTS TO THE COMMUNITY

Therapy gives directly to the community in two direct ways: through persons and through knowledge. If the church or other religious community has discerned the therapist's gifts rightly, and if it has trained and guided that individual faithfully, the therapist's spirituality will be discernible in the exercise of the gifts. The therapeutic arena will be a place of awe and wonder for the therapist, a place wherein he or she both experiences God directly and gently introduces clients to the Holy. In Bion's language, the pastoral psychotherapist will be functioning as a mystic, one in direct communion with the Other, one who is formed for that communion by the faith group, and one who enters it on behalf of the faith group. The therapist enters it knowing that, though he or she is bound by vocation and contract to seek first the interests of the client, there is no way to transmit God's healing power without being open, before and during the encounter, to being healed personally as well. Both God and the client speak to the therapist in the moments of deepest contact, as well as the other way around. If the therapist is not open to the healing, it stops for the client as well. But if the therapist is faithful to the calling of mystic, as one who encounters God directly, with the client, on behalf of the community, then the client also is schooled in mysticism as well. Clients are led into direct encounter with the healing power at the core of the universe, and heal insofar as they admit that power into their lives. When this process works, it releases into the world another individual (or couple or family) who loves, respects, and knows his or her dependency upon the God, named or not, who has transformed suffering and confusion into direction and hope. This graced recipient is now available for alliance with others seeking to advance that healing in the world.

The process also returns knowledge to the community. By its selection, credentialing, training, and support of pastoral psychotherapists, the church and its institutions have equipped them with tools for discernment of data available nowhere else in ministry, and placed them in a position to utilize those tools. It is an enormously privileged position, carrying unique responsibilities. The privilege includes the fact that most human beings are informed only about the lives of persons very like themselves, and even then only about the publicly acceptable parts of those lives. They know little about the complexities of the wounds, temptations, opportunities, joys, and terrors of one another's lives. They are shielded by racism, classism, and sexism from knowledge of people less comfortable, more marginal, than themselves. In the process of participation in the healing of those the society has harmed (sometimes en masse, sometimes one by one in their families and through their own decision making), pastoral psychotherapists are blessed and cursed with the knowledge of how people are broken and how they heal. Therapists experience viscerally what it does to a person to live through the humiliation of a family's eviction, the disorientation of forced migration, the terror of sexual abuse, the day-to-day numbing hopelessness of racism and denial of economic opportunity. We get to hear things that other people do not hear, and what we hear needs to find its way back into our communities to confront and reduce the sources of pain. Our knowledge of the psychological and spiritual effects of combat, of satanic ritual abuse, of incest, of family violence, of divorce, are crucial sources for the whole community as it seeks to respond to the lure of God. Our writing, teaching, preaching, and conversation can be avenues through which the pain we have been privileged and compelled to witness can be refined into revelation and judgment for the institutions and persons who create the pain. To do so makes the healing circle one level more inclusive, and adds meaning to the pain of those who come to us. It puts us in a position to address the ecological problem that cannot be solved at the level of individual pathology.

God lovingly, playfully, invites us into our own growth, tempting us further into our anxiety and possibility, like a mother urging a newly walking toddler to try one more step, or a supervisor supporting a student therapist to endure his or her own fear of the client's freedom for a few more minutes. God always uses communities at both human and nonhuman levels to make creatures safer, to offer them courage and hope, to create environments in which they can experiment and develop their capacities. The unique community that is the church channels an energy in the world inviting us to emulate Jesus Christ in becoming human. It strengthens our attempts to do so. That community and every community are flawed, transmitting creative good, but also restrictions, prejudices, and hatreds. Different communities bearing radically different cultures, values, and loyalties compete and always have competed for human commitment. Those communities, built by the partial and imperfect commitments of past generations, have formed us and our clients and continue to offer us new possibilities for faithfulness and failure. In response to the lure of God, among other lures transmitted both within and outside the church, many of us have committed ourselves to the ministry of pastoral psychotherapy for the sake of the world and those who seek God's healing. Their pain has come from broken community. As we seek to restore them, we will need to look closely at how our communities get inside us, how we are formed into selves, and at how that process goes awry.

Chapter 3

God in the Creation of Selfhood

We have seen how God lures communities into existence and uses them to provide the content of meanings, the language in which those meanings are exchanged, and the network of relationships that protect and enrich life. Our attention now turns to the process by which those communities get inside human beings, creating the elements that form their core, and to the role of God in this ongoing creation.

THE STRUCTURE OF EXPERIENCE

Every culture, like every household, develops what Bernard Meland calls a "feeling context," that set of discernible but nonconscious moods, emotions, values, and explanations that constitute the character of a family or a people.[1] You could think of it as the dominant mood of a place, which in turn makes it evident what other moods and affects are compatible and appropriate, and which ones are completely out of place. It is the body of experience that makes being on the street in San Francisco feel different from being on the street in New York, Managua, Manila, or Madras.

Meland describes this "structure of experience" as the most elemental level of meaning in any culture, giving form to our collective valuations. It functions very much like Erikson's group identity. Formative strands of religious myth and faith run through this structure and are diluted, modified, and combined with other elements, much like the meat base that gives the dominant flavor to the soup but would be impossible to separate from the flavors supplied by the spices, the vegetables, and even the wine served with the meal. It is "an organic inheritance that is greater in depth and range than the perceptions of any living persons," a "context of feeling and awareness that is always beyond their grasp, emotionally or cognitively."[2] God is one of the factors to which persons are responding as they generate the layers of this structure in any setting, as God offers to successive individuals the best option the moment makes available, sometimes in the form of explicitly religious elements, sometimes not.

Within the space occupied by a given culture, subcultures with slightly different structures of experience can be discerned, separated along lines of region, climate, ethnicity, generation, economic class, religious subgroup, or industrial base. Yet the thematic similarity among them can be discerned, much as a piece from one jigsaw puzzle is usually recognizable as belonging in that box and not some other, even if one does not know exactly which space it should occupy. And within each subculture, the structure of experience within its various extended families and friendship groups again will vary slightly, while partaking of the thematic unity of the whole.

A crucial part of the structure of experience in any place is its specific practice of and lore about child raising. There are distinctive, predictable interactions between parents and children, repeated thousands of times in the life of every growing child, that differ strikingly from culture to culture, and to a noticeable extent between contiguous subcultures. Many of the behaviors are so subtle as not to be noticed by the person performing them. Others are noted and surrounded by layers of explanation and mythic history, some of which change more often than the behaviors themselves. They are nuanced differently in every home, change subtly in response to the temperament and age of each child, and are modified further by life cycle crises in the development of particular families.

Cultural and psychoanalytic anthropologists have catalogued these particles of the structure of experience in detail for most known communities. Erik Erikson, Stanley Kurtz, Alan Roland, and Sudhir Kakar have linked the way mothers and other caregivers transmit behavior and meaning to children, the way broader families support and free mothers to do so, and the kind of children the culture wants to produce.[3] Monica McGoldrick and her colleagues have detailed how that process creates ethnically distinctive family structures and personality types within American culture.[4]

Our knowledge of this process has been greatly increased by contemporary infant research. Daniel Stern has documented that infant learning begins at or before birth, is culture specific (for instance, babies learn to recognize particular musical patterns in the womb), and proceeds in predictable sequences of increasing complexity.[5] He identifies that all learning, especially infant learning, is affect laden, that affective and cognitive processes are not separated, and that infants combine experiences across different sensory modalities without appearing to differentiate the modality (i.e., they respond to a sound that rises, peaks, and descends identically to their response to a felt physical surface that rises, peaks, and descends).[6]

THE TRANSMISSION OF EGO AND CULTURE

Two findings here are particularly important. One is that infants, from birth, are always constructing cognitive "islands of consistency" in their experience, noticing that certain originally discrete experiences dependably occur together: mommy's "oooOOOOoooo" when baby stretches for the mobile over the crib, the sensation of something impacting the foot and the mobile jumping and shaking, etc. It is clear that the first few times each of these happens the connection is lost on the baby, but there comes a point where it becomes clear that this sequence is not coincidence. Anyone who has thrilled at the acquisition of a new skill or the thinking of a new thought can imagine both the baby's and God's excitement at this piece of the "emergent self."

Now think about God's role. The correspondence between these events has existed from the baby's birth, and God offers the idea, the possibility of recognition, from the first. On the twentieth, or the fiftieth, or the five-hundredth repetition, the baby's self leaps in response to this gift, and his or her behavioral-cognitive repertoire has grown.

A second crucial finding is that the primary caretaker functions as a self-regulating other to the infant. In games such as peek-a-boo the intensity of the infant's affect is regulated. The baby is excited more and more, then calmed. A wide range of experiences are regulated in the same way. Sleep-wake cycles are learned in this way. This interchange marks the boundaries of any given "structure of experience" by describing an allowable spectrum of affects the caretaker shows and responds to. Hunger and thirst and their satisfaction are regulated in a manner that becomes predictable, etc. The infant's participation in the process is eased or obstructed by his or her skill at constructing the islands of consistency and storing their cognitive markers, what Stern calls "Representations of Interactions that have been Generalized," or RIGs.[7] Obviously, the caretaker, in playing that role in the dialogue, is enacting and transmitting core cultural values:

1. What affects should an infant have, in roughly what proportion?
2. How much frustration should an infant be subject to?
3. Who should be the agents of satisfaction and frustration?
4. How much control should the infant accept from outside?
5. How should the world respond to the infant's crying? or laughter? or terror?

Each culture has answers to all these questions and a thousand more, and these answers are either implemented in child rearing or defied in ways that have predictable alienating consequences. We have already established that God has helped the culture cohere and transmit itself to caretakers of children. We now see how God's encouragement of new infant realizations furthers the infant's becoming a member of a particular culture. As that culture achieves more and more integrity, it is available as a partner in play for both God and other cultures.

This process is the formation, not only of the cognitive mind, but of the broader ego. The infantile ego's processing ability produces the RIGs, the content, and is itself being learned, just as the process of walking will be learned by the infantile body a few months later. Most of the acquisition of ego process is outside consciousness. Its acquisition depends enormously on the mother's (by "mother" I mean caretaker of either gender) aesthetic of life, again a version of the cultural ethos, the structure of experience. Christopher Bollas has described the mother's spirit, which informs her "logic of care," as the hand of fate. It determines the shape and structure of the infant

ego long before the infant is aware of the shaping.[8] "He is being transformed according to the mother's aesthetic" in a way that will affect
all future ways of being with the other, and that begin to establish the
"grammar of his being" long before he has words to describe it. It establishes an internal unconscious cosmology, a vision of how the
world is and how beings are arranged in it, that Bollas refers to as "the
unthought known."[9] Infants know both mother and themselves as objects before they know them as subjects (hence *object* relations theory), as their internal geography is already firming up before they are
aware it exists.

Perhaps no one has helped us understand this aspect of infants' internal experience as clearly as Wilfred Bion. He differentiates between the mental experience of the infant who can take the data from
the environment and represent it symbolically, and the one who cannot. The former experience Bion terms "alpha-function."[10] If the individual, in earliest infancy or thereafter, is willing and able to allow
an experience to persist in awareness, to be felt, to be represented in
some way that will let the person remember it, think about it, dream
it, etc., alpha function is at work. The raw experience has been transformed into alpha elements. But there are experiences for the infant
(and the rest of us) that he or she (and we) wills not to exist, recurrent
patterns he or she wishes to deny because they are envied or hated.
They are denied representation, not stored, not recognized, not dreamed,
and can only be extruded, projected, imagined not in one's own experience but in that of the other. Such elements do not link together, are
not suitable for thinking or dreaming, though in close relationships
they can actually be felt by the partner—particularly the mother.[11]
They are beta elements. If only beta elements exist, they block the experience of the live other. Another way to describe this event is to say
that God's offer of the experience of connection, the emergence of
new knowledge, is repulsed because the knowing would be too painful. This represents a choice to evade frustration rather than to modify
it. The intolerance of frustration forces immediate evacuation of beta
elements, blocking the divine offering.

But this blocking can be prevented or reversed if the relationship to
the caretaker has the needed quality. If the mother can endure it, a

mental space is created between her and the baby, a container in which the child's experience can be held, detoxified, and given the chance to evolve connections with both the world of language and other elements of experience. That process begins in the primary relationship. Winnicott terms it "primary maternal preoccupation."[12] In that state, the mother has a heightened capacity for "reverie," the intense focus on the infant's experience that enables both imaginative participation in the infant's inner life and the reception of his or her unconscious communication. Bion writes that reverie expresses the mother's love, which acts as a sort of psychological receptor organ, "that state of mind which is open to the reception of any 'objects' from the loved object and is therefore capable of reception of the infant's projective identifications whether they are felt by the infant to be good or bad. In short, reverie is a factor of the mother's alpha-function."[13] What happens here is crucial. The mother (or other caretaker) communicates to the infant through her muscle tone, the security with which the infant is held, the tone of her voice, the way she meets the infant's eyes, that she will receive and hold in reverence whatever communication comes from the baby. If the baby is having incomprehensible, unacceptable experiences, pain, rage, or hate, those emotions will be felt by the mother, i.e., evacuated into the mother by the baby. The mother then communicates back to the baby, through the same physiological means (though words are often included) that she has received a meaningful communication from the baby, sometimes quite precise (I'm hungry), sometimes inchoate (I hate you because you haven't satisfied me). Sometimes her response is to remedy the immediate distress, but more important is her receiving, unscrambling, and returning to the baby as meaningful and manageable the original beta elements, now linked with a discrete perceivable form (a look on the mother's face, the way she clucks her tongue, the tension in her arm as she feels the baby's pain). She has taken the beta element, metabolized it through her own alpha function, and returned it to the baby as an alpha element—which the baby can tolerate, store (in the newly expanded mental space), think about, dream with, etc. In the process, she has made the experience available to the baby in a way previously impossible, contributing to the baby's sense of being an emerging self, part of the joy of God. Bollas describes the mother in this process as a transformational object.

This parallels a Christian understanding of God's receptivity to our cares, and is precisely what Whiteheadians mean by saying that God prehends the experience of every actual occasion. The event enters the experience of God and changes it, and God wills for that to happen. It is reminiscent of Kakar's observations about the devotional practice of the Radha Soami sect, a major Hindu religious movement. The devotee, upon initiation, is to spend four hours a day gazing at the picture of the Guru,[14] internalizing and idealizing him much in the way that Stern describes the infant taking in the mother with his or her eyes.

A mother (of either gender) can only provide this reverie and preoccupation if certain conditions exist. She must be able to tolerate her own psychic distress, to contain it and symbolize it. That, in turn, is made more possible by her position in a safe relationship, supported by a broader structure which provides her physical resources, offers her a shared meaning for the sacrifice of self into the baby, and provides her physical protection. These are cultural and family functions, available at optimum levels only when both contexts are functioning well.

THE ROLE OF INTERNAL SPACE

The internal space hopefully created in mother and baby has much in common with Winnicott's "transitional space," totally controlled neither by the infant nor the environment. It has its first full-fledged occupant in the "transitional object," that special possession of almost every infant: personified, imbued by the child with a psychic life, offering an arena for the development of the child's powers of fantasy. The object is neither wholly objective, since the child experiences it as having personality, will, and vitality that no other observer recognizes; nor wholly subjective, since absence or destruction of the object creates a massive sense of loss, disorientation, and outrage. The child does not simply transfer the investment to another available object. It is tied to the blanket, the teddy bear, the ball of fuzz. In relation to the transitional object, the baby develops a repertoire of play, story, and attachment that complements the behaviors being developed with the caretaker and other family members. The acceptance and designation of a transitional object is a further step in the growth of the personality, and represents another response to the lure of God. Again, this requires cooperation by the family and culture: retrieving the object when it is left behind, respecting the child's wishes about washing and transporting it, not insisting that the child be "realistic" in talking about it or evaluating it. Ana-Maria Rizzuto's classic work on the formation of the God-representation observes that God functions as a transitional object in early life, and forever resides in the transitional space.[15]

The transitional space comes to contain many objects and experiences. In Winnicott's famous paper, "The Observation of Infants in a Set Situation,"[16] he shows how a metal tongue depressor, always attractive to babies, is admitted as a play object in the moment of hesitation that occurs after the child seizes the shiny object from the table, checking out with the adults whether it is OK before mouthing it, gesturing with it and making it his own. In that moment of hesitation, the object is changing in character for the infant, going from an unambiguously objective inanimate thing to a lively part of the infant's play (transitional) universe. Winnicott understands the whole of humanity's creative expression as having this quality: art, religion, humor, and play.

Bion speaks of the transition into this space as providing a contact barrier, allowing facts and emotions to survive in the presence of one another. The barrier "marks the point of contact and separation between conscious and unconscious elements and originates the distinction between them."[17] Across this boundary moves all contact between conscious and unconscious, a contact indispensable to human health and the activity of God within us.

There is a tightly involved relationship between transitional space, internal space, the creation of inner objects, and the relationship of container and contained. Two empirical phenomena appear to coincide. As Stern has pointed out, there is a point in the first year of life when infants appear to notice that both they and other people have feelings, and to show concern about hurting the feelings of those they love. By this point, as Winnicott has observed, they have already noticed that very important things move in and out of their own bodies: food, breath, feces, urine. Concepts of outside and inside develop. Children also notice that, before they realized that other people have feelings, they had caused mother real pain and had wished to cause her more. They had bitten, devoured, hated, scorned, and wished her dead on as many occasions as those on which they adored, doted, reassured, and confirmed her. The roomier a child's mental space (inside), the more access the child has to alpha elements, and the more able we can assume the caretaker has been to absorb the child's projective identifications and return them as manageable and symbolizable data. With that in place, children can allow intensely contrasting emotions to co-exist within them and to cohere around the internal picture of the mother. That is the biography of an internal object, the amalgam of visual images, emotions, physical memories, sounds, and smells that together make up children's stored experience of each of the important persons in their psychic lives, including themselves. The mother's reverie opens the space to let the elements in, then functions as glue to help them stick together. But if the reverie is impaired and/or other events compromise children's ability to let those impressions rest within themselves, unified representations may never be generated, or may include only pieces of their experience, and the construction of self God seeks for us all will be impaired. Fragments will persist, unavailable for contrast and harmony, instead working actively to cancel out, trivialize, and inhibit other elements of self, marring the beauty of our individual adventure.

By this point a child has a psychological inside, where images, words, feelings, and memories live by a logic different from the external world's. That inside overlaps but is not identical to the transitional space, which functions as an experimental arena where the child's internal productions encounter the rules and objects of external reality, much in the way that an object of art results from the conjunction of the artist's vision and the physical limits and properties of the medium—paint, marble, violins, words. There is give and take between the transitional space and the internal space, but in health neither is tyrannized by the other, just as there is a comparable give and take between the transitional space and the logic of the outside world. The child cannot will the transitional object into existence if it has been destroyed by a fire, but as long as it exists it has enormous plasticity at the bidding of the child's imagination.

Return your attention to the inside and the outside. Bion observed that several kinds of relationship are possible between the two, the container and the contained, and that individuals consistently favor the same style of relationship. He names them parasitic, symbiotic, and commensal.[18] The crucial variable is whether the content is contained in a way that is destructive to it and the container; mutually satisfying but irrelevant to the context; or strengthening to the container in a way that enables a contribution to the context. As persons develop, those in whom beta elements typically predominate host a war between container and contained. Their internal object representations constantly seek to devour and attack each other and the ego, and the ego is constantly working to control, restrain, shrink, and starve its contents. Such persons inadvertently yet consistently relate to others in the same way, either seeking to control and diminish them, or struggling to escape and counterattack against the other's real or imagined control. The same correspondence exists for persons who contain their objects in a symbiotic way, hosting them congenially and feeding off them exhaustively, so that the relationship yields little for the surrounding world. It is self-contained, though comfortable. Persons who relate to their psychic contents in a commensal way seem to grow from the experience, and, like their contents, have a gift for making their growth available to the broader community, as the mystic does with the group. Bion names these relationships hate, love, and knowledge (H, L, and K), and they have great significance for the self's ability to function as a vessel for the love of God.

INTERNALIZING THE OTHER

Taking others into the core of our psychic life is a critical part of growth, perhaps the most important use we make of the resources God gives us. We take them in by building internal objects, but we do not simply swallow them whole. We internalize a version of them marked by our half of the relationship. The psychic niche where we install them is shaped by who we have already become, by virtue of our prior creativity with prior materials, just as they become part of the structure into which any new person fits. Winnicott describes such internalization as "use of the object," in which children exercise their total appetite on their caretakers without hanging back out of concern for the other's vulnerability. What children want or need is seized from the one who wants to make it available, though healthy children take it, at first, without reference to how big a hole it may leave in the caretaker. For all children know, they have ripped the mother limb from limb and devoured her, out of their own hunger. But, miraculously, she survives, and surviving continues to relate to her child and to the pieces of herself the child has taken in. That relating heralds children's beginning ability to be concerned for the caretaker, but only after they have already revealed and exercised their own voraciousness. That appetite is a child's own, without admixture,[19] and exercises the reality of the self the child already is.

A theological discussion of the same process is offered by Gordon Jackson. He emphasizes the Whiteheadian concept of subjective aim, that each actual occasion has its own slant on things—it wants what it wants, in response to God's making known the universe of things it could possibly want. It has selected from those divine offerings a direction, always shifting but always its own. If the child took in the other without modification, the past would merely be repeated; no novelty would occur.[20] But since the child's access to the other is always mediated by the child's perception, and that in turn is directed by the child's wishes, it is the other as relational partner who is internalized. Reams of the other's raw data are available to the child, but the child only digests what has emotional power and relevance.

Bernard Loomer can be helpful at this point. In his classic paper "Two Conceptions of Power," he introduces the concept of size in internal relationships. He observes that we are internally related to those persons who have influenced us, who have become part of us, and that "size is fundamentally determined by the range and intensity of internal relationships one can create and sustain. The largest size is exemplified in those relationships whose range exhibits the greatest compatible contrasts. . . ."[21] God wishes to create souls of maximum size, combining the greatest possible range of contrast and intensity, without mutual interference and cancellation. The task of all infants is to take from their environment the maximum range of influence they can successfully integrate—a range established in part by the caretaker's capacity for reverie—and as such be an active participant in God's ongoing creation of species and ecosystem. As we will see in the next chapter, some introjects greatly interfere with the capacity for compatible contrast and contribute to evil, while others draw richly contrasting forces into their orbit.

In this mix of unconscious and semiconscious internalization, an infant begins to be a subject in his or her own right and to experience others as subjects. As Tom Ogden writes, from the very beginning babies oscillate between different modes of experience. They struggle to maintain physical cohesion, to keep their insides in and their outsides out, with acute sensitivity to the danger of shattering (the autistic-contiguous mode).[22] They soon begin to notice seemingly opposite emotional experiences of the same person, falling into dichotomized either/or thinking to prevent their rage from destroying internal goodness (paranoid-schizoid mode). They labor to maintain their morale after bringing the two halves together, realizing the pain they have caused before coming to grips with the fact that the mother they hate is the same person as the mother they love (the depressive position).

From the advent of toddlerhood and for the rest of our lives, "experience is always generated between the poles represented by the ideal of the pure form of each of these modes."[23] Experience in any of the modes is constantly challenged, corrected, and deepened by experience in the others, and the loss of any is a severe impoverishment. The balance we create among them is the hallmark of our individuality.

Ogden extends these insights in later writings to the dialectic between conscious and unconscious, and the dialectic between persons (and we will suggest it fits the dialectic between the self and God). He understands Freud as meaning that "consciousness and unconsciousness are . . . mutually dependent, each defining, negating, and pre-

serving the other. Neither exists nor has any conceptual or pheno-
menological meaning except in relation to the other." It is "by means
of the discourse between conscious and unconscious qualities of experience, the illusion . . . of unity of experience is created."[24] He argues that the existence of each is dependent on the other, that each
takes the other as its object and is subject in relation to it, and that any
attempt to identify the "I" exclusively with one or the other falsifies
reality. We are constantly decentered by input from the other side of
their shared membrane, providing a constantly shifting triangulation
in which the path of central self can be loosely charted.

The developing intersubjective movement within psychoanalysis,
of which Ogden is a part, also extends this observation to interpersonal contexts. Having understood that projective identification allows us to displace parts of our experience into one another, and that
the development of internal objects makes us a walking plurality, it is
a short step to recognition that our psychic experience is different
when we are with different persons. The I that is evoked in the presence of one is different from the I evoked in the presence of another,
and the "real" I, the subject, arises "in a dialectic (a dialogue) of self
and Other,"[25] whether the other is another person, another mode of
experience, one's conscious or unconscious, or God. It is not identifiable with any fixed position.

This has been well illustrated in the personality theory of Robert
Kegan. He describes development as a progression of decenterings.
In each, the developmental task being mastered and the community
within which it and the self are relevant, shifts.[26] One is always partly
embedded in one culture (such as the mother-infant relationship) and
seeking to master the tasks it requires (biological regulation, development of attachment), and simultaneously moving toward the next
larger culture and its tasks, in an unending set of concentric circles.
As soon as one clearly defines oneself as "about" something, the very
ability to name it paves the way for its becoming less central and
problematic, as something else from a yet wider world becomes
available and demanding. Ogden and Bion would contend with

Kegan that those stages do not so much replace one another as they successively recede to become less salient parts of the repertoire, always available and reasserting themselves as they are evoked by changes in the environment or psyche.

THE REARTICULATION OF SELF

In the theological realm, this same alertness to repeated decenterings of the self is offered by David Tracy. His magnum opus, *The Analogical Imagination,* is organized around the assertion that any position in which one imagines oneself is at best shallow and usually false if it speaks univocally. It alerts us that theologians themselves are defined differently and define themselves differently in relation to different publics: society, academy, and church. It considers the dialogue between theologies of manifestation and those of proclamation. This psychoanalytic observer notes that the God of the theology of manifestation has much in common with Winnicott's "environment-mother," the provider of structure and bounty who more generates a world than exists as a demanding or gratifying presence within it; and that the theology of proclamation's God bears a similarity to Winnicott's "object-mother," the loved and hated personal figure who rewards and punishes. James Ashbrook has further noted that the religion of manifestation is largely a right-brain religion, the religion of proclamation largely a left-brain one.[27] Tracy concludes with an exhaustive discussion of the inadequacy of any one theology, language, or perspective to capture the core of Christian experience. He argues that all our language at best points to similarities between realities we understand and the imperfectly intelligible God, and that we need a wide array of "similarities-in-difference," organized by the response to a central event, to keep from falling into oversimplification, triviality, and boredom.[28] He moves, in a way comforting to a Whiteheadian, to the centrality of the negations (could we say contrasts?) inevitably contained in the mix of perspectives. "The negations with their disclosure of radical dissimilarity in similarity . . . will also manifest the genuine similarities disclosed by means of the defamiliarizing difference exposed in the event."[29] The event remains uncontrollable, having more potential and energy than can be contained in any of our constructions. Only our maturing internal contradictions and para- doxes preserve us from identifying it with some partial expression of itself.

Maturation proceeds by means of the constant rearticulation of ourselves in relation to the objects (ideas, media, persons, activities) we invite into our lives. We are guided in the encounter by the partic- ular idiom (form, aesthetic, subjective aim) we find ourselves recur- rently preferring, just as an orchestra is guided by a conductor and a score. "To live life fully, the self must be open to its objects," Christo- pher Bollas has written.[30] Our own idiom, the aesthetic taking shape among the different others of our experience, draws us to new objects that we must be free to encounter with all our appetites roaring if we are to dignify the object by truly receiving it (enjoying it, in the Whiteheadian sense), and enrich and elaborate the self in the inter- change. Bollas writes,

> Because an adult seeks objects of desire, and his use of objects under the terms of this principle must be necessarily ruthless, he develops a profound gratitude toward life—for what it offers and for how it can be taken. Such an individual conveys not ra- pacity in the choice and use of objects, but almost exactly the opposite: a kind of pleasure in being, a knowledge that there is sufficient experience to go around.[31]

The self becomes more itself in this play with its objects, and more able to contribute commensally to its ecosystem. Similarly, God plays with the world—throwing Godself into the experience of the cosmos, offering it possibilities, delighted or appalled with the out- comes.

THE PROBLEMS IN OUR GROWING

Though this is inevitably the way we grow, it brings several prob- lems. For one, in our drive to become ourselves through play with the objects that excite us, we always choose some candidates over others. Some, for the moment, are excluded from the partnership. Some theologians, McFague and Graham among them, appear to see this as

very close to the core of evil.[32] Our horror at discrimination and our
awareness of the damage it does is crucial, yet it has made it appear
shameful to honor our natural choices. McFague's argument for
God's impartial striving for continuation of life in all its forms, because all are equally valuable,[33] can complicate our awareness that not
all are equally valuable to us. Our experience of moment-to-moment life,
as we struggle to become who we are by choosing objects that arouse
energy, imagination, and commitment, makes us aware that those forms
being equally valuable to God marks an inevitable, not necessarily sinful, difference between God and us. We will choose the poetry crafted
by the finer wordsmith, the lover we find most beautiful, the faith that
resonates with who we find God to be. We should, because not to do
so means our energy will not be evoked, not be available to the world,
not enhance the play of God. And to do so carries the certainty that
we will leave people out, and obligates us to minimize the damage to
them—but not by pretending they were not chosen against. We must
be free to choose what we choose, and there must be limits on our indifference toward those we choose against.

  The second problem it generates is a political/epistemological one.
Any configuration of objects we choose privileges specific boundaries between our conscious and unconscious experience. Choice of a
given object brings certain things to our consciousness and leaves
others beyond the periphery. Our choice to remain unconscious of
particular things, such as the impact on Central American workers of
our enjoyment of bananas and cheap textiles, or the impact on women
of men's fondness for certain hair and clothing styles, influences our
behavior. Those choices, in turn, support and/or undercut the political
interests of competing groups in the society. Any configuration of objects and interests, hence any location of the boundary between conscious and unconscious, represents a choice among competing political interests; some groups become more powerful, some less, because
of the objects we choose and the way we array our minds in response.
That, in turn, has a profound effect on what we can know and the style
with which we know it (the manner in which we contain our objects).

  For instance, many of us in academic life noticed early on that not
much satisfaction was available from relating intimately with our

families of origin. We developed solitary, disembodied pleasures, insulating ourselves against noticing that intense closeness with parents and siblings was either unavailable or unpleasant. We learned to work well and hard, and to expect the bulk of life's pleasure to come from solitary work and little of it to come from enjoying the people in our households. That interferes with our adult ability to enjoy the people we live with and for them to have the experience of being enjoyed. It passes to the children the sins of the fathers, and the generations before them.

Like any other habitual structure, this one works better if unconscious; and it has consequences. It and others like it serve the economic and political interests of people with freedom to move workers around the country without considering their familial ties. It strengthens the hand of those who want faculties to forego family time to be consistent in committee attendance; and of those who do not want public discourse cluttered with emotional appeals. Such leaders, whether they know it or not, have a political interest in the boundary between conscious and unconscious, since workers who put that boundary where the power wants it will be more manageable and cooperative. They see only the rewards they obtain by going along with the program.

I am not arguing that any one set of locations is the right one, but am contending that there is a deep resistance against any individual or group's seeking to rearrange those boundaries in and beyond themselves. All our choices in this area are subject to political influence and have political effects. Our choices are inherently corruptible, and our moral and spiritual health require dialogue with those whose political and personal choices are different.

THE POTENTIAL FOR ABUSE

A final problem with honoring our choice of objects is that, as James Poling has written, "Every desire has abusive potential."[34] When we love a thing or a person, we do not want to lose it to someone else, not even in a fair competition. We do not want her, him, or it to be inaccessible. We are deeply ambivalent about supporting the right of persons to choose against us and of the due process that allows others to outcompete us. Women have made it clear to men in the last twenty years that men's need and desire for them often damages them, since men have been willing to brutalize, rape, and kill when women do not choose to be with a particular man. As men have validated the intensity of their need, in itself a good thing, their power has often led them to invalidate women's need for a comparable freedom—a very bad thing. If men want a world in which they can continue to honor the intensity of their own passions, they must do it without suppressing the right of others to do the same. If they succeed in the oppression, they lose the free response of the other, and suffer the spiritual blow of being responsible for the other's pain. Further, those who are suppressed will always counterattack, and the counterattack will destroy peace and prosperity, even for those with apparent power.

In sum, we become selves, and by becoming selves become part of a culture through repeated interactions with enculturated persons who care for us. We take them inside our conscious and unconscious experience. We become selves in response to the lure of God, to God's active, constant invitation to us to take in and integrate the rich multiplicity of life, and to assemble it internally in response to the subjective aim we have selected from the options God renders available within a given culture. That aim increasingly takes the form Bollas calls our "idiom," that repeated response to individual cultural expressions selected from the structure of experience around us, and is nourished by our intense, passionate experiences of objects—first our primary caretaker, our transitional objects, and finally the whole realm of created existence. As we continue to respond to God and world in the adventure of self-creation, character expands, including intensifying harmonies of contrast and beauty. All of that is regulated and enhanced by the culturally sponsored receptivity of the relationships that contain us, and furthered by our energetic incorporation of the objects and persons that we love. It can bring us to full flower and an exciting give and take with God, others, and ourselves, though the same processes that make that possible also can enable profound abuses of self and other. In the next two chapters I examine life impacted by evil and life lived in faith, before moving to a consideration of pastoral psychotherapy in mitigating the one and expanding the other.

Chapter 4

God's Obstacles: Sin and Evil

In the area of sin and evil, the classical witness is "the wages of sin is death."[1] Everything human in us is jeopardized, for this time and all others, by life situations that make evil inevitable and by our individual and collective choices to do evil. Sinfulness has been understood in various ways. Some emphasize our collusion with dehumanizing social structures, which then turn back and attack our faithfulness; some proclaim an ontological reality that our being itself is flawed, predisposed in every instance to choose against God in a deluded attempt to choose for ourselves. In all theologies, sin presents a rival empire to God's sovereignty, with we humans and our communities occupying a border territory that receives emissaries from both powers, whose internal agents seek to move the selves between them to one loyalty or the other.

Paul Tillich's version of the nature and shape of sin, sin as fact and act, has been particularly helpful.[2] It reminds us that "sin is a universal fact before it becomes an individual act, or more precisely, sin as an individual act actualizes the universal fact of estrangement."[3] Our individual acts begin in a network of relationships, some external to us and some internal, shaped in part by our own and others' previous sinful decisions. We are never free of the temptation to either continue or attempt to rectify our own mistakes and those of our communities. We reap the anger of others at our ancestors' exploitation, and direct our rage at those seeking to recover what they feel cheated of by those ancestors. In the process of becoming selves and part of a culture, we internalize values that damage the earth and our neighbors. We learn a standard of success that rewards greed, and inherit so

complex a world that we cannot be certain where creative self-assertion leaves off and culpable exploitation begins. Our individual
choices are tragically consistent in missing the fullest possibilities
that God makes available. As I have argued elsewhere, we do sin dependably, if not efficiently.[4] Beyond the corporate and ontic obstacles
to faithful life, we choose the individual and deadly sins of pride,
vengefulness, sloth, avarice, envy, lust, and gluttony with numbing
consistency.

THE RUPTURE OF COMMUNITY

Other theologians, more community focused than Tillich, have
identified sin with ruptures in the integrity of human community.
Meland, making a passionate case for the sensitivity of one being to
another as our hope against chaos, describes sin as the "assertiveness
of force over sensitivity."[5] He speaks of it as "disregard of the persuasive good revealing the lure of God's working."[6] He argues that to
consider the influence from another is an act of faithfulness,
sacralizing the willingness to receive subtly transmitted data that discloses realities our conscious minds fail to comprehend. For Meland,
empathy is a primary mark of our ability and willingness to be in relationship with God or culture. But individuals can choose to refuse to
be influenced, at least consciously; or, within the limits imposed by
earlier events, can choose to receive the other's experience, let it take
shape within them, and learn from it. Refusal leaves one doubting
(and perhaps stems from doubting) that others can understand one's
experience, and gravely diminishes the likelihood that any persuasive
attempt to influence the other's experience can succeed. The choice
of force springs from that impoverished position, and further sunders
the cohesion of the body.

Many contemporary pastoral theologians are aware of the pragmatic consequences of insensitivity. James Poling refers to a specific
and widespread example when he calls rape "touch without vulnerability."[7] If we refuse to accept vulnerability (either because we were
taught that it is weak and wrong, or by virtue of having our own vulnerability abused or neglected) but still crave touch, some form of co-

ercion is the only way to get it. In choosing coercion, one places one-self against the community, refuses to accept one's position as part of that body, and falls into what McFague terms the very center of sin.[8] This act elevates our own chosen plan in total disregard of the needs and good of the other. It ignores data that might inform us of the other's nature and seeks to impose terms that preclude the possibility of love.[9] God's terms always involve a balance of justice between the goods willed by the parties in the relationship. The good we will, based on the data we have and the needs we feel, "is a good intermingled with evil, a precarious good: a good often bordering upon depths of terrifying evil,"as Meland has written.[10] It is "the good not our own" from which redemption comes, and it is precisely our reliance on our own good, what we plan and structure and protect, that often walls us off from God.

In the battle to protect our own good, we often protect a created good that has become an obstructive evil. All created good has a limited life span. When God interacts with human beings and communities, new structures are formed at every level. If they are good at the moment of their creation, they enhance the greatness of soul of persons and the viability and holiness of their communities. But that goodness is situation specific, and what is good in one situation may not be good a few years later or in another place. Yet our investment in any created good is not alert to the precise point in time or place when it becomes an obsolete or misplaced obstruction. New efforts, human and divine, will appear that are directly competitive with the good we have cherished. Wieman points out that the destruction of created good may or may not be evil, but will always be opposed, "because men . . . are more disturbed over the evil that attacks what they have in their hands than over the evil which opposes the creation of what they cannot envision and do not yet specifically want."[11] Our fidelity to created good, to our own chosen plan, to the good we can envision and hold, places us against God time and again, even when we are defending good that God helped create in a former time and/or another place.

Our attempt to preserve the good we know is an attempt to control events and outcomes that we cannot and should not control, and as such is the very center of sin. This demand for control and predictability is ultimately an effort to control the freedom of God, though it begins in our less obviously sinful intolerance of frustration. To the extent that we choose to avoid frustration rather than modify it, a temptation to which all are vulnerable, we will seize facts and store them in the containers we call our minds. We will seek to preserve them unchanging, and keep the world as we had known it. Bion calls this –K (minus knowing), the attempt to hold information in a static, unmoving, unchanging form.[12] It aims to prevent the discovery of new meanings for the data, new relationships among its various elements, by maintaining that everything that needs to be known about the realities under consideration is already known, and that the knowledge is codified finally in the words and symbols stored in our memory. It strives to saturate every symbolic expression with content, so that no new content can be added or discerned. A –K, saturated, idea of God would be that God is precisely a male, vaporous, being, composed of atoms and molecules, who dictates literal sentences to human scribes appointed from before the beginning of time, etc. It would not include phrases such as "God is like . . ." or "God may . . ." or "God is becoming." Such (–K) "knowing," Bion indicates, becomes a substitute for living, and protects us from the terror of dealing with life among living, changing beings, including ourselves.

THE PRETENSE OF CONTROL

We have many ways of pretending that we are in control of the world. The common phenomenon of obsession is one such method. In its simplest form, preoccupation, it is an attempt to "rush into a space before it is dominated by the other," to have the dimensions of the mental space under control, to have it so fully furnished that there is room for nothing else.[13] It often proceeds to full-blown obsession, "aimed at maintaining a terminal object that ends all unconscious use of the object."[14] The actual living thoughts are too unsettling, too impinging, so we fill the mental space with consciousness so that nothing can quietly recombine, newly inform the other, move the furniture around while we are not looking. It is a frantic attempt to get

Why do we control?
Is control inherently sinful?

things nailed down, internally and externally, with nails of our own design.

The truth such negative knowing generates "is too often a cover word for conquest," David Tracy writes.[15] It attempts to identify truth with what we are capable of controlling and defining. It is a truth that denies the simultaneously revealing and concealing properties of language, and the relativity of language communities themselves. It pretends that language is a neutral vehicle of expression, disregarding that the "same" conversation is a different experience in English, French, Hindi, or Swahili. The values embedded in each culture are expressed in the grammar and vocabulary they have constructed to present and organize meanings. For instance, the English "tomorrow" and "yesterday" are represented by the same word in Hindi. Imagine the difficulty of attempting to communicate seemingly identical meanings about time, its reversibility, the relative importance of linear narrative, between those two languages. The choice of the language in which to have a conversation partly determines the outcome of discussion, the possibility of establishing a given "truth." Since few of us have the luxury of choosing equally among several languages, the givenness of the languages we are born into means that every truth we store linguistically is marked by the biases and commitments of our own culture, and as such is both deeply, and not at all, true. Every claim to truth, as Tracy points out, is a disclosure and a concealment.[16] Our attempt to deny it is an understandable accommodation to our own anxiety, but a distortion nonetheless.

Tracy's theological contentions mirror a reality that Daniel Stern and other infant researchers have approached through the last decade's psychological inquiry. Babies have experiences, feelings, and concepts before they have words. The simplicity and repeatability of words is enormously useful, but the usefulness has a price, since the words only approximate the experience being represented. Something is always left out. Something is always shifted slightly to fit a linguistic category.[17] What cannot be represented, either because the logic of the language does not permit it (a response to the culture's values) or one's family will not allow it (it disrupts the politics), always goes underground and perpetuates itself in the individual unconscious and the culture's structure of experience. We always omit what we can least control, what will make us most uncomfortable when it seeks to reemerge. To keep ourselves comfortable, we always pretend that what we can verbalize (hence structure and control) is all there is, and the effort always separates us to an extent from the reality of God and the world. The more intense our commitment to the precisely verbalizable, the more vulnerable we are to the "danger of our own chosen plan," and the more difficult it is to respond to change, to the other, and to God.

Language, and our ambiguous commitment to it, is one of the most powerful tools in the social structuring of reality; hence a dominant element in the culture's ability to advance good and perpetuate evil. Each competing interest in the society seeks to govern how language will be used. Witness the politicized struggles over how phrases should be defined: family values, freedom fighters, budget cut, equal opportunity. The shape of language in any generation, like the dominant character type, is a social and political creation.

PREFERRED SINS OF THE POSTMODERN WEST

As we see, each generation creates its own characteristic obstacles to the work of God, and each generation's theology seeks to describe them. The late nineteenth century identified its enemies as moral and physical weakness, drunkenness, and prostitution; by the mid-twentieth century the major danger was the hubris of humanity's attempt to build social utopias, the belief in human perfectibility, and the hopelessness of authoritarian structures as contributors to the good. Major contemporary analysts, theological and secular, identify the major obstacles to human growth and divine pleasure as privatism and the resulting loss of community.

As Bellah and colleagues have alerted us, and Stephanie Coontz has spelled out in detail,[18] we have built a massively organized society that individuals believe they cannot control. In our fear and frustration about its unmanageability, we try to control every molecule of the small pieces of space and time that do fall within our sovereignty. Until recent decades, the majority of every society knew almost nothing of privacy. The combination of poverty, communitarian ideology and architecture, and the technical necessity of performing tasks in common meant that people did know one another's business. They lived close together; they could hear what happened in one another's houses (no central heating or air-conditioning, hence the windows were often open). The crowding of homes meant that most recreation and pleasure was sought in public space. Citizens had a shared stake in control of open territory, since there was no place else to go.

With the opening of the American frontier and its ideology of independence (despite its reliance on government entities such as the U.S. Army), the dispersal of communities into isolated farmsteads (unlike the New England colonial pattern, which was copied from Europe's villages), and the late-twentieth-century explosion of technology and affluence that frees us from party lines, the community well, and walking to work, the American propertied classes have developed the most atomized, isolated style of living in human history. We drive to every destination in closed vehicles. We can select from dozens or hundreds of wired-in televised diversions at any hour. We can bank by phone and at machines, shop through catalogues, inform ourselves via the computer, and make conversation unnecessary by the fax machine and e-mail. I have lived in the same house for ten years, and know the names of only two other families among the twenty or thirty houses I can see from my windows. Yet I have people I consider friends on at least three other continents, and am more likely to have conversations with them than people who have lived within 100 yards of me for a decade.

This is true because we have made it so, and it appears to be what we want. It is not intrinsically bad. But it has major costs. Maintenance of all those private resource bases, all that technology, is very expensive. For people of only modest affluence, it requires more work hours per household, typically two incomes per family. It diverts time from many other valuable activities: child care, marital companionship, volunteer activity, worship, and play. We see the results in the increasing severity of psychological disturbance we are called upon to treat, the acceleration of marital violence and abuse of children, the difficulty maintaining marriages, and the incredible sales volume of psychotropic drugs. It creates fearsome economic pressures, since the increase in cost of an "average" middle-class lifestyle has occurred during a period of falling real income, especially for the young, the poorly educated, and minorities. Those changes are producing a restratification of the society, with clearer boundaries between those who can afford to fully participate in privatized technological enclaves and those who cannot.

With sharper class boundaries has come a weakening of shared citizenship, shown in everything from a decline in charitable giving to a drop in election turnout. We have diminished the amount of public space while increasing the cost of private space, thus siphoning time and money away from every public use. Institutions that have traditionally counted on volunteer time and contributions are weakened across the board: churches, the United Way, youth athletic programs, scouting, political parties, public education. As structures that traditionally mediate between private and mass life have been outcompeted by the apparent needs of the private sphere, overarching super-organizations have stepped in to provide the resources and structures needed to sustain so much "private" life. Government and corporations have assumed functions once handled in the voluntary sector, but we have little trust in them or the people who manage them. Furthermore, they are expensive, and as a people we bitterly resent the taxes, prices, and impersonality they require. We are in a desert time for institutional and community life and must find ways to revive them without sacrificing our freedom.

That is our overarching malaise. It works itself out in identifiable wounds to which particular parts of the creation are extremely vulnerable. At every point in history where privacy has increased, protection for the weakest members of self-contained households (and other communities) has decreased. As Poling has eloquently pointed out, our protection of family privacy and parental power has enabled a major increase in sexual abuse of children, the battering of women, and abuse and neglect of the dependent elderly. "There is more sexual and physical violence, including homicide, in the family than in any other social location." He attributes that to three factors: the social legitimation of violence in interpersonal behavior, the increasing privacy of the family, and the "stubborn inequality of women and children in relation to men."[19] By confining small groups of people in residential enclaves, we remove sources of social control that used to come from neighbors, church, the police, extended family, and other community agents. The more isolated the nuclear family, the higher the incidence of abuse, making clear the links between the increased privatization and the intensifying violence. Poling leaves no doubt that organized, systematic male dominance both profits from and intensifies the fragmentation of society, and combines with militarism, the excesses of individualistic capitalism, and the exploitation of women to create a mutually reinforcing fabric of oppressive structures. It obstructs people's validation of their internal experience and denies them access to the individual experience of others.

THE ORGANIZATION OF SINFUL POWER

Where Poling leaves off, Larry Graham's pastoral theological analysis begins. He draws heavily on Poling, McFague, Loomer, Rita Nakashima Brock, Ashbrook, and the family therapy tradition, identifying the principalities and powers noted in the previous section as a network of oppression that requires a contextual, not primarily an individual, response.[20] He contends that expressive individualism invites us to see relationality and individuality as opposed, and argues that if we are to provide meaningful care, we must recognize that reality is interconnected and organized, and that that has implications for how we practice. He observes, with McFague, that our present level of privatized technology uses resources at an unsustainable level, in turn fueling a violent competition for those resources, threatening warfare at a level that could destroy all life.

He names networks of imbalanced and unaccountable power as the primary evil. "Victimizing and chaotic power exists when . . . one person or group is coerced into becoming the receptor of the influence of others quite apart from their own desires, needs, and aspirations."[21] It results in the targets of power being invalidated, unfulfilled, and stigmatized, their symptoms being seen as their own failure rather than the results of evil structures. Note recent court cases in which the psychological instability of abuse survivors is counted not as evidence of the severity of their abuse, but of their unreliability as witnesses. Holders of such power typically deny their influence and its consequences, while stubbornly retaining their hold on it and identifying some outside force—God's will, national security, the natural order, the free enterprise system—as requiring and maintaining it. This is power as domination, self-perpetuating, other-demeaning. It denies the reality of internal relations, mutual responsibility, and unconscious meaning, and works in a structured way to keep the society privatized and hierarchically controlled. It seeks a specific, unmoving pattern of boundaries between conscious and unconscious process, keeping our attention on external products and eliminating awareness of the consequences of its impact. When it does not succeed in eliminating the awareness, it seeks to restrict it to persons who can be easily disqualified. It favors the interests of those who "sell the needy for a pair of shoes," who see profit and well-being as the same things, and who garner governmental and military support worldwide to seek profit without regard to other visions of how life might be organized.

Graham at times appears to join the argument that individually focused psychotherapy supports this structure, helping it perpetuate the oppression. Advocates of this view maintain that privacy, confidentiality, and exclusive therapist loyalty to individual clients help blind clients to all broader responsibilities. Certainly this is true at times. Even if that claim is rejected, there is no question that good psychotherapy makes it possible for individuals to better tolerate societal distortions, creating perhaps more ability but less urgency to change them. Yet the broader question is whether any other model of treatment can thrive in a society that has produced history's first proclamations of a right to privacy. Is psychotherapy a spearhead of fragmenting individualism, or is it one of the few outbreaks of our deeper craving for intimacy and unconscious meaning, offered in the society's preferred trappings of autonomy and secrecy, while covertly working to break down those very structures? This is a central question for both pastoral psychotherapy and this book. I believe that Graham is wrong, that realized individuals are indispensable to breaking down individualism, and that individualism is most powerfully maintained by persons unable to break through the demands for conformity to the present pseudoindividualistic ethos. But even if I am right in this, psychotherapy only escapes the accusation if it empowers persons to resist the community-eroding power of mass-yet-privatized society.

EVIL'S INVASION OF THE SELF

Graham, McFague, and the Bellah group deal primarily with these evils' external impact on life: how economic, ethnic, and political forces combine to build an impenetrable obstacle to the aspirations of individuals and groups. But the more damning effects of these forces are inside the character structures of the persons whose experience is shaped by them.

Poling, following Loomer, gives an indication of the power this process holds. "Children internalize relationships with their abusers so that these experiences become a part of the very structure of the self."[22] This is not unique to relationships with abusers. Children internalize all their basic, formative relationships, taking in first the feeling tone, the emotional ecology of the relationship, and establishing it as the backdrop against which more finely delineated features are later outlined. The child senses a certain mood, a specific nuance of feeling, as the expectable ambiance of the family or a subsystem within it. The child develops a strategy for living in an environment dominated by that feeling, a way to survive and cope with the balance of resources and dangers daily present. When the feeling tone is invasive or constricting, the child learns to live as though that were the expectable environment of the entire world, and seeks the most workable patterns for preserving hope and life in that situation he or she can imagine, choosing among the options God makes available in imagination. Hence Poling can write, "abuse is not over when it is over," because the abusive environment persists in the patterns and expectations the child develops in response to it. The child "constructs a defective self from the inside out."[23] Of course, that is true for us all to an extent, abused or not, but the colonization by evil is particularly dramatic when the parenting is exploitative.

American theologian Horace Bushnell was one of the first to recognize the theological import of these realities. He argued in the 1840s that more was done for a child's soul before the age of six than ever after, observing that

> all family transactions and feelings, acting thus together, take a common character. Their character, feelings, spirit, and principles, must propagate themselves, whether they will or not. Hence the odor of the house will always be in the child's garments, the spirit of the house is breathed into his nature, day to day. If the house subsist by plunder, the child is swaddled as a thief, the child wears a thief's garments, and feeds the growth of his body on stolen meat.[24]

In describing the same realities, Poling reminds us that the emotional attachment of abuser and abused guarantees that the abusive experience itself will be internalized. "The consequences of the smaller moral size (in Loomer's sense) of the abuser are reproduced in the victim."[25]

This affective and ethical background precedes and supplies the substance for the child's construction of internal images of the parents. It constitutes the structure of experience, in Meland's sense, out of which specific memories of parents and their ideals are created, and stands ready to correct or augment every flawed representation of those persons and their effect on this developing child. Whatever picture of the parent the child forms has to be consistent with this inner emotional ethos.

When Gordon Jackson wrote that evil is part of what struggles to constitute us,[26] this is what he meant. It has a particular opportunity in early childhood. Into the child's not yet formed psychic space flows an enormously complex mix of elements, images, emotions, and events. Some represent the heroic response of communities, and parents representing those communities, to God's leading through the circumstances of their lives. Others represent the reality of limited resources and opportunities, providing only a narrow spectrum of vision for the child to appropriate. Others represent flat societal and parental failure to respond to the lure of God: the choice to abuse a child, to abandon a family, to be indifferent to need. Children's own energy and imagination, their own subjective aim and response to God, guides their choice among these elements. But a child cannot take something that is not there, and in most (though not all) cases will take what is there in greatest abundance. As the evil done to the parents and grandparents finds its way into their character, and is elaborated and often intensified by their own choices, it is available to the child as a piece of a personal stance toward life.

We return to Bion and Bollas for an understanding of the details. The crucial variables have to do with the ability of the mother-infant dyad to process frustration and the effect of that capacity on the development of psychic space within the child. All children are born with a unique individual level of frustration tolerance, which I will label "x." If a child is forced to wait longer for food or comfort than the time required to reach "x," while he or she is still too physically undeveloped to do anything to modify the situation, the child will be unable to remain conscious of the distress. Part of it will be split off, harming psychic integrity, then projected as undigested "beta elements."

What happens then is crucial. If the mother or other caretaker in her reverie can allow her experience of self to be modified by the baby's pain, can take in the projective identification, give it a name, and make decisions about it, it becomes for her an alpha element which in turn is offered back to the baby, in tone and gesture and gaze, communicating that life can be good and safe even in the presence of this misery. That gift of the mother's mental space functions as a temporary annex for the baby's inner space, helping contain the painful stimuli and making them available for representation and meaning. Bion puts it, "projective identification cannot exist without its reciprocal, namely an introjective activity intended to lead to an accumulation of good internal objects."[27] But that depends upon the mother's capacity for reverie, her ability and willingness to have her internal experience changed by the infant. If her own fear of failure, of reproach, of competition is too great, if her own envy of the baby too intense, she will turn a cold eye back upon the infant, and there will be no reception of the infant's feeling, no modeling of how to hold a painful stimulus, only a learning that indeed this terror is too great to keep in awareness (the mother's or the baby's).

If the load of pain the mother is already carrying is too great for her to take any more, the baby will be left alone with her or his own pain, which must be maintained as undigestible beta elements, fit only for externalizing into the experience of others, with consequent confusion and retaliation. The greater the proportion of such unsuccessful transactions, the more the baby is blocked from developing empathy, the more he or she depends on splitting, polarization, and fragmentation, and the greater the danger of both interior psychopathology and external antisocial behavior. Thought is impoverished, since it requires the fullest possible range of symbolization, acting out (to discharge unacceptable feelings) is intensified, and the capacity for ambivalence diminished. It collapses one or more of Ogden's modes of basic experience, leaving the developing child with an incomplete repertoire of voices (in Tracy's sense), more dependent then on autistic-contiguous or paranoid-schizoid processes, less able to construct a history, to acknowledge the many-sidedness of mother's reality, and to accept the world's imperfections without retaliation.

The paradigmatic response of the parent without a current capacity for reverie is abuse, an acting out of the parent's frustration over his or her inability to comfort or control the child. It is the probable response when the parent is unable to accord reality to the child's inner experience, instead behaving as though the parent's own need-determined fantasy of the child's internal state were the only truth about it. The abused child is denied a portion of what Bollas terms "generative innocence," the state which creates "a continuously renewed 'blank screen' upon which one can project one's desire. . . The abusive parent has muddied the screen and it will never be blank again."[28] Bollas' discussion bears striking resemblance to Tillich's account of the loss of "dreaming innocence" at humanity's fall, or its individual loss in maturation. For both writers, the deepest loss is the freedom of desire, the recognition that one's desires can and probably will be used against one, that they cannot be offered freely to the world (parents) without the risk of violation, manipulation, and repudiation. This results in the hiding of desire from oneself and the other, and the resulting loss of the opportunity of adventure, beauty, and full partnership with God.

THE ENTRENCHMENT OF SIN

Sin takes up residence in us, first through what we prehend from a damaged world, conveyed externally through danger, poverty, and disruption of relationships; internally through the insensitivity and indifference of our overburdened caretakers; then through our own symbolizations, habits, and survival techniques, adopted in an attempt to deal with what has come in from outside. It leaves us less available for play with God and the other, limited in our ability and willingness to feel the full existence of the other or to offer our own to them, thus more vulnerable to the false promises of fulfillment offered by the explicitly sinful substitutes the world will make available. Both through those sinful substitute gratifications and through our diminished capacity for faith and playful response to God (and the other), we inflict the consequences of our sin as fact and act on those who come after us, visiting them upon and beyond the seventh generation.

With this being true, it is still important to remember Meland's observation that sin is a mark of spiritual potency,[29] and hence cannot be dismissed as sheer evil. The same capacities that make us vulnerable to sin fit us to be relational partners for God or any creature. To remain in dreaming innocence when invited by God to know and desire the world is also to fail God, to leave God and the other without a partner. In this sense, McFague's recasting of the classic tradition is in error when she names the "desire of the self for the self" as disrupting the body of God, hence central to sin.[30] The self must desire itself to become itself, and without becoming itself it cannot be a full and contributing member of the body. We also fail God by remaining in the false self, the camouflaged attempt to evade responsibility for our own desires by constantly seeking to please the other, without recognition that the good we see is also real, though only partial.

Over time, each cultural age has unique ways of disrupting the harmony of the creation and its components. Freud, Tillich, and Meland wrote in an era marked by highly organized, structured violence and domination: world wars, colonial imperialism, massive institutionalized sexism and racism, and a nearly universal claustrophobic, self-limiting, frightened neurosis. Tracy and Poling, Bion and Bollas, Graham and Ogden speak more from a world where the massive structures have lost coherence, where world war and state socialism have given way to terrorism on one hand and corporate downsizing on the other, and where the relatively stable, stifling structures of neurosis have diminished, being outcompeted by the more chaotic, less predictable, wilder explosiveness of personality disorder. Discrimination is giving way to incest, claustrophobic parenting to the failure to provide structure and order.

But in this and every other era God is not left without a witness. Though evil on a global scale and its counterpart in individual psyches are very powerful, in every moment we are also presented with the possibility that things can be different. God does offer us, again and again, glimpses of life as fulfilled that stand in stark contrast to the evils around and within. We are repeatedly called to assess whether our present way of doing things is taking us toward the intimacy that we crave and the world needs. Every wave of pain, every twinge of anxiety, is also a witness to the imperfection of our chosen plan, the good that is our own. At critical points, the cost of those sorrows, perhaps intensified by the outbreak of a dramatic symptom or the loss of a cherished relationship, can break through and convict us of the bankruptcy of the path we were first offered and subsequently elaborated for ourselves. In those moments of defeat, when we cannot go farther in the direction we have been heading, there is the chance for the in-breaking of the Spirit that can turn us around. Many sufferers use that horrifying defeat as an opportunity to seek out psychotherapy for the first time, in hopes that it can help them discern their sin and seek out a way of living in greater harmony with God, the world, and themselves.

It is to that possibility that we now turn.

PART II:
PASTORAL PSYCHOTHERAPY AS THE PLAY OF GOD

Chapter 5

The Hope of Pastoral Psychotherapy

That piece of sin that is also psychopathology, the sin which generates pain that leads clients to pastoral psychotherapy, is identifiable by rigidity. Its essence is a repetition of unsuccessful solutions, continued because other tactics promise to produce even more pain than is now suffered. The repetition, this unsuccessful but loyally maintained pattern, is sustained by constrictions at every level. Thought content is delimited: the person thinks about the same small array of mental contents. Thoughts follow the same routes in dealing with one problem after another. The same overfocussedness, or vagueness, or evasion of responsibility for outcomes, crops up in response to every situation. The body participates in the rigidity, tightening some muscle groups, atrophying others, to keep unwanted impulses out of awareness and make sure available energy does not exceed what the controlling structures can manage. Facial expressions become habitual, limbs are awkwardly cramped, tension is frozen in muscles, posture is distorted to the point of structural damage, all in service of the required stasis.

Relational systems also become fossilized, losing the flexibility that allows interactions to range broadly across emotions and activities, so that the link with person A only allows certain kinds of scripted behaviors, with person B a different set, and so on. Marriages confine themselves to limited repertoires, parent-child interactions have fewer options than the task demands, and work relationships gradually eliminate either play or productivity, and often both. Larger networks are also restricted, as domination by any single behavior patterns will produce choice of and by a narrowing range of partners, excluding those who offer or demand either more or less than the system is calibrated to accept and extend. Those networks, which support and inform value choices, require maintenance of the established level of inflexibility, the current range of awareness, the currently allowed set of feelings. They require a specific boundary between experiences allowed into or excluded from consciousness, making it unnecessary to cope with frequent unacceptable impulses, disobedient thoughts, unsettling visions.

The more tightly we restrict ourselves to any set of patterns, the more likely we are to feel the distress of psychological symptoms, physical discomfort or illness, and relational sterility. We lose our freedom to pursue objectives, as though someone else, somewhere else, had locked us into a frozenness that keeps us from doing what we want to do. But the compulsion stems directly from the restrictions in relationship, affect, and thought we have, with the complicity of others, imposed upon ourselves.

BEGINNINGS OF LIBERATION

Sooner or later, we are startled into noticing that our lives are not what we had hoped. Sometimes it takes a series of distressing dreams, the disruption of a valued relationship, a psychological symptom such as insomnia or depression, an arrest, a job loss. The spirit cries out with a plea for the self's attention to its own pain. Everything depends on how it is heard. The pain witnesses to our hope that God wills and can enable a different life, a fuller state of grace. In the contrast between what is and what could be, pain motivates change.

Often that combination of pain and hope is focused by, or accelerates in response to, a fragment of memory. The freeing memory can be hideous or beautiful, something that helps make sense of the chronic pain or something that identifies a resource for changing it. Anyone who has had much contact with survivors of abuse has witnessed the profoundly disorganizing, subversive power of the first slivers of recollection of the abuse. Those primarily concerned about the dangers of false memory notwithstanding, these emergent scenes with their physical sensations of horror and violation typically shatter

Pain is the witness to the hope

survivors' sense that they reliably know the relational world. But abuse is only the grossest of the memory-burying impacts on young psyches. Even in benign families, normal developmental events, historical intrusions such as war or natural disaster, and private crises such as the birth of a sibling or a parent changing jobs create stresses that a particular child (with a given combination of strengths and weaknesses) cannot integrate. Whatever the cause, strategic forgetting will temporarily protect the integrity of every psyche, at the cost of the continuity of individual or community historical knowledge.

Memories typically reemerge when the person creates a situation safe enough to allow the collapse: a move away from parents, a marriage, the pending or recent birth of a child, a time lapse between jobs. The memory trace functions like a prophetic oracle, proclaiming simultaneously that "the axe is laid at the root of the tree" and "the Kingdom of God is at hand." It inevitably is experienced as a call to "prepare ye the way of the Lord," promising that things will radically change, that the present order will come under judgment. Later, a new and straight path through the desert begins to emerge. It exploits some tiny crack in the barrier between conscious and unconscious, and pours life through that pinprick, life that grows and strengthens, stretching the gap and ultimately ripping it so broadly that floods of memory come pouring through, providing raw material for the construction of a new picture of the world, correcting many old omissions and ushering the knower into a new, more fluid space.

The space is frightening, both for the one remembering and those remembered. It more resembles Jerusalem in 586 B.C. than first-century Rome or Calvin's Geneva. But it must happen if the old rigidities are to be reexamined and the old ways modified. It must be followed by months, often years, of further deconstruction, at a more controlled pace, and then by a comparable period of patiently building one stone upon another. But the initial opening of the seal on the unconscious, the repository of memory, is a gift of God—even in the midst of the pain. As Karen, the woman Poling describes in the extended example in *The Abuse of Power,* writes, "I really began to heal when I began to remember."[1]

Trauma blots out memory, as Ashbrook reminds us.[2] The traffic victim who cannot remember anything from five minutes before the accident until he wakes up in the hospital is protected from the horror of the fear and pain. The combat veteran who can only revisit the burned-out village in his nightmares, and distributes his unremembered horror through his family and community by exuding the beta elements of that experience, is protecting consciousness from implication in guilt and destruction. He fears both the enemy sniper he went in after and the punitive superego that accuses him of murder. The abuse victim has used her God-given power to dissociate to protect against the inadmissible horror that her daddy, her brother, her minister touched her in painful and forbidden ways and/or demanded she perform acts they had earlier said were wrong. To deepen this protection, the rigid patterns I described previously are established: using personal distance, refusal to engage authority (deference for women, defiant distancing for men), rejection of love, and the truncation of life. The first slivers of memory promise to undo this powerful, stabilizing, insulating protection, and in the process bring both hope and horror.

MEMORY AS AN OPENING FOR GRACE

Memory is thus a vehicle for the grace of God. I believe God wills human beings and communities to be in constant dialogue with an orienting narrative, connecting them to history and describing a trajectory into the future. If those lives or communities of lives are to maintain coherence and connection, both internally and with God, they must keep the events of that narrative in conversation with the community. One effect of evil is the disruption of memory, whether in the individual situation of a childhood abuse victim or the corporate horror of the British burning of Beijing's library during the Boxer Rebellion. The disruption limits the inclusiveness of our stories, their capacity to make a place for the events of our lives. The cost of the self-protection offered by forgetfulness is the shrinkage in applicability of our stories, a diminishing of the size of our character. There is a

God-given mandate and drive to remember, activated as soon as the danger of remembering has passed.

Christians experience this most powerfully in the classic language of the communion table, "do this in remembrance of me." Jews do it in the Passover rituals. We are to remember Jesus or Exodus, with all they promise of judgment, forgiveness, community, and hope. We are to reencounter Jesus and God through revisiting the tradition, as Tracy and many others remind us, entering the intense particularity of the experience.[3] Our memory is aided by many lives, books, sculptures, pieces of music, and events of celebration that call us from a numb indifference to the past into a lively, urgent encounter with the Reality disclosed in and through them. Such encounters produce what McFague calls a "destabilizing, inclusive, non-hierarchical vision." She cites the parables as paradigm, those stories in which Jesus maneuvers the sensibilities of his hearers into direct confrontation with their own tradition and the realities of their lives. She describes how parables take the vague and muted awareness of history and community, particularize and intensify it, casting the hearer as part of the story in a way that makes remembering inescapable.[4]

God is always working to bring the life of our personal and communal histories into demanding contact with the habitually half-conscious patterns of daily experience, in the process breaking the hold of principalities and powers who work powerfully to keep us asleep.

A historical and social manifestation of memory's power was seen in the waves of Latin American revolution following Vatican II and the subsequent bishops' conference at Medellín. When legions of missionary priests and lay catechists brought the "preferential option for the poor" to the attention of the poor themselves and led them in reading the Gospels and discussing their meaning, organized forces of power and privilege were shaken, and freedoms developed in societies that had been oppressively static for centuries. That piece of societal memory is still working itself through, but the power of the remembering stands as evidence of the intensified energy that emerges when memory is recovered in cultures and in selves.

When memory is unsafe, as in an abusive family or an oppressive society (and all societies and families are abusive or oppressive in some ways), it is compacted and hidden away. It goes into the muscle tensions of the body, the symbol structures of the unconscious, the encoded literary traditions of a society—to await the time of safety. Freud taught us that the unconscious always seeks to escape this confinement (repression), seeking to bring its urges into contact with the world where they can be gratified. In a similar way, God works unceasingly to create safe situations where we are prompted to remember, accessing the Divine power and grace as it moves through communities and psyches. A previously stifled protest emerges, carrying the conviction that this horror was not and is not God's will, and that something in us remains alive to seek a more abundant life.

THE THERAPIST'S CONTRIBUTION

The memory and the protest require a partner outside the psyche, a sign of God's faithfulness, a warrant of the current safety, a function that therapist, church, spouse, or friend can often play. The memory is always necessary and is often evoked by a stimulus new to the sufferer. That is one reason the power of the pathology (sin) is intensified when it keeps the patterns of daily life unchanging. If a person is always presented with the same environment, the same combinations of stimuli, there is always a familiar and available response. The most isolated systems are the most resistant to change. It is when new factors—persons, art, scripture, economic changes, migration—reach the self that novel responses are called forth, carrying a greater hope for freedom. At a minimum, the therapist functions in this way, what Keeney calls "a source of the random."5 Simply by talking in a different way than the usual relational partners, talking about different things, the therapist creates a different environment, which increases the chances of a different response. As such the therapist performs a prophetic function, regardless of that person's skill, theoretical base, or personal style.

Obviously one hopes the therapist will do much more. One of the crucial arenas for therapist activity, and the most powerful stimulus to memory, is transference—the universal tendency to respond to the present persons in our lives on the basis of the emotional needs, hope, and pain left over from earlier relationships. We are created so that a neutral, safe, and intimate environment will often evoke the same feelings we had known as children in relation to that epoch's key persons. At first we do not notice the similarity, but if the therapist works skillfully, the transference functions as a spillway for memory's reservoir. The once unsafe memories, compressed into a set of feelings and sealed by repression, are released by the combination of the safety of the setting and the hopefully discerning transference interpretations; once released, they trigger a series of previously unavailable responses.

THE THERAPIST AND THE SPACE

The space in which this happens is sacred, and the therapist has a critical role in making it so. Keeping the sacredness discernible and consistent is our most necessary responsibility. The crucial territory is the relational space, defined and maintained by the covenant between therapist and client, though the physical space itself is crucial for some clients. But wherever the hour happens, the space the therapist presides over takes on the quality of "the center of the world," the *axis mundi* around which the rest of the world revolves. Following Mircea Eliade and Victor Turner, Tracy writes of the key events in sacred space as "an eruption of power of some manifestation of the whole now experienced as the sacred cosmos."[6] He, like other students of ritual, emphasizes the separateness of this space from ordinary space and time, and the way this time reenters the "sacred time of origins." In language resonant for psychotherapists, he describes "retelling the myth," "creatively reinterpreting the symbol," and allowing this present moment to be saturated with the time when the cosmos (for our purposes, the cosmos of this person or system) was first taking shape. Tracy's interpretation of Eliade also describes what happens when psychotherapy is sacred. The power of God, which organizes and energizes the sacred cosmos, erupts into a particular moment in this sacred space, seizes and mutates a piece of the sufferer's myth, restoring that person to community with an unshakable sense of authorization to participate and contribute, typically with a newfound and crucial gift to offer.

I have argued elsewhere that Turner's concept of liminal space, closely allied to Eliade's concept of the *axis mundi*, sheds light on the pregnant possibilities of therapy space.[7] Turner, focusing on initiation rituals, describes the preparation, the carefully demarcated boundaries of the "liminal vessel," the different rules within that vessel and without, the highly specific role of the ritual elder, and the newly attained status of those who pass through the experience. Particularly important are the signs of the numinous quality of the space and the events within it. Its boundaries serve that function, as do verbal formulas and physical gestures that accompany entering and leaving, semiscripted transactions that occur within it that would never occur outside. These heighten all participants' awareness that something special, something of unusual power, happens in this particular setting.

The rules governing exchanges between the same persons outside do not apply here. Those applying here prescribe something more essential, more basic, than the world's ordinary space. That is also true in pastoral psychotherapy. The importance of the parallel is this: God and the community have an investment in the effectiveness of the transformation, and the effectiveness is maximized when it is clear that we are together on holy ground. God best uses the therapist as a vehicle when the therapist conveys that this is a special place, and that we are together in a different way, for a different purpose, than we could be in any other context.

Henri Nouwen contributed another useful set of images of sacred space. He wrote of "the places set apart for the Holy One," of "beautiful frames around empty spaces, witnessing to Him who is the quiet, still center of all human life." Though Nouwen understood himself to be writing about celibacy, he was adding richly to our imagery for understanding pastoral psychotherapy. He speaks of spaces without "loud noises, hungry movements or impatient gestures," places that "want to invite us to be silent, to sit or kneel, to listen attentively and to rest with our whole being."[8] He quotes St. Thomas' description of celibacy as a "vacancy for God," in ways that remind us of therapists' continual call to abstinence, the refusal to fill the space that must be kept open for the client's exploration.

There are many ways to wrongly fill it, and we are called to avoid them all: sexual exploitation, talking to hear our own words, demanding the client accept our interpretation or act in the way we deem wise or faithful. Bion urges the analyst to enter each session—and each moment within the session—with neither memory nor desire, no compulsive attempt to recall a previous hour or to evoke a particular response, no "irritable reaching after fact or reason,"[9] but rather with an attentive readiness to hear from the client and from oneself. If one believes (as I do and Bion came to) that God enables the client to communicate with the therapist in "sighs too deep for words," through all the preverbal and even prestructural pathways available to human beings, then we believe that by hearing from/through oneself and the client, one is also hearing from God. Of course, we are hearing not only what is needed for the client's freedom and transformation, but also for our own.

THE GROUND RULES AND THE FRAME

This sacred space, this undemanding, liminal availability of two persons' attention to the movement within and between them, overlaps greatly with what Robert Langs calls the therapeutic "frame" and what Winnicott describes as the "container."[10] The repeated processes by which therapist and client establish that this is different space from social or business territory accomplish the same objectives as two familiar religious processes: the introductory phases of ritual, and the state of preparation or readiness to receive revelation. Every theology of revelation describes human situations and attitudes that increase the likelihood that God will reach human beings with saving knowledge here and now. The studies of ritual establish that the power of the experience is multiplied when the boundaries of sacred space are well-demarcated, when a person is thus rendered cognitively clear and emotionally alive to moving from outside to inside and vice versa. Jerome Frank's classic, *Persuasion and Healing,* documents that healing is far more likely when the situation is structured so that the sufferer expects to be healed.[11]

It is thus an act of worship and faithfulness by the pastoral psychotherapist to establish the boundaries of the therapeutic space, the life-giving frame or container. Not that the ground rules must be as rigid and unforgiving as those proposed by Langs,[12] but it does matter to God and your client that there are clearly different expectations for what happens in this relationship and what happens in all others. It demands that each of us seeks to identify, reflectively and prayerfully, what in the moment-to-moment texture of our client relationships most enhances God's play with those clients, and that we structure those relationships so that optimal amounts of time are available for the sacred play to happen, minimally impeded by other types of interaction occurring in and around the hour.

Minimally, this requires a signal to the client that we are entering a space where the rules are different. I prefer a visibly attentive silence; others may use a standard question or a neutral observation. It requires that notice be taken when the client attempts to blur the boundaries of the sacred space. It requires us to expect that, in the early stages of the work, clients will always attempt to blur them, both as a way of communicating the nature of their pathology and out of ignorance for what enhances the process. They are being introduced to a world we hope they will carry outside the session, and they need a way to identify when they are in that world and when they are not. In this sense, pastoral psychotherapy is always evangelism and/or religious education, whether or not there is explicit reference to faith. It is not kind or faithful to withhold these behavioral teachings, though it is necessary to design the signs of the space in subtly different ways for different clients.

One client, a yoga teacher and healer, reflected on the differences between my ground rules and her own. "You don't go to dinner with your clients, do you?" "I've noticed that when I say something, you don't just come right back with something. You give me some time to think about it." This same client, years earlier, had related a history of being sexually involved with other religious therapists. I responded with a ground rule that seemed necessary for the work with her (though not with everyone): "I will never touch you." The point of that, and all such regulations, is not primarily morality, but to create a space in which something can happen for this person that has not happened before, something that can be carried beyond the therapy relationship into broader life. She knew much more about how to seduce and be seduced than how to be respectfully loved.

The ground rules are the behavioral markers of the sacred space. Within the space we can catch our breath, the *ruach,* in both a symbolic and a literal sense. Ashbrook reminds us that the brain uses far more of our oxygen supply than is proportional to its size. It requires a lot of breath to do the work of monitoring and imaging our lives and relationships. The constrictions described earlier, like all anxiety, reduce our oxygen supply.[13] When we catch our breath in the sacred space, our brains are fueled for the work of reuniting our disparate pieces in a unifying narrative.

THE CONTEXT FOR PSYCHOTHERAPY

So therapy begins in this context. Each of us is birthed into a family and community in conflict between the lure of God and resistance to the lure. Particular persons and systems, due to their history and structure or to random events, are pulled into and maintained at a level of unease containing both sufficient pain to motivate seeking a major change in life and sufficient aliveness to God and self to notice deprivation and maintain the hope to relieve it. The world, external and internal, encourages us to continue the patterns that have "brought us (un)safe thus far." Those demands and offers provide a constant smoke screen, obscuring the poverty of present life and the cost it requires of self and others. Yet glimpses of hope sparked by the lure of God occasionally penetrate the haze of activity, fed by random (or providential) events that awaken the memory and remind us of the wounds that produced the present pain and of a story that leads to redemptive possibility.

Out of this ambivalent dividedness, people choose pastoral psychotherapy. They enter it in all their ambiguity. As with any new meeting, their hope and fear are powerful; they enter with a lively sense of both danger and possibility. There is the awareness of the possibility of the prevenient grace of God, as Christy Neuger has argued.[14] God has prepared a community that sponsored and trained the caregiver, placed that person where he or she is available, and created the means to compensate the caregiver. When the therapist is able to present congruently with this preparation, the client can open to the healing potential in relationship and community—connecting through the therapist to the faith group that calls and sustains him or her, and beyond both to the God who enables all healing.

But this preformed positive transference, this organismic acknowledgment of the goodness of creation, is never unambiguous and rarely dominant in the seeker. Wilhelm Reich argued seventy-five years ago that "there is no genuine positive transference at the beginning of the analysis."[15] Simply put, if the structures of reality had presented themselves to the client as dependably benign, the constriction and pain that necessitated the therapy would not have occurred. The symptoms themselves are the client's way of dealing with the perceived barrenness and assaultiveness of reality. So the therapist's assumptions must include a God who, however gracious the therapist may deem God to be, allows the seeker to experience the Divine as a mixture of promise, gift, seduction, and betrayal; and the therapist must be prepared to be experienced as such also.

Ashbrook teaches us that the client first enters the sacred space focused primarily on survival.[16] The sympathetic nervous system is aroused, the dominant cerebral hemisphere is in charge, and the behavior patterns trusted to make safety out of ambiguity are deployed. For most, that will be an attempt to connect to stave off the horror of isolation, but for others the greater felt danger will be loss of autonomy, of emotional control, or of status and position. Clients will attend carefully to signs that the therapist represents danger in the way their world is dangerous, holding their breath and guarding themselves against the relational space. But they also will be alert to signs that the therapist incarnates the Spirit of the holy-but-not-yet-trusted community, that the culture they are creating with the therapist has room for the language in which they can best express themselves, and that their ways of being safe will be respected while the necessity of their use is being gently challenged. Only when negotiations about how we are going to be together are successfully concluded will the client shift from wariness to alliance (never completely and forever), will the survival behaviors give way to the effort to be known, will the strict hemispheric dominance be relaxed and the multivocity of sacred play become available, and the middle phase of therapy be achieved.

God wills the lively, stimulated safety of the client, the client's growth, hope, and trust. But the client cannot know that at the beginning. The therapist seeks a reverent, transformative encounter with God on the client's behalf, but the client cannot help but doubt it and look for signs that this doubt is or is not justified. The therapist knows she or he cannot be a vessel of grace for the client unless she or he is willing to be touched and changed by both client and God; but the client expects, and may need for a time, the therapist's superiority, expertise, responsibility, and professional judgment, with all the dangers they carry of violating the human bond between participants. Any fixated, unchangeable meaning client or therapist assigns to those terms will produce survival behavior and keep both parties outside the liminal vessel. Only as they sense their common fealty to the transformative love surrounding them both can they accept that each is judged and judging, that each has an area of expertise crucial for this endeavor, and that they are equal before God yet distinct in their responsibilities for the creation and use of the sacred space they share. When that is achieved, the sacred play of psychotherapy is well underway.

Chapter 6

The Hallowing of the Space

God enters psychotherapy's sacred space through the broader community, the therapist, and the client. The active participation of all is required for God's power to be fully actualized in any therapeutic encounter. Each can obstruct God's will to be present.

THE COMMUNITY CREATES THE SPACE

The community functions as both environment and object, in Winnicott's sense. It is the all-encompassing, largely implicit source of structures, values, habits, language, meanings, and safety (environment); and the ally/adversary that confronts us intimately in the persons of loved and hated others such as parents, siblings, teachers, clergy, employers, supervisors, and therapists (object). Further, God lives in the calling together and ongoing life of every primary community, as described in Chapter 2; and every one of its representatives has the community inside himself or herself, as described in Chapter 3. God leads the community to create the settings in which its members, seeker and healer, come together in the sacred play of psychotherapy.

No part of the process is free of the mark of the community any more than it is free of the influence of God, but there are discernible points where the community is noticeably transparent to God's power and grace. They include at least the following:

1. The communal belief that God wills the healing of psychological and spiritual suffering, and that psychotherapy is one of God's ways of healing it
2. The network of philanthropy, administrative skill, and traditions and technologies of training and compensation for those who have taught and/or are teaching us our craft
3. The web of private associations and governmental bodies that promote excellence in this work and attempt to certify when it has been achieved
4. The ephemeral, informal constellation of sources that constitute our referral networks, sharing information about who does psychotherapy well, and with whom they do it best
5. The processes by which we are called into this ministry, through discerning our gifts and graces as awakened by life in community, through relationship with teachers and counselors, in our pilgrimage through literature, and in our own experiences of healing

Communities create the space for psychotherapy, pastoral and otherwise, at particular points in their own histories, responding to an identifiable combination of opportunities and needs. Though all cultures have ways of defining and treating illness, the unique combination of (primarily) Christian theology and the various streams of the psychoanalytic and behavioral traditions that form the skeleton of pastoral psychotherapy is largely an American creation. It was unknown before 1900, recognizably emerged in the 1920s and 1930s, began creating a literature in the 1950s, and had a substantial institutional presence by the end of the 1960s. It grew rapidly in the 1970s and 1980s and has currently spread beyond the institutional boundaries of the American Association of Pastoral Counselors and far beyond the United States, spawning alternative organizations with differing theological and/or theoretical foci in this country and regional groupings in literally every part of the world. If you include the total body of psychotherapists who see their vocation as a response to the call of God, its share of total worldwide psychotherapy activity has been increasing steadily since the 1950s.

This growth is empowered by the community's belief that God does not will the suffering of God's creatures, and that suffering we define as psychological or spiritual is as important to God as is physical suffering, or the kinds of community suffering we might label political or economic. It is consistent with a belief that psychological or spiritual suffering has an impact on and is influenced by the more tangibly physical or communal sources of pain. It does not deny the existence of appropriate suffering, such as punishment for crime or guilt over harming a neighbor, but understands that kind of suffering as a direct consequence of one's own action rather than God's choice for human life. It is flatly different from the stance expressed by one Hindu thinker; "The problem with you Christians is that you believe problems are supposed to be solved,"[1] and some expressions of the Buddhist tenet that suffering can be abolished by abolishing desire.

The core of this belief is expressed by Paul Tillich: "Spiritual healing is the depth-dimension of mental healing; it is potentially, if not actually present, whether it expresses itself in the seriousness and profundity of the psycho-therapeutic situation, or in explicit religious manifestations."[2] Tillich also argued that mental healing follows from spiritual healing, and that bodily healing contributes to and is affected by the others. The extent to which the human self is centered, in loving relationship and rich integration with its component parts, directly influences its capacity for intimacy with God and neighbor; and, as we have argued earlier, is deeply influenced by the intimacy it achieves with both. Tillich's words are not evidence that these assertions are true, but they are evidence that the community that made him a spokesman accepts them as plausible. The community believes that painful failures of psychic health obstruct the relationship with God, and believes that God wishes us to be in intimate relationship with Godself. That creates a place for pastoral psychotherapy as a vehicle for the relation to God. Further, the community has created the space for the therapeutic vessel as sacred space; has hallowed it and made it available for healing.

It makes this hallowing tangible through the creation of institutional structures, which channel energy and money into this effort. Hospitals have created chaplaincies that have created pastoral counseling centers; freestanding centers have been funded by local churches, foundations, and businesses; universities and seminaries, funded by a wide range of church and nonchurch sources, have created faculties whose time has been freed to specialize in this aspect of ministry; great teachers have been prepared by those structures, have developed teaching methodologies and been authorized to utilize them on behalf of both the churches and the broader community. Those teachers, in turn, have produced a literature that has helped new generations of spiritually based therapists avoid repeating the mistakes of their predecessors, and aided them toward integrating their technical expertise with spiritual and theoretical commitments. Each step in this institutional development has required the community's response to the lure of God, has required the decisions of hundreds of donors, board members, hospital administrators, deans, bishops, and foundation executives. Each such decision has been an attempt to be faithful to an understanding of the will of God and the needs of a constituent community. Without that community and those decisions over the course of the last seventy-five years, there would be no pastoral psychotherapy.

Another way the community has hallowed the space is through creating organizations and agencies dedicated to deepening, defending, and purifying the growing tradition of thought, technique, and faithfulness. The Institute of Pastoral Care, the Council of Clinical Training, the Association of Clinical Pastoral Education, the American Association of Pastoral Counselors, the National Association of Catholic Chaplains, and dozens of other voluntary groups in this country and increasingly around the world, have been (at least occasionally) successful attempts to deepen the connection of practitioner, practice, faithfulness, and God. Independent sections within basically secular organizations, such as the American Psychological Association and the American Counseling Association, fulfill the same function. Further, almost all states now license providers of mental health care, many of whom have specifically pastoral orientations— as licensed professional counselors, as psychologists, as marriage and family therapists. A few states specifically participate in the community's setting aside the space through the licensing of pastoral counselors as such: Maine, New Hampshire, South Carolina, and

Kentucky, among others. In these ways, the community identifies the healing as important and helps persons gain access to it.

A less formal but very powerful community participation operates through referral networks. People send us clients; they give out our names and in the process witness to the importance of the suffering that elicits that giving, and to the givers' confidence that what we do deepens the life experience of those they refer. Those who make referrals perform a prophetic or apostolic function, pointing to what they hope and believe is a locus for the activity of God. As such they become part of that great cloud of witnesses whose prayers enhance the power of our work and to whom we are accountable for our practice. They also stand with us and for us, testifying to those referred that they put their own credibility on the line in the work we do. It is a holy and mutual commitment that links the client, referral source, therapist, and God in a hopefully healing encounter.

The community further invites God into the space for healing through participating in calling us to do this work. None of us finds psychotherapy as a vocation without being invited into it by the direct leading of God, of course, but also by a network of persons who participate in a variety of ways. People sensitize us, for good and ill, by putting us in a position to know pain, theirs and our own. Others speak of their pain to us and respond to our response. Their response guides us about returning to that or like situations. If they find our response helpful, it confirms something in our wish to be found valuable. Further, they speak of it to others, which assures we will or will not have further opportunities to exercise our skills and test our investment in this aspect of ministry. At some point the dialogue finds its way to persons with official or advisory importance: educators, judicatory executives, our own pastors and friends, certification committees. They ask if we have considered such a ministry, or respond with interest when we volunteer that we are thinking in this direction. On each of these occasions, God is luring us toward a space where we can join a sufferer in healing, and using the community to participate in the creation of that space. If we ultimately find ourselves in the room with a client, playing with God and the other, it is because a long series of encounters has carried us in that direction. In a sense, the whole community, and the God who calls and holds it together, is in the room with us.

HALLOWING THROUGH THE THERAPIST

As God has worked through the community to call and inform the therapist, and to create the institutions that provide the structure undergirding the relationship, God also works directly in and through the therapist to hallow the space. To say it differently, there are particular things that the therapist must do and be, in response to God, for God's access to the therapeutic space to be powerful.

Phenomenologically, this begins in the therapist's expectations of what is going to happen in the therapeutic space. It identifies the space as a locus of God's action, as a point of transition between different worlds, as an arena that will reward the most constant and hopeful attention. Meland describes the attitude as wonder, "undoubtedly the most elemental expression of spirit in the human creature, . . . the spontaneous play of thought not focused by any functional purpose."[3] He calls it the primordial moment of every creative act, and identifies it as characterized by levels of receptiveness to the data of experience. While conceding that open, unstructured awareness is probably not available to human beings, he focuses on the middle level, which he terms "appreciative awareness." "It implies further an open awareness toward the end of knowing the reality out there in its own right."[4] There is a reaching, a readiness to establish an interchange of meaning, a willingness to submit one's own construction of meanings to modification by what comes in from the other. It is reminiscent of, though deeper than, the traditional psychoanalytic "evenly hovering attention."

This is a readiness to be impacted that shows up in almost every theology of revelation, and is understood there as a gift of God. It is closely related to what Tillich describes as "ecstasy," the subjective side of the receipt of revelation.[5] It is a condition of readiness to be grasped by the mystery, a readiness deepened and intensified when the grasping itself occurs. The therapist's presence in the hour, in a state open to the new, results from the combined preparation of community and Spirit, and is indispensable to the hour's transparency to the Holy.

Bion on Intimacy with O

Bion, uniquely among psychoanalysts, identifies this readiness as directly linked to therapists' openness to contact with, even intimacy with, the Other. He writes of "O," "that which is the ultimate reality represented by terms such as ultimate reality, absolute truth, the godhead, the infinite, the thing-in-itself."[6] He says that O "can be become, but it cannot be known." Analysis itself, in Bion's understanding, is an attempt to relate to O through the link that he defines as K, a particular form of open awareness or knowing. O "is darkness and formlessness but it enters the domain K when it has evolved to a point where it can be known, through knowledge gained by experience . . ."[7] In another passage, he describes O as "The absolute truth in and of any object; it is assumed that this cannot be known by any human being; it can be known about, its presence can be recognized and felt, but it cannot be known. It is possible to be at one with it."[8] He contends that the religious mystics have probably come closest to describing how it is experienced.

In a particularly insightful passage that captures the prayerlike quality of a realized pastoral psychotherapy, he writes that "the analyst must focus his attention on O, the unknown and unknowable. The success of psychoanalysis depends on the maintenance of a psychoanalytic point of view; the point of view is the psychoanalytic vertex, the psychoanalytic vertex is O. With this the analyst cannot be identified: he must be it."[9]

He contends that every object, including the human person, is an evolution of O, and when it encounters the K capacity of the relational partner, especially the analyst, those evolutions of O are known in a uniquely complete way. Analysis is one of the many processes by which O evolves in the world. Each effective interpretation is an event in the evolution of O, by which O evolves into K, and knowledge about how O expresses itself in and through a particular person is increased.

Bion describes the state of mind that enables the apprehension of O, the K of O, as faith: "faith that there is an ultimate reality and truth—the unknown, unknowable, 'formless infinite.' "[10] Good analytic practice, per Bion, consists of a succession of acts of faith, of the lived confidence that the Real will present itself in and through the client's material if the analyst does not obstruct the evolution and transmission. Hence, the analyst's preparation consists of an experiential deepening of this faith, much as the mystic learns to trust the self-disclosures of God.

My contention, following Bion, is that the space is hallowed by the therapist's quiet readiness to receive, and help the client experience, God's self-disclosure in each moment of the process. It is a state of expectation, of undemanding readiness, of unquestioned certainty that what the client does and says expresses a truth central to but extending beyond the client, from which both parties present can learn all that needs to be known. This expectation increases the likelihood that God will reach into the present to intensify the divine effect on—and in—the world.

The Therapist's Preparation

The therapist's hallowing requires preparation, as does any encounter with the sacred. Pastoral psychotherapists have known of that preparation largely in academic and psychological terms, and have named it as the need for degrees and for one's own personal therapy. The latter has been justified in terms of client protection, as in AAPC's Fellow standard: "give evidence of having undergone sufficient theological and psychotherapeutic investigation of one's own intrapsychic and interpersonal processes so that one is able to protect the counselee from the pastoral counselor's problems and to deploy oneself to the maximum benefit of the counselee."[11] But I see the pastoral counselor's own therapy, and the analyst's training analysis, as more importantly a move into the sacred space for one who needs its healing and, in fact, receives it. The criterion for adequacy is not primarily whether one's neurosis is resolved, or one's symptoms have diminished to a specifiable extent, but whether one has redemptively experienced God's saving power in psychotherapy. If that has happened, the mental health benefits will be visible and client protection enhanced, and the therapist will have moved toward the faith required of a dependable vessel for the grace of God.

We must now address the preparation that enables the therapist to meet Bion's central demand that the analyst forego memory and desire during the therapy hour. He specifically advocates exercises in "discarding memory and desire" as "preparatory to a state of mind in which O can evolve,"[12] reminding the reader of the preparatory exercises in any training in mysticism. There is a period of asceticism or self-mortification, the deliberate foregoing of available satisfactions. It has the function of proving to the candidate both that he or she can do without them, but more importantly that being without them opens the way to other, greater satisfactions. Depending on the mystical system, the preparation may involve deprivation of sex, sleep, food, personal though nonsexual intimacy, approval, and admiration. It often requires concentration on particular moral behavior (analogous to our demand that people read the code of ethics) and concentration on passages of scripture or theological dogma. But the goal is always the same: bringing the candidate to the point where faith is possible, where the gratification longed for and achieved is the emergence of O, the manifestation of God, rather than any relational or material substitute.

This is analogous to psychoanalysis's historic demand for abstinence by both therapist and client. The demand is not for the sake of morality in the conventional sense, though it has good effect at that level. It is primarily a prohibition against idolatry, a behavioral recognition that this relationship is a quest for the vision of God. Any pursuit of or settling for lesser, more tangible goods would represent failure, accepting less, and less lively, satisfaction than we had set out to get. Faithful practice requires the discipline of bypassing the possible sexual, financial, or egoistic rewards beyond the contract, in the faith that the joy of participating in the evolution of O is far richer than these, and that pursuit or acceptance of these lesser gifts hopelessly compromises the search for the greater good.

Supervision and training, then, are ultimately spiritual formation. Through the candidate's own therapy, through reading and interaction in the classroom, the therapy done and the supervision received, the candidate is being ushered into the experience of the Holy as it manifests itself in the experience among these persons. As in the training analysis or other personal therapeutic experience, there are also more mundane objectives that must be reached. There is one's own pathology to be brought under control (for every therapist), theories to be grasped, protocols for managing predictable crises to be integrated, and dozens of rules of thumb and their exceptions to be learned so thoroughly that they need not be thought about. But all of that is to bring the student to the humbling exhilaration of sensing that one is part of the realization of the will of God in a particular human setting. Once the student has experienced God being born to him or her through the exchange with a therapist, supervisor, teacher, client, or colleague, the possibility that the student too can be that vessel is an adequate lure for continuing faithfulness and, potentially, a lifetime of stewardship of self for the sake of the clients God loves. The continued hope of repeated intimate encounters with the Divine establishes itself as the primary motivation for professional excellence.

The heart of the therapist's hallowing of the space is the approach to the therapeutic moment with neither memory nor desire. Quoting Bion: "The first point is for the analyst to impose on himself a positive discipline of eschewing memory and desire. I do not mean that 'forgetting' is enough: what is required is a positive act of refraining from memory and desire."[13] This is necessary because memory and desire block attention to the emerging experience in the present. If K of O is the aim, and it can never be possessed but only reexperienced to varying imperfect degrees, the therapist who approaches the hour focused on what he or she wants from or for the client, or what he or she remembers from the previous hour, is already partly filled up with and preprogrammed by data that is imprecise and outdated. "The more successful the memory is in its accumulations, the more nearly it resembles a saturated element saturated with saturated elements. An analyst with such a mind is one who is incapable of learning because he is satisfied."[14]

As with any mental, and particularly any mystical, discipline, practice strengthens some habits and weakens others. So preoccupation with what is remembered or what is wanted, in or out of the session, increases the capacity and predilection toward memories and desires, and weakens the capacity for faith that the next clinical moment will provide the needed illumination. "If the mind is preoccupied with elements perceptible to sense it will be that much less able to perceive elements that cannot be sensed."[15] Further, if the therapist wants some specific content from the client, whether it be dreams, or admiration, or affect, the client will feel the wanting and feel possessed by the therapist's desire. That in turn inhibits the client's attention to O within self, which obstructs God's access to the space.

Freud wrote at one point of blinding himself artificially to some realities in order to heighten his sensitivity to others, which otherwise would be particularly obscure. If all else is darkened, that which is trying to emerge has a better chance of being noticed.

For our purposes, the hallowing of the space requires readiness to be alive to what appears in the space, which requires the choice to not bring in avoidable elements of our own past or future experience that block awareness. That accomplished, if our exchange with the client evokes a piece of memory or desire, we can explore that, silently or through conversation, knowing that it is emerging through and elicited by the client. It is not an attempt to make ourselves comfortable through relying on a "known" fact from yesterday or a gratification desired for tomorrow. In that lively present, the client's reality as a piece of God's revelation declares itself to us and to the client. It requires our relishing the experience of not yet knowing, attention to the chance thought as disclosure of the new, maintaining the unsaturated status of our preconceptions so they may be realized anew in this hour.

Another important piece of preparation to forego memory and desire, and thereby to hallow the therapeutic space, is to permit the natural cycles of rest and dreaming. God comes to us from beyond conscious deliberations, offering data for us to use but never pausing long enough to be captured, photographed, or diagrammed. Hence consciousness is never an adequate container for God, and access to unconscious experience is crucial if our lives are to faithfully support our vocations.

Ashbrook encourages "sabbathing" as the core of soul making. He describes sabbathing as "the integrating and transforming activity of stories and soul, of meaningful memory and each person's own unique identity in the service of community."[16] He joins the products of brain study, psychotherapy, and theology, seeing the reorganization of the mind in dreaming as critical to the elaboration of a lasting, satisfying personal narrative. Sabbathing is an integrating activity, a "means God uses to connect heaven and earth." It is a suspension of conscious activity to allow the unconscious to do its work. It consists, in our daily cycle, of a period of nondreaming sleep when brain information transfer is blocked, followed by a REM (Rapid Eye Movement), dreaming cycle in which information is rearranged. Blood flow to the brain increases in REM sleep, while new information is excluded, and muscle output is blocked. In Ashbrook's description, dreams "take stimuli with low-recognition value and turn them into high-information narratives."[17] Waking and sleeping, we go through unending ninety-minute cycles of holding on and letting go, of intense focus on external data and reflective reorganization of self.

Forming and Reforming the Therapist's Self

Bollas describes the same process as a constant reformulation of the self in the condensed experience of the dream, then a scattering of the fragments of the rearranged self through the next day's experience, as though to test the newly formed constellation in a range of settings, returning the next night for another opportunity to realign the structures.[18] We are always trying to perfect the form we sense as truly our own. We are always about it, day and night. God is our partner in that play, an uncontrollable source of hints for the direction of our dream, of the pattern for yet another rearrangement.

When this process is allowed to do its work, when we as therapists allow space for dreaming and for dialogue with our dreams, we are readier to respond to the environment—and the Other—on its own terms, free of the need to force it into our image. The dreamwork has relieved us of that urge. We can then play with it, as God plays with us, tasting it for both its own raw deliciousness and for how it does and does not satisfy our desires. The play does not push us to greedily consume the world to stop the appetite's tormenting us, as would be true if the appetite were out of our vision, but allows us to watch it shape itself in relation to the selves that we are, as one would watch two dancers in a ballet move in relation to each other. But when that rhythm of holding on and letting go is disrupted, when the space for our waking and sleeping dreams is filled (with compulsive productivity, with physical pain, with overfocused desire), there is a perpetual backlog of unfiled experience, of untested self-reconstructions. In that state we are overwhelmed by temptation to make the other only the foil in our self-creation, as the medium for our attempt to ascertain the truth of our lives. Clients may perform that role well, but our placing them in it blocks their chance of gaining what they entered the therapy to get. They will nonetheless try, just as the child always attempts to heal the parent. If the therapy is working, each party will have a sense that the other is helping work out a piece of his or her own healing. But when the therapist has other personal arenas for reflective encounter with self, the client's hour can be shaped by the client's encounter with God and self, with therapist growth being a byproduct rather than our central and compulsive preoccupation.

This back-and-forth exchange between therapist and God, therapist and client, God and client, is participation in what Rita Nakashima Brock calls "erotic power" and Larry Graham terms "bi-polar power." Both stem from Bernard Loomer's identification of "relational power," the capacity to sustain an internal relationship with and in the other.[19] Graham elaborates Loomer's concept into that of a systemically connected universe in which all entities must have the power to shape their own environments in order to endure; and also have the ability to be influenced by their environments "in order to be enriched by the fullest set of possibilities for their own growth and becoming."[20] Exchanges of influence are necessary for any system to remain sufficiently informed about its environment to survive, and to keep its neighbors informed enough about itself to cooperate. Brock, like Graham, relies on the process tradition and sees this "power of our primal interrelatedness" as a "fundamentally ultimate reality of human existence."[21] It is the antithesis of power as dominance, instead regarding power as the capacity to engage relationships, both to affect and be affected. The stronger the flow of influence in both directions, the more the individual or system functions as a fertile meeting place for life.

For the therapist, a commitment to this playful, mutual power, this power God lends us to perpetuate the other's influence in us and ours in the other, is indispensable. It is the sensitivity Meland tells us is the only guarantor of ongoing life for the planet and every individual. It allows us to sense the shape of life in the other, and to let our own be shaped, for the moment, by the other. It allows God's relationality to be effective in the sacred space of therapy.

This process produces what Bion calls a sharpening of the sense of O as one moves toward union with O. As one knows the other as other, not containable by any concept or image of God or person, as constantly escaping the details of every prediction, the experience constantly heightens our awareness of complicity in the world's pain and the pain of this particular other, along with our participation in its, and their, achievements and joy. This is the cost and reward of actual contact with live objects. It is always uncertain, always carries risk, always requires a recasting of the knowing of self and the certainty that our view of the human and divine other will be proven wrong over and over again. The willingness to embrace intimate contact with such intense ambiguity is central to hallowing the therapy space for God, and thus is totally necessary for redemptive pastoral psychotherapy.

THE CLIENT HALLOWS THE SPACE

The third agent in the hallowing of the space is the client. This other (like ourselves) always approaches the sacred space ambivalently, hoping against hope that his or her pain can be removed by some simple mechanical, behavioral, or pharmaceutical manipulation that neither requires nor offers personal transformation; but also always craving a reshaping of the self that allows richer, more intense, more impactful experience, while doubting its possibility. None of us ever pursues this quest purely, nor is any of us faithful to it, even imperfectly, in every moment; but to the extent we pursue it, we are open to God's presence in the therapeutic hour.

Of the three—community, therapist, and client—the client is the one whose participation the therapist can least predict. We cannot compel the client's openness to saving change any more than we can effectively will ourselves to be free of sin. But there are important aspects to the client's hallowing of the space that we can identify here and cultivate in practice. They include (1) the client's identifying pain as a sign that fuller redemption is both possible and needed; (2) the client's seeking us out, a response to the community's identification of psychotherapy and us as vessels for God; (3) the client's response to our locating an option for greater growth and offering routes into it; and (4) the client's joyful embrace of a piece or pieces of achieved growth as a gift from God, who wills to give without end.

The client's hallowing of the space begins with his or her ascribing a particular meaning to pain. We all hurt in some way every day. Insofar as we notice the pain—which is a part of giving it meaning—we categorize it. Some we identify as fated and immutable, just a part of getting old or being young or having the body we have or living in the part of the world we are in. Other pain we identify as requiring a speedy, almost automatic, physical response: we need to walk around the block, eat something, or take an aspirin. Yet other pain requires a prompt and available relational solution: I need to stop working for a while and talk to my wife; you need to call those friends you have meant to invite for dinner before the gulf between you expands; she will feel better if she breaks off that relationship. Yet there are pains for which no obvious remedy is available, but nonetheless cry out to be removed. We sense there is something in the way we are living, the way we have organized our minds and our relationships, that generates this particular pain. Our community has taught us that this particular feeling means something more, represents an invitation or even a demand, perhaps from God, to change something basic about ourselves. It is a call for repentance, though we do not immediately identify it as such. It is a challenge to the way we presently live and a sign of hope that living differently is possible. Our linking this meaning to the pain begins our search, at first unconscious, for a sacred, healing space.

Different communities identify different spaces as the appropriate refuge for one so pained. Much of the Western world has come to see an intimate connection between the sacred, how we experience and think about ourselves, and how we are related to other people. We see God as reflected in and influencing how we organize our minds and how we structure our relationships. We see those variables as influencing how others experience us. When we have pain in those areas, we often see ourselves as needing greater harmony with God or whatever we see as sacred. The community has evolved this structure of beliefs as an option we can consider when we are in pain, and we can accept or reject it. If a person accepts it, seeking a pastoral psychotherapist is one of the options. (Often people who reject it also find themselves in our offices, either because they did not realize their own rejection or they did not know who we were.) Their quest, explicit or implicit, leads them to someone who offers our name. The giving of the name, with whatever description goes with it, is part of the community's hallowing of the space. The client's accepting it and making the connection is his or her contribution, all in response to the structuring and enabling grace of God.

Clients' next steps in hallowing the space are part of therapy itself, and will be considered in the next chapter. At this beginning point it is a function of any therapy to identify, in and with clients, in bite-sized doses, the points at which they must choose between the quick mechanical reduction of pain and the risks and hopes of exploring it and themselves more deeply. If clients choose to avoid engaging the pain, to demand its removal from their consciousness, the space itself will be small and God's access to it quite limited. Of course, most clients committed to that stance will not choose us in the first place, except by error, but there is some of it in every client and in every one of us. Our task is to help clients notice the choice—typically they have built a way of life around not noticing—in a way that lets them sense the balance of risk and safety in the leap they are considering. If they were not considering it at all, they would not be present. As they move away from the safety of defense and avoidance, they further the hallowing of the space.

There comes a point in the therapy where the hallowing is as much theirs as ours. This is the middle phase, the fullness of time, the immersion in ongoing revelation. They have felt the spark of joy in their play with God in the beginning phase, and have come to trust that if they move into the place of fear again and again, they will be met by One (and one) who will not abandon them, who will offer new meanings and new possibilities, who will offer energy for linking these discoveries with the self and communities they have always known. At this point the therapy is a celebration of hope, though not of ease. Horror after horror, failure after failure, sin after sin, are brought forward in the never-quite-complete certainty that new strength, hope, and joy will be found if one stays present to the pain until its deeper truth reveals itself.

By this point therapist and client are partners in faith (though the object of faith may never be named and will never be totally understood), and it is a partnership and a faith journey that is, in principle, unending. It continues in the newly hallowed space that grows within the client long after the therapist is not needed to sustain the play. This playful journey moves to the center of our focus in the remaining chapters.

Chapter 7

Sacred Play in Hallowed Spaces

We have described the sacred spaces where pastoral psychotherapy takes place. We have identified the means by which God is invited into those spaces. We now explore what happens there in terms of God's role and stake in the process.

There are holy moments in psychotherapy, times when the discipline and work of study and restraint flow into divine play where truth is encountered, elicited, and enjoyed. In those moments, participants open sight lines beyond the barriers, cognitive fields are reorganized, new actions become possible, and new worlds come into being. In those ecstatic bursts of energy, the beauty of human souls is intensified and the joy of God expands. How does it happen? What are the decisive events? How is God's grace manifest and in which actions is it incarnate? We now turn our attention to these questions.

CONNECTION, THE CONTAINER, AND REVERIE

Ashbrook has described the rhythm of pastoral psychotherapy as involving connection, response, sabbath, exploration, and action. The opening stage of therapy is the effort to produce dependable and effective saving connection. Ashbrook names the therapist's critical contributions as presence, invitation, and immediacy. The client comes warily, hoping against hope that the therapist will see through the disguise that has been the key to the client's survival. The subterfuge is itself a valued artful creation, the best the client could craft out of the resources God and the world have made available. But, like any human creation, it also blocks the growth of intimacy with God and others as it simultaneously helps the client be safe. It is the self the client knows how to be, and none of us is lured out of it without fear.

Clients' choice to move ahead despite the terror requires them to believe several things. They must believe that the cost of their present way of being is no longer worth paying. They must have faith that there is something of self that will endure even if this form is lost, and a hope that grows out of their perception of the therapist's ability to nourish and protect. God has acted through the community and cosmos to inflict the cost (judgment leading to repentance), to be the gift needed to generate the faith (trust in the goodness of creation), and acts both through the community and directly on/in clients and therapists to enable the hope. Those therapists must be seen as both safe and powerful: safe so clients know their vulnerability will not be exploited; powerful so the reward for disclosure is quickly apparent (though not often quickly harvested). God cannot yet be known to be, but must be hoped to be, both loving and effective.

Winnicott's concept of the good enough container can help us understand the therapist's contribution. That containment was first provided by the womb, well-sustained by blood and breath and insulated from environmental shocks by the mother's body. Then it was extended by "primary maternal preoccupation," the temporary but intense focus on the newborn that lets the mother be so aware of subtle shifts in the baby's body, psyche, or spirit that she can provide an environment that rarely impinges, allowing continuity to the infant's fragile experience. That in turn is only possible if the community—mainly the spouse or other intimate partner—supports the caregiver with material and emotional supplies that make it unnecessary for the primary parent to fend for herself. This provision communicates in word and act that she nurtures on behalf of the community. The container evolves, with more players taking a role in establishing its boundaries and its culture, as the child's developmental levels expand. The broader the container, and the wider the systems that constitute it—extended family, church, ethnic group, nation, God—the more secure its holding and the safer its guest of honor.

It is the rupture of that container, from outside or in, that limits growth and sows the eventual need for therapy. It is the rupture from outside (that has become internal through creation of internal objects) that creates clients' fear upon entering therapy. People have made promises of help before, so the quality of the container will be carefully examined before clients give themselves over to it.

The decisive factor in its passing the test will be the quality of the therapist's reverie. Reverie is the object-relations word that includes and transcends Freud's original concept of evenly hovering attention. It is the state the therapist creates within the sacred space, rooted in the faith that truth will appear. It is an actively receptive state, but not an insistent one. For Bion, it is the condition in which the therapist's mind is totally unsaturated, satisfied with nothing in its present knowledge of client and relationship, utterly open to such material as may be offered by contact with the client. If the reverie is sufficiently deep and open, the transmission happens as much through the mysterious link between the two unconscious processes in the room, or the one jointly created therapeutic subject, as by any words that either says to the other. It is specifically not generated by the deductive thought of the therapist, based on careful attention to the notes of the previous session or how the material coming forth fits the theories therapist and client have created together. It is a waiting to receive a gift, but waiting without "the irritable reaching after fact and reason" that would demand that the gift come now and the knowing be completed. A gift from where? From the unconscious, from the other, from God, from any and all of these.

Bion's reverie refers specifically to the mother-infant bond and is described as "the psychological source of supply of the infant's needs for love and understanding."[1] But it extends beyond infancy as "that state of mind which is open to the reception of any 'objects' from the loved object."[2]

Reverie could also be seen as containment, though with a slightly different meaning than Winnicott intended. He used that language in a specifically physical and social sense. The infant was within the mother, the mother within the family, the family within the community. In each case, the spatial arrangement provided physical safety, nurture, resources, and guidance in a context of nonimpingement. The one held, the contained child, experienced the freedom "to be alone in the presence of the other." Bion, to whose meaning we are closer, takes Winnicott's image and shifts it slightly, so that it refers to the contents of a human mind, though not in a narrowly denotative sense. While Bion also uses physical imagery, his concern is primarily with the relationship between a thinker (imaginer, discerner, observer, etc.) and the contents of his or her thought.

THE THINKER AND THE THOUGHT

The relationship between the thinker and the thought is decisive. Bion saw three basic links, three ways of relating, between all containers and all contents: L (love), H (hate), and K (knowing). He also found it relevant to identify their opposites, –L, –H, and –K.

In the condition of H (Hate), for instance (which Bion also termed the parasitic relationship), container and contained seek to destroy one another. The thought seeks to erode and disorganize the mind; the mind seeks to banish, crush, blur, confuse, and strangle the thought. This is the relationship between container and contained, mind and thought, that exists in psychosis, when the mind so hates and fears sequential thought, because of the feeling it carries, that it refuses to think it. A whole pattern of "attacks on linking" develops, showing itself in thought disorder, hallucination, and delusion.

If we return to Ashbrook's discussion of pastoral psychotherapy, we can see how this operates. Suppose a receiver of care seeks to connect with a generic statement, "I'd really like to do something about my anxiety." If the therapist refuses to let the anxiety into her mental space, responding, "You don't seem anxious to me," then she has refused the reality the client has claimed as his own. An "H link" has been created, as the therapist seeks to annihilate the client's experience. Similarly, H links could be created by a judgment on the client's feeling, "you're foolish to be anxious here," and by a wide range of other nonreceptive responses. Conversely, if the therapist is frightened by the client's anxiety, but unconsciously wishes to hide that from self and client, she might seek a –H link by diverting attention both from the anxiety and her response to it. A –H link in this situation could be established by changing the subject, by mishearing, or by asking a question about some detail that takes the client's and therapist's attention away from the anxiety.

L (love, or symbiotic) links are less destructive and more comfortable. Though they do not move directly toward the client's liberation, if created sparingly they may pave the way for later and more redemptive links. With an L link, the container and contained affirm one another's present reality, claiming a positive affection for it. One might see an emphasis on L links as central to supportive therapy, to community affiliations, to the casual moments of friendship and other chosen personal relationships. In Ashbrook's connection phase, an L response to the client's opening gambit about anxiety would be, "I'm glad you've decided to work on that," or "that's a wise decision." A –L link is established when what could honestly be expressed is love or affirmation, but the therapist chooses, usually unconsciously, not to do it. The therapist may sense that inquiry into the client's anxiety will lead to a discussion of sexual feelings toward her, and be afraid of that discussion, so steers the conversation in another direction: "Tell me about your mother," etc.

The same words can create a –H link or a –L link, depending on what underlying feeling is being avoided. The energy in the room will be different, the contained will feel differently held by the container, but the words may be identical.

The central link for pastoral psychotherapy, as for psychoanalysis, is the K link. It refers to knowledge, but specifically not to the possession of information. Bion expresses it as "the state of getting to know the object."[3] K requires the presence of emotion, permeating both container and contained.[4] That is what makes it alive. When the container seeks to reduce the contact to the possession of information, it becomes –K, a mechanical, dead relationship. But as itself it is commensal experience, in that "container and contained are dependent on each other for mutual benefit and prevention of harm to each other."[5] Both mutual benefit and, specifically, psychic growth are the products of K links. Unlike L or H, it requires as its basic medium tolerated doubt. It allows the container to increase flexibility yet remain integrated. It is "the foundation of the state of mind of the individual who can retain his knowledge and experience and yet be prepared to . . . receive a new idea."[6]

If the client opens with the observation about working on his anxiety, and the therapist responds either with a receptive silence or, if something has truly crystallized in her thinking, with a statement such as "you've come to believe that something can be done about it" or "the anxiety has pushed you to change the situation that creates it," then establishment of a K link may be in process. There is neither a warding off of the reality of the client's statement, nor a flat-footed affirmation or repetition of the reality as stated, but an *idea* of anxiety that comes from the therapist's *feeling* of the client's *feeling* of the anxiety. For Bion, this is the only way mental growth occurs in anyone. There is a precognition, an emergent belief that something may be true of a situation, which then "mates" with a realization, a piece of data that supplies the substance that had been, in less specifiable terms, imagined. Though it is not directly sought—that would saturate the precognition and close the mind—there is a perceptible readiness to find it. This process parallels Winnicott's description of the hypothetical "first feed," in which infants imagine that there must be something like a breast somewhere that would satisfy their hunger, and at the moment they begin to look for what has been imagined, the actual breast appears. The interplay both confirms and stabilizes the previous, more open category. It saturates the precognition, satisfying the container and opening the way for a new cycle of need, imagination, discovery, and growth. It is by such microsteps that the mind grows and the self becomes.

THE ENTRY INTO SABBATHING

Returning to Ashbrook, the initial moments of the therapy—both the first session and the beginnings of each subsequent one—are marked by the client's tentative attempt at connection and by the therapist's response. At all the beginnings, the client is assessing the link with the therapist. When it is consistently enough K, the client's trust deepens, relaxation occurs, and we move into what Ashbrook calls "sabbathing."

Sabbathing is a very complex physical-psychic-spiritual experience. Ashbrook relates it both to God's command in Exodus to "remember the sabbath," a demand that is also a gift, and to REM sleep, that nightly experience during which meanings are redistributed, interpreted, and reintegrated. The link between Ashbrook's thinking here and Bollas' description of the function of dreaming is helpful. Our daily experiences are concentrated in the newly compressed symbols of the night's sleep, so we might live them out and explore their meaning the next day. Ashbrook relates this to the psychic and spiritual movement between sessions, and even to the silences within the therapeutic hour.[7] "The soul requires 'sabbathing' to take in new experience and make it part of itself. Change requires breathing space, time, sleep, inattention, incubation, retrospective reflection in order to be bone of our bone and flesh of our flesh."[8]

My assertion here is that the reclamation and integration of being, of both protoplasm and societies, requires a cessation of striving. That cessation shares properties with REM sleep—the process of redistribution and reintegration of meanings that follows the profound rest of the deep sleep phase. It is equivalent to what often happens between sessions of a therapy or during the silence in the midst of the therapy hour, when the removal of an obstacle in the previous moment or hour clears the way for the mind's generation of new meaning. It is what Ashbrook understands to have been intended in the command to "remember the sabbath," to recall, which is also to remember. The sabbath is a prayerful process, in which interaction with the holy transforms by creating space where reintegration can occur. My claim is that God acts in the space created by our observance of sabbaths, and that the sabbath command was given to create space for the reintegrating of selves, community, and God. It claims that God particularly lends energy, removes obstacles, and is more accessible in those times when our focus on doing and achieving is suspended. It echoes the traditional claim that worship, prayer, meditation, and stillness are created by God and actively used by God to re-form us, calling us into community, making a saving truth available. It is an event in what Winnicott called "potential space," that territory marked by the moment of hesitation in which the infant—and all of us—take the resources of the outside world and make them our own.

Another aspect of this sacred process is evident in Bion's (at least vaguely Kantian) incredibly useful distinction between two elements of the process of knowing. He identifies raw sensations, uncategorized signals of external and internal reality, as beta elements. They have collided with our perceptive surfaces, but are not yet classified, named, or even truly experienced. In that form, they are suitable only for evacuation, for being got rid of as sources of nameless discomfort. They cannot be thought about, dreamed, or remembered (because they have not yet been made members). But they can be transformed into alpha elements by the process Bion terms alpha function, which is most noticeable through its absence in psychotic process and other primitive forms of thought.

Alpha function for each of us is first enabled by mother's reverie, which attends so openly to our infant experience that the chaotic and disorganizing flow of beta elements is welcomed in her psychic space. At first she does not know it is happening, and even after she knows, it does not disclose its full meaning to her. She is aware of it incrementally, perhaps first through a shift in physical sensation, as the baby's emotion impacts her. Even before she has given the impact a name, she has begun to feel differently, to shape her containment in a way that helps the baby—if her reverie is deep enough—to tolerate and survive the distress. The baby notes the shift in her, still before it is named, and attributes a meaning to the changed emotional gestalt between them. Soon enough, she identifies the constellation of the change in appearance, sound, and feel of the baby, plus the shift in her own emotional experience that accompanies those changes, as a repetitive pattern with constant conjunction. She gives it a name— "sleepy," or "hungry," or "angry," or "frightened," and so on. She begins talking to the baby in those terms: "You're sleepy," "You're frightened," accompanied by the unique tones of voice and body she attaches to that image. Her reverie has enabled her to take in the beta elements, undigested sensations, and make a gestalt of them; the baby's projective identifications, unusable for symbolization, memory, or reflection in his or her mind (because so disorganizingly, unintelligibly intense), are given a title, responded to in a consistent way, and formed into a vehicle for a quality of interaction that calms the baby's fear or enables him or her to rest. In this instance, the mother's alpha function has produced alpha elements that are returned to the baby and become available for the building up of the baby's mind. When that process has been repeated dozens of times, so that mental space is building up inside the baby, he or she individually begins to perform alpha functions, at first on a limited scale.

Bion described alpha function as operating on the raw material, "beta elements," largely sense impressions and emotions not yet experienced as phenomena, but as "things-in-themselves."[9] They cannot be dreamed, or thought, or remembered, though they are stored in the muscles and emotions as raw data. When alpha function operates on them, they are digested and can become dream thoughts, or symbols; they can be made conscious or unconscious and become usable to the mind. (One of the things that apparently occurs in trauma is that alpha function is suspended, so the overpowering events that happen to the person do not acquire the alpha-element handles that enable them to be processed, but persist in a state that can only be evacuated or re-enacted.) If alpha function is absent, sensory impacts are not translated into meaning-laden symbolic structures. Hence we cannot dream. Since the dream functions to protect sleep, without alpha function we cannot sleep. After a time, we are able to be neither effectively asleep nor awake. Sabbathing is prevented, and with it the meaning-full psychic digestion that lets the mind be different from day to day. A psychic rigidity, the hallmark of pathology, ensues. The individual functions like an automaton, not quite alive and not able to adjust to the constant flow of changes in the world.

The therapist's function with the client is identical to the cognitive-affective part of the mother's function with the infant. The therapist offers reverie to the client, waiting to receive whatever emanates from the client, as free as possible from memory and desire. Those parts of the client's psychic space that are most rigidified, least alive, those where the client keeps himself or herself from knowing present reality, will eventually call the therapist's attention to themselves. They produce the most pain when encountered, being the places where the client's ignorance has been placed in command. They will be the areas where the client's function is most impaired, since images of experience will be unformed, not available for the cognitive work of being dreamed or felt, thought or imagined. Feeling will instead be acted out, externalized, evacuated, especially into the space that client and therapist share. When the therapist encounters this experience, the tenor of the work changes dramatically.

THE FERTILE MIDDLE PHASE

In the middle phase of therapy, therapist experience typically alternates between the sense that the client is "doing the work," that nothing much is required of the therapist but to track the process and take in data for further use, and the feeling that something is "off the track," that the client's productions are not governed by K links, that a flood of beta elements is infiltrating the shared mental space. Those latter times are marked by therapist unease, a sign that the therapist is hosting an array of projective identifications, beta elements, along with whatever positive work is going on. These will be times when the client invades the therapist's sleep, disturbing it or producing dreams that refer to the client. At those points, the psychic space of the therapy hour is not containing the shared mental field.

The most crucial work of therapy, in this situation and more ordinary ones, is analogous to mothering. The therapist must take in the diffuse excitement, let it find words, symbols, a containing response, and give that back to the client in a way that names the experience the client had not yet been able to name, or perhaps even to notice. The therapist's alpha function works on the client's behalf, building up a new layer of psychic structure (an idea) for the client. From the relative security of that new cognitive structure, the client can afford to be curious about the feelings, rather than simply to externalize them.

The therapist's ability to do this depends on his or her capacity for reverie, for K links and alpha function. To put it another way, therapy is done in an intrinsically meditative state, the client functioning as the object of contemplation. As Bollas describes it, "we often disappear from the world of thought itself; into what Bion refers to as 'O,' a state of meditation, in which we seem to have no particular thoughts. These moments of inner stillness are continuous intermissions in the otherwise mentally productive world of inner experience."[10] Bollas maintains that such moments are incredibly productive, because the unconscious of the client speaks most powerfully and discernibly to the unconscious of the therapist during them, even though no new thoughts are being stated. During such sabbaths for the therapist, the Reality that wills to break through has the greatest access, and the therapist becomes more a part of O, of God, a vessel for redemptive energy in the space he or she shares with the client.

In that space a shared psychic experience is generated, enabling transmission, reintegration, and memory. As Ogden has written,

> We ask of ourselves that we be unconsciously available to be subjects in the unconscious experiment of the other. We as analysts attempt to render ourselves unconsciously receptive to being made use of in playing a variety of roles in the unconscious life of the analysand. This unconscious receptivity involves (a partial) giving over of one's separate individuality to a third subject, a subject that is neither analyst nor analysand but a third subjectivity unconsciously generated by the analytic pair.[11]

What happens here is that parts of the self of both client and therapist flow into one another, through the medium of the sacred space, and both are changed in the process. Elements beyond the analytic couple are also present. Each of the players is constituted by communities and histories that extend beyond the walls of the consulting room or the boundaries of this century. Both consciously and unconsciously, clients carry internal, constitutive visions, attitudes, memories, and stories of their parents, their teachers, their previous therapists and clients, and all the sources of humanness that have been available to them. This is an encounter with the communion of saints, pulled together in a sacred time and location by the reverie of the therapist and the grace of God.

The therapist acts as a mediating presence, whose ability and willingness to endure the client's pain and longing allows the client to do so as well, and in the process to appropriate that experience for psychic and spiritual growth. Joan and Neville Symington tell a story that illustrates this. The client was a thirty-three-year-old mentally handicapped man, who asked his analyst to give him a verbal picture of who he (the patient) was. The analyst refused. The patient then asked why it might be useful for him to continue. The analyst's answer was to move across the room, stand beside the patient, and say, "It is like this. There in front of us is thirty-three years of waste, nothing, and emptiness. It is like sitting on a train and opposite sits a man with a wounded and diseased face and it is so horrific that you have to hold pictures up in front of you because it is more than you can bear. But the reason you come to see me is that there is just a possibility that if you have me beside you then you can look at it."[12] The clinical experience of many individuals, by no means all of them analysts, confirms that people will allow themselves to remember, think about, and endure realities about themselves in our presence that they are unable or unwilling to experience alone.

The therapist functions like Whitehead's vision of the consequent nature of God, by which the events of our lives are taken into the divine reality and preserved forever as part of the ongoing store of meaning and energy for all other beings. It is a sacred function, achieved only by virtue of the therapist's immersion in reverence for the sacred within the other, accepting into the therapists's own self the reality of another individual and holding it there for recovery, if and as the Spirit calls for it. The client is often terrified to allow different pieces of memory to come into consciousness or into contact with each other. As the therapist is enabled and allowed to take in and integrate the isolated pieces, to preserve them as a unity in his or her own conscious and unconscious minds, the therapist both sits in the place of God with the client, and transmits the essence of the client through his or her own symbolization into the broader community of saints and the very life of God.

TO EXPLORATION AND ACTION

Once sabbathing has done this sacred work, Ashbrook asserts that therapy moves first to exploration, and from there to action.[13] While meanings are being shifted and new structures are coming into being, those structures become the basis for new perceptions of and behavior toward the world. The therapy relationship shifts incrementally from passive-receptive to active-exploratory. Ashbrook likens it to a discovery of one's own reality, a discovery that leaves the client profoundly curious about what the world looks like in his or her own new terms. The crucial therapist activity at this point is the respect offered the client's new sense of reality and the support offered—through Presence—to move on the basis of the newly owned initiative into reclaiming and redefining the environment. This is Abram's call from Ur, the Exodus from Egypt, the crossing into Canaan, the coming into one's own—often experienced as following "a pillar of cloud by day and a pillar of fire by night." The sabbathing has produced a call to follow, but the leading seems to come not from a demanding external source, but from a liberating, empowering inner voice carrying its own sense of validation. People often refer to it in language similar to that which they use to describe an unspoken yet clearly experienced answer to prayer. It is a claiming and owning of the right to assign meaning to experience and to act on that meaning.[14]

After ten years of work, a borderline man reported, in deep distress, that he did not know himself. His family had defined him for over forty years in terms of a handicap that had just been surgically corrected. The family's definition had been experienced as disabling, compelling the apparent acceptance of a self-identity as profoundly defective if he was to maintain membership. Over a period of weeks, he realized that not only was that self-portrait false, but that it obscured the healthy self-exploration and discovery that might otherwise have been going on. Now well into middle age, he struggles with the possibility of self-definition, of looking at the world on terms that are his, once he ascertains what they are. He also, of course, is tempted to avoid the pain and uncertainty of that task and resign himself to resentment and blame. He fears the depth of the sadness, the possibility that it may be greater than his capacity for hope, but also senses an ambivalent safety in the presence of the therapist (ambivalent because he senses both safety in the companionship and terror that the felt safety might tempt him to move ahead into the unknown) and longing to know what lies beyond his personal lake of tears.

He is experiencing what Whitehead terms the lure of God, the fledgling awareness that the possibilities opening out from this moment could create new beauty, new hope, new community. Ashbrook reminds us that unlike some earlier points in therapy, this is not a time when the therapist can define the reality. The task, as he puts it, is "to connect with and respond to another's essence," requiring us "to put one's own self—one's heart and soul and mind and strength—at the service of the other's own self—her or his unique heart and mind and soul and strength. Instead of telling the other what reality is for them or what they 'should' do, our call is to risk being open to their perception of what is and what might be."[15] Our reverent presence can lend the safety that undergirds the courage required for movement, while at the same time adding to the risk of real external conflict. Response to the lure of God is enabled by the safety in the sacred space, and leads one to excitedly risk moving into new and more promising dangers.

Ashbrook observes that we come finally to action. The client embarks on the great adventure, the attempt to create new beauty on the basis of the options the Lure has disclosed, in making the exploration. This transition takes the client from the discovery of a newly meaning-rich cosmos back into the life of the world with focus and intention. It is an experience of communion, coherence, and engagement with a new world, known by direct experience for the first time. "Behold! I make all things new."

The product is action bringing the individual into engagement with the broader community. All this verbal and spiritual exchange is aimed at enabling life in and on behalf of the world. Bion makes a decisive distinction between language that prepares for achievement and language that substitutes for achievement, and names the meeting of analyst and analysand in the sacred space as language that is "both a prelude to action and a kind of action."[16] This language is a particular kind of action, aimed to "effect the transition from knowing about O to becoming O."[17] O, which cannot be known but can be become, is variously termed "ultimate reality," "the Godhead," and "truth" by

Bion. His meaning is clear, if difficult. As the individual is emboldened by being known, led into the sanctity of reverie and alpha function, made ready to notice the lure of God and possibility of communion, he or she is led by Knowing to act in concert with the therapist in joint participation in the life of God for the ongoing transformation of the world.

Creating new beauty through the work of the Holy Spirit

Chapter 8

Transference, Intersubjectivity, and the Holy Spirit

The essence of therapeutic work and all ministry focuses on and is enacted through relationship. The reality and fantasy of psychoanalytic and other therapies are identifiable by the relational structures created. Empirical studies have repeatedly identified relationship quality as the crucial variable in client improvement and satisfaction. The deeper one gets into psychoanalytic study, the more focus is placed on the handling of transference and countertransference, the interacting constellation of fantasies that provide the texture of the therapy relationship.

Few aspects of psychotherapeutic thought have changed as often or as decisively. Freud originally thought of positive transference (when the client experiences positive feelings [once felt with a loved parent] toward the therapist) as therapeutic leverage. "If the client likes you, he's more likely to do what you suggest." Many nonanalytic therapists continue to work on that basis. Soon Freud recognized that transference could function as resistance, noting that the blurring of realistic feelings about the therapist prevented a clear focus on the patient's problem. Next came recognition that the shape of the distortion was itself an expression of the problems and a pointer toward them. From that grew the classic psychoanalytic doctrine that the transference neurosis, the psychic configuration forged from the interplay between these archaic feelings and the therapist, provided the decisive arena for analytic work. Freud's mature technique, with its focus on anonymity, abstinence, free association, etc., was designed to remove the barriers to and contaminants of the transference unique to each particular client.

As attention to the management and interpretation of transference grew, the recognition emerged that the analyst has a feeling response to the client and the client's feelings. This was named counter-transference, and analysts (with therapists of all persuasions) were implored to continue their training analyses until all vestiges of this frailty were eliminated. Debates developed over the proper definition of the condition, whether countertransference included the feelings generated by the analyst's own character that found their way into the therapy hour, or if the term should be limited to responses directly elicited by the patient's transference. Whatever it was, it was to be minimized, so the therapist's rational capacities could control his or her response to the patient. Only then could the patient be protected from exploitation or misperception stemming from the therapist's own problems.

COUNTERTRANSFERENCE AS AN ASSET

The beginnings of respect for countertransference marked the split between object relations theory and ego psychology, the previous American and British psychoanalytic orthodoxy.[1] Beginning with Melanie Klein's awareness of projective identification and its effect on the therapist, Winnicott's paper "Hate in the Countertransference," and Bion's recognition that Freud blinded himself to some facts about the patient to create space to receive unconscious communications, these leaders worked to heighten the trust in the well-analyzed therapist's use of feeling responses as a therapeutic tool.[2] These shifts contributed to growing distrust among "orthodox Freudians" toward these less rationalistic, more relationally immersed analysts. Separate groups developed, the British middle or independent school, self psychology in the United States, intersubjective psychoanalysis in both countries, and institutions such as the Tavistock clinic in London (the mother church of the object relations movement).

Soon it was clear that transference elicited countertransference, which changed the transference, which influenced the countertransference, and so on. The two structures could not be definitively separated, nor could either remain constant in the presence of the other. The reality of the *intersubjective field* had been identified, the unique structure generated between and within the unconscious minds of people intimately connected in a psychotherapy (or other) relationship. Though we have hinted at its presence and action in the previous two chapters, it remains for this chapter to spell out how it happens and what it means from a psychoanalytic and theological perspective.

Within therapeutic circles, the new intersubjective awareness had united therapist and client on the same plane. It altered the previous perception that the analyst was a detached scientific observer scrutinizing and impacting a relatively inert client. It challenged the belief that the transference was an utterly individual creation of the analysand that would unfold in precisely the same way with any competent analyst. It made the analyst's personality and the contents of his or her unconscious part of the treatment equation, and made it clear that the analyst was impacted and changed by the client—and that the analyst's very capacity to be so impacted and changed was indispensable to the healing power of the therapy. It produced a more real, balanced, and mutual relationship between the parties in the analytic hour.

During the same decades, similar observations stimulated other therapeutic movements. Family therapy's challenge to psychoanalysis relied on the discovery that each of us is slightly different when we are with different people, and that when we are in the presence of family, its relational web calls out and reinforces its particular version of our person and possibilities. Unfortunately, family therapy has remained largely ignorant of contemporary psychoanalysis, so its critique applies more to ego psychology, which object relations theory and self psychology are also defining themselves against, than to current analytic work. Current psychoanalysis emphasizes the constant interplay between the intrapsychic fields of therapist and client, husband and wife, parents and children, and the mutual influence of the participants' real relational behavior, their conscious and unconscious fantasies, and the communication between these actors. Family therapy and psychoanalysis have grown toward one another, though many in both camps have not noticed.

THE CLASSIC DOCTRINE OF THE HOLY SPIRIT

When we enter the theological circle, we find the development of similar perspectives. Classically, when theologians have encountered healing relationships and communities, especially when those situations involved subtle reciprocal influences of dramatic redemptive power, they have seen evidence of the Holy Spirit. The Spirit has been described as that aspect of God most directly involved in the generation of community. As Clark Williamson has written, "The Spirit creates community between and among human beings, and between human beings and the nonhuman beings with whom we are in a covenant of moral obligation."[3] Yet in the existentialist-phenomenologist tradition of the middle part of the twentieth century, language about the Holy Spirit was cautious. For instance, in Tillich's *Systematic Theology,* the term "Holy Spirit" rarely appears (twice in the 425-plus pages of Volume III), with "Spiritual Presence" or "Divine Spirit" being used instead. It is clear that Tillich intends to describe a divine impact consistent with classic Holy Spirit language, but he does not assume that Christians know or revere that linguistic tradition. The Spiritual Presence, he writes, "does something the human spirit could not do by itself. It creates unambiguous life."[4]

In *The Analogical Imagination,* David Tracy avoids trinitarian language altogether. He bypasses many opportunities to use terms relating to the Holy Spirit, choosing instead to focus on God and Christ. Yet he views human fulfillment and community as God-empowered events, speaking of grace (rather than Holy Spirit) as the power by which "we are finally freed to embrace a fundamental trust in the whole, to demand of ourselves, by that trust, a hope for the sake of the hopeless, to risk a life in the impossible gospel possibility of a faith and hope working through a love given as pure gift and stark command."[5] It appears that this whole theological stream had lost confidence in the meaningfulness of traditional language for the way God unites persons in community. This tendency parallels the cultural emphasis that promoted the rigorous individualism of ego psychology. Tillich and Tracy cry out for Christians to see God as the energy of relationship and community, but their philosophical bases will not allow them the typical Christian rhetoric.

The process tradition, in which Williamson stands, takes a more communitarian position. It picks up the classic language, seeing the building of a particular kind of community as the central work of the Spirit. Meland describes the Holy Spirit as a resource of grace that enables the church's self-realization as a community of the forgiven, releasing us from the sense of alienation and dissociation.[6] Daniel Day Williams argued that "love is that expression of spirit which has communion in freedom as its goal," and that "since his being is love itself, He is always the Holy Spirit, the spirit of unqualified love."[7] Love, community, freedom, and forgiveness are the continuing themes regarding the Holy Spirit in these process theologies, and before them in most of Christian history.

Rebecca Button Prichard argues for a systemic, rather than a systematic, theology of the Spirit. She points out that Holy Spirit language is always relational, circular, a system of systems.[8] As is also discernible in the discussion of contemporary psychoanalysis,

> systemic (theological) thought circles back upon itself, but within an open system. For a systemic theologian, the circumference of mystery is ever-expanding, defying reduction, deduction . . . . Rather than concentration, which focuses on a still point at the center, systemic thought is eccentric; it moves outward, flirting with mystery, a spiral. Yet it is centered in particularity—embodied, indwelt, creaturely existence.[9]

As in contemporary analysis, the closer you look at any given phenomenon, the harder it is to separate the influences of one on the other, from those of the other on the one. Given the symmetry of these panoramic views of psychoanalytic thinking about intersubjectivity and theological thinking on the Holy Spirit, we expect a deeper insight from closer examination.

TRANSFERENCE, COUNTERTRANSFERENCE, AND INTERSUBJECTIVITY

In the previous chapter, we saw Bion's description of how the reverie of mother and therapist contains and detoxifies the unsymbolized distress of baby and client. We introduced Ogden's account of the client's occupation of the therapist's psychic space. Our task now is to detail that mutual occupation, leading to clarification of God's stake and role in the process.

We begin with projection, a major part of transference. Therapists of many persuasions have understood that all of us, when experiencing anxiety beyond our ability to contain it, will unconsciously split our experience, move into the paranoid-schizoid position, and experience a piece of our emotion as residing in someone else. "It's not I who am angry enough to kill you, it's you who are angry enough to kill me." This is projection. Jill Scharff describes it in this fashion: "In projection, a part of the self—either a part of the ego or its internal objects, or a feeling or an idea originally connected to the self or objects split off from them—is expelled from the intrapsychic domain and displaced to an external object during an unconscious mental process."[10]

Everybody does this, and we do it in relation to a wide range of persons, objects, and groups. When a particular person becomes an important part of our mental life, he or she becomes an attractive target for projection. The projections onto or into a particular other, combined with the consciously owned feelings of the self toward that other—which always include inner constellations of feelings originally developed toward previous others—add up to transference. It is widespread for each of us, especially but not solely in therapeutic relationships.

A crucial variable in transference is the recipients' willingness and ability to receive it. If a mother's reverie fails to receive and metabolize the infant's projection of beta elements, the infant's capacity for tolerating frustration is harmed, and the level of confusion and thought disturbance rises.[11] If a prospective spouse refuses to entertain our projections, we typically lose interest and seek someone else. If a therapist insists too quickly that clients take back their projections and own their own feelings, clients are left feeling lonely, rebuffed, and alienated. Supervisors call this poor transference management. Clients' opportunity for (holy) play, in relation to their own fantasy elaboration of the therapist, has been foreclosed.

A further step in understanding transference involves projective and introjective identification, which in turn lead us to consideration of countertransference. When projection occurs, and it is occurring to some extent in every moment, it can affect the therapist in a range of possible ways. It can be consciously noticed and rebuffed. It can be consciously noticed, silently acknowledged, and allowed to stand unchallenged for the moment. That is typically a conscious transaction, based on therapists' recognition of clients' spoken or unspoken display of affect. Quite often though, that is not the way it happens. Instead, therapists simply begin experiencing some emotion or thought that would be uncharacteristic for them in other situations or with other persons. If therapists are alert, and the intensity of the feeling does not exceed their own capacity for containment, they will notice the difference and be able to use it as information. But several times in every practicing therapist's day, they will only notice that they have had their minds invaded after they have acted on the projected affect. This is projective identification (when recognized either before or after being catapulted into action), and it is the aspect of countertransference not primarily governed by therapists' own personality structure.

A couple of examples will illustrate. Consider two clients who could be classified, in Masterson's terms, as lower-level borderlines.[12] Each of them periodically reaches a position in a therapy hour where they feel an intense unwillingness or inability to speak. It is a silence unlike any other silence these clients produce at other times. On several occasions, I have experienced myself descending through levels of ability to think, from ordinary thought, to sentence fragments, and ultimately into a stupor from which thought is banished, into brief moments of sleep. I do not have to be particularly tired or find what the client had been discussing uninteresting. My ability to think has been attacked and temporarily defeated, in what Bion calls an "attack on linking." My only (or first) knowledge of clients' inability to tolerate thought at those moments is my awareness of having my thinking process immobilized. It is an intimate, powerful communication of the client's inner reality, and typically has produced changes in my behavior before I am aware it is happening.

A similarly compelling example occurred in a supervisory hour. I was seeing a male supervisee, a very cognitively structured man with excellent intellectual abilities. He was presenting his experience of discomfort with the erotic transference of a pair of female clients. As he discussed his constant temptation to shut off the transference with premature normalization or interpretation, he discussed his fear that if he allowed the feelings to continue he would be seen as, or would actually be, seductive. I, a consciously thoroughly heterosexual male, began to feel aroused as he explored the dangers of experiencing his strong emotions at the same time the client was experiencing hers. Alerted by the arousal to his difficulty containing these women's sexual feelings, I explored possible contexts from which that difficulty might arise. I was told of his own family history of the sexualization of most emotionally intense situations and suggested that his technique in these situations would probably be more improved by further involvement in his own therapy than by supervisory exploration of therapeutic gambits. He asked for names for referral, and I offered them. The projective identification of his uncontained sexual feelings into me was an indispensable communication of the actual nature of his experience. My countertransference was informed by the projective identification and used to enhance his learning and his clients' safety.

Though these examples describe situations in which the countertransference embrace of projective identification has been helpful, that is not always the case. Therapists, especially those with incomplete therapy experiences of their own, occasionally participate in major disasters when lived by a client's projective identification. On the other hand, some near-disasters have redemptive possibilities.

Patrick Casement writes of clients creating countertransference in their therapists in order to relive and revise specific childhood traumas. He speaks of "using the analyst to represent an element of parental failure from the past."[13] Citing Paula Heimann and Donald Winnicott, he argues that the countertransference is a creation of the patient, and often maneuvers the therapist so that the therapist's errors will mirror those of the parent. The patient's unconscious cues then alert the therapist how to "recover from an element of his own failure in the analytic relationship," which recovery occurs if the analyst observes and responds to the client's unconscious leading. The key here is that the patient leads the therapist into representing the "traumatic experience as it had been,"[14] rather than trying to be a better parent than the original one. When the client and therapist together have recreated the original drama and trauma through their play, the client can then experience the therapist as willing to confront it without evasion.

In discussing a case, Casement notes an accumulation of his errors, followed by this conclusion: "there began to be an uncanny parallel between how I was behaving with this patient and how her mother had been at the time of the accident," the original trauma.[15] He cites Winnicott, who alluded to the patient's hope for the coming of a day when "the failure situation will be able to be unfrozen and re-experienced, with the individual in a regressed state, in an environment that is making adequate adaptation."[16] For Casement the crucial thing is that the therapist does not try to reduce or undo the trauma, but is led precisely into replicating it. The redemptive difference is the therapist's ability to stay with the client in the horror of the original situation without emotionally withdrawing.

At another point, Casement recounts how the (typically very prompt) therapist of a client often abandoned in childhood overslept, so the client arrived at the office to find the door locked. The therapist had "unconsciously reproduced a real failure in the therapy . . . close to the experience of her patient's own childhood trauma."[17] That, in turn, generated the patient's memory of the parent's death after such an unexpected separation had left the client raging. It led to the patient's ability to experience "her own obliterating anger that belonged to the original trauma."[18] The therapist was used to represent the failing mother, and became the first person who could tolerate the intensity of the patient's newly reexperienced rage. Without the mutual unconscious leading that generated the therapist's error, the discovery and reworking could not have happened.

Stephen Mitchell states that patients utilize the therapist's pre-formed personality and shape the therapist's unconscious in powerfully intersubjective ways, to arrive at a healing place. "Unless the analyst affectively enters the patient's relational matrix or, rather, discovers himself within it—unless the analyst is in some sense charmed by the patient's entreaties, shaped by the patient's projections, antagonized and frustrated by the patient's defenses—the treatment is never fully engaged. . . ."[19] Again, we hear the theme of analysts being structured by the patient's intrapsychic process, giving themselves over to it. They must be captured by the transference-countertransference interplay, before they can find their way out of it and use it as data. We are here in intersubjectivity proper, where during the therapy hour the therapist and client are jointly creating a psychic structure.

This reality is most fully expressed in the contemporary work of Thomas Ogden. He presents a lengthy account of a session, complete with his own musings, illustrating how his noticing an envelope on his desk, the preoccupation with picking up his car at the garage, and the feeling of being suffocated are visibly shaped by the client's material. He argues that "no thought, feeling, or sensation can be considered to be the same as it was or will be outside of the context of the specific (and continually shifting) intersubjectivity created by analyst and analysand."[20] He reports being changed by his reverie (reverent reception) concerning the client, both in thought process and emotion. He reminds us that the other's projection is processed through our psyches, changing both us and the projected content, and returning to the patient, where it further changes the patient. He holds that the separate I-ness of the two is converted into two aspects of a single interpersonal event.[21]

> The projector . . . has unconsciously entered into a form of negation of himself as a separate I and in so doing has become other-to-himself; he has become (in part) an unconscious being outside of himself who is simultaneously I and not I. . . . The outcome of this mutually negating process is the creation of a third subject. . . .

[P]rojective identification involves a type of partial collapse of the dialectical movement of subjectivity and intersubjectivity resulting in the subjugation (of the individual subjectivities of analyst and analysand) by the analytic third. The analytic process, if successful, involves the reappropriation of the individual subjectivities of analyst and analysand, which have been transformed through their experience in the newly created analytic third.

. . . [T]he individuals engaged in this form of relatedness unconsciously subjugate themselves to a mutually-generated intersubjective third . . . for the purpose of freeing themselves from the limits of who they had been to that point.[22]

Here we have the core of intersubjective experience. Therapists, by virtue of becoming therapists and choosing to do it well, have given up such control over their own inner experience as any of us ever get. By offering their reverent attention to the client, they allow the client to infiltrate and modify their own inner contents, as that same process works to modify the client's internal object representations and change the client's life. But it is not only the client who is never the same again, as the "new subjectivity stands in dialectical tension with the individual subjectivities of analyst and analysand," making modifications in the internal experience of both.[23] This is a task that humans are not routinely willing and able to perform. As we shall see, some sense the work of the Holy Spirit when it occurs.

David and Jill Scharff have written extensively about the interpenetration of therapist and client. They speak of therapists presenting themselves to be used by the client, for the client's psychic process to utilize therapists' internal structure as a play apparatus, simultaneously lending itself to the client and retaining its own consciousness of how it is being used. In a case illustration, David Scharff writes,

> It is I who am bottled up, seduced and abandoned by Albert. He is my tantalizing and unsatisfying object. . . . Albert and I are caught in a perverse web of interchangeable self and object. While I am with him, taken over by my concern for him, he is in me, and being in me, he keeps me from having access to parts of myself for which I actively long.[24]

The therapist gives self over to the power from beyond self, freeing both members of the dyad from the structures that had been inhabiting them, so both can be made whole for the encounter they are presently pursuing.

Although object relations theory has emphasized the way the patient's intrapsychic structure shapes the countertransference, hence contributing to the intersubjective mix, it should be noted that intersubjective theory originally began in a different branch of the psychoanalytic family tree: self psychology. The original intersubjective theorists, Robert Stolorow, Bernard Brandschaft, and George Atwood, also emphasized the reciprocal movement within intersubjectivity, but especially emphasized the way the analyst's character structure and responses shaped the patient's transference. Beginning from the perspective that the patient's subjectivity is the primary field of analytic observation, they noted that "the analyst's attitudes and responses will influence which dimensions of the transference predominate at any given time."[25] They contend that analytic responses which fail to recognize the actual sources of patient feeling will evoke transferences reminiscent of the originally traumatizing figure, which will change quickly if the therapist's responses begin taking patient feeling more accurately into account. For them, "transference and countertransference together form an intersubjective system of reciprocal mutual influence."[26]

Jessica Benjamin, another important voice in the intersubjectivity discussions, pointed out that the key difference between this perspective and those preceding it is that it assumes the analytic encounter is always between two subjectivities, rather than a subject and an object. Each is equally an actor upon the other. Each must recognize the other. The other is influenced by my feelings, which, in turn, deepens my trust that I can reveal tender aspects of selfhood to the other.[27]

For each of these thinkers, the critical events are the admission into one's own experience of very subtle, perhaps unconscious, elements of the other's, and the nuanced communication back to that other, often outside of consciousness, that the communication has occurred. On some occasions, therapists find themselves acting in a way that feels forced upon them, based on mental contents that seem not their own. On others, they only notice themselves thinking a thought or feeling an emotion that appears to belong more to the client than themselves, though as time passes they are less and less sure of the boundary. The experience stems from clients' desperate yet hopeful need to make themselves known to therapists, especially those parts of self not yet well enough understood to be put into words. As therapists follow the leading of the intersubjective third, they are presented with new information. It dislodges established ideas, creating the basis for a freedom that intensifies therapist vision and produces a new relational situation for the client, allowing behavior and insight not previously available. As is also true of mothers, therapists can refuse to allow this client material into their experience, but the cost of doing so is the continued imprisonment of both parties in the constructs of the past, and the resulting failure of the therapy.

THE ENABLING OF THE HOLY SPIRIT

The reader will have noticed the congruence of theological and psychological themes. An examination of contemporary works will make it unmistakable that these constructs are describing very similar realities. There has been a resurgence of serious theological interest in the Holy Spirit in the past decade, and its accomplishments will make the points of intersection clearer. Two works from divergent theological streams will aid us in identifying the primary marks of the Spirit's presence and action. We will identify phenomena associated with the Holy Spirit, explore their congruence with comparable therapeutic events, and ascertain what theological claims can be made.

We draw primarily from the work of David Cunningham and Michael Welker. Cunningham, an American Episcopalian, relies heavily on Barth, Balthasar, and Aquinas, and is deeply influenced by concepts recently rediscovered in the classic rhetorical tradition. He is particularly concerned about audiences and what theological statements do in relation to audiences. He contends that the doctrine of the Trinity is a compressed expression of the differing ways the Christian story was told to its immediate postbiblical audiences.[28] He is particularly concerned that Trinitarian belief evince itself in Trinitarian practices of Christian life.

Welker, a German biblical theologian, is mercilessly thorough in identifying biblical material from both testaments that proclaim the Spirit, also citing liberation and feminist theologies to create "a realistic theology of the Holy Spirit."[29] Though the two thinkers come from different theological ancestry and utilize divergent sources, their conclusions are remarkably similar, although Cunningham focuses more on the Trinity's role in constituting realities from the beginning, and Welker pays more attention to the way the Spirit intervenes in realities that already exist.

A basic finding in both theologies, one that resonates deeply with object relations theory, is stated by Cunningham: "Personal identity is communally constituted."[30] This assertion is crucial to his doctrines of both God and the human person, and follows his initial argument that the word "person" is inappropriate for the members of the Trinity. He prefers "movements" or "relations."[31] They are never as separate as "person" would suggest, either now or in the original language of the creeds. Otherness is internal to the life of God, and the human subject is equally multiple. We are particular because we have allowed ourselves to be shaped by different combinations of the influence of others.[32]

Welker is similarly critical of the notion of the human person, the free individual.[33] He decries the illusion of narcissistic individualism, exemplified in the person who "seeks to constitute himself in the futile search for himself."[34] He focuses on what happens between selves, how God's Spirit impacts their already existing realities. Hence, "the granting of the Spirit . . . of God is attended by an exchange of hearts. Specifically, the heart of stone is replaced by a heart of flesh."[35] What happens between selves, under the power of the Spirit, is that one offers a resource (a heart of flesh) to replace the implacable heart that previously existed. For Welker the Spirit is an active agent at specific times in the self's radical and redemptive revision. Welker speaks of this change of hearts as a "change of identity" that evokes public astonishment (à la the biblical Samson), a simultaneous empowerment and disempowerment of the same person, and always for the sake of the broader community.[36] He sees this Spirit action as God's response to collective situations of danger, a Divine gift of unexpected deliverance.[37] He focuses on the time-specific intervention of the Spirit in moments of distress, through and for the community, while Cunningham stresses how "we are (at all times) products of communicative activities," have our particularity in ways that are "neither an individual achievement nor personal possession," and always have their highest expression in the Eucharist.[38]

THE SPIRIT IN THE THERAPY

In light of these accounts of our being constituted of and for our contact with others, and of the Spirit's central role in that construction, let us return briefly to the therapeutic arena. In a recent series of three sessions, I was with a middle-aged single woman, whose very demanding mother recently entered a nursing facility with Alzheimer's disease. After the first session, which had been full of exciting discovery, she left during an intense snow shower. In the second session, she reported that for perhaps the first time in her life she reached home feeling that the drive in the snow had been pleasant, even beautiful, and not at all frightening. Earlier in our relationship, she always canceled sessions if there was a hint of snow. She had been very pleased with herself and with the work. She arrived home to find a message waiting, telling of a potentially serious setback in her mother's condition, and immediately recognized that throughout her life, when she has felt really good, something—very often her mother—has interrupted to return her focus to unpleasantness.

In the third session, she began telling me of her belief that her mother was never pleased with a single thing her father had done. Surprisingly, I felt a yawn coming on (she is extremely sensitive to my yawns). I fought it off for a couple of exchanges, then said, "I notice that I'm struggling not to yawn. It seems like your mother's energy has leaped up between us, and yours has shifted to attend to her. It's almost as though she couldn't tolerate your being focused on this relationship, here, with me." She responded, "I'm remembering a scene in the kitchen when I was five. Dad was eating breakfast, and my brother and I had wandered into the kitchen. I was sitting on one of his knees and my brother on the other. He'd give one of us a taste of bacon, the other a sip of coffee—we were laughing and having the best time. Then Mother came in and was really angry, yelled at us, and chased us out of the kitchen. She turned a good memory into a very painful one." I answered, "So the mother you carry around inside you notices when you are focused on another relationship that's giving you pleasure, and kicks up such a ruckus that your energy moves to calm her down, and the person you're with feels dropped." She followed with another set of memories, this one recent, of a visit to the nursing home. Her mother had jealously demanded her attention when she began a conversation with the son of a woman her mother had been talking with.

We see here how she had been equipped with the heart of stone, in the interactions with her very deprived and depriving mother. We see her using the transference to reenact and dramatize her maternal object's obstruction of the relationship with me and that object's entering into me, reconstituting me, first disempowering and then empowering—rendering me sleepy and annoying, on one hand, and then giving me the information I needed to sense the triangular pattern and her collusion with it. She responded with the memories, as she used her experience of me to reconstitute her internal object structure,[39] modify a piece of her internal mother (á la the Scharffs), and become more able to relate both to me and her mother in the present, and potentially to her wider community. As Welker had suggested, this discovery arose from a situation of distress—she was pained by the sense that her mother could always prevent pleasure. I was embarrassed and frustrated by the developing yawns. It produced an unexpected insight and revealed how both of us were the products, in that moment and every moment, of interpersonal processes.

Another set of concepts from pneumatology (doctrine of the Spirit) will be helpful. Cunningham, following communications scholar Calvin Schrag, refers to subjectivity as being more a space than a point. Both contend that there must be such a space if we are to use human action and discourse. The other must be able to come into the space with his or her own subjectivity, and we need to enter it to play with the other. Welker seems to be discussing the same phenomenon when he writes, "Free self-withdrawal for the benefit of others gives fellow creatures open space and possibilities of development that surprise and delight them."[40] He writes of the self that freely withdraws itself, becoming the good seed from which springs diverse fruit, finally claiming that "this action of the Spirit reveals the unbreakable interconnection between free self-withdrawal for the benefit of other creatures and the reflection of God's glory."[41]

As therapists and as partners in every human relationship, we have the power to either fill and saturate the space that we and others could enter and encounter God, or step back from dominating that space, so a free, uncontrollable, playful event can happen. Transference and countertransference can fill the space so there is no room for anything else,[42] "we already know exactly who this other person is"; or intersubjective dialogue can reopen the space as a gift of the Spirit, in which new selves can be discovered. This intersubjective space and its contributing components in both selves mirror the sacred space of the therapy room, and is a gift of the Spirit.

Another common action of the Spirit cited by Cunningham and Welker is to join widely divergent sources of input, stimulation, and knowledge in a comprehensible whole. Cunningham relies on musical imagery to make this point. He challenges the typical assumption that oneness and difference are mutually exclusive categories, claiming that the Truth that God gives us to know is polyphonic, with "its chief attribute [being] simultaneous, non-excluding difference; that is, more than one note is played at a time, and none of these notes is so dominant that it renders another mute."[43] This resonates with the Whiteheadian belief that the goal of God is to produce contrasts of increasing intensity and harmony, without canceling each other out. Cunningham calls truth "symphonic," and argues for musical unities of differential flux, "not a fusion or synthesis that is achieved at the expense of their diversity."[44]

He comes back to this theme in his discussion of authority. Authority should require "multiple voices to be heard (polyphony). Secondly, the lives of those whose voices are considered authoritative need to be woven into the lives of others. . . ."[45] He speaks directly of the polyphony of bishops.

Welker addresses the same reality with his use of the image "the force field of the Spirit."[46] He also employs musical imagery, saying that the force field of the Spirit "immediately forms a domain of resonance."[47] He moves to exegetical and historical examples, with particular emphasis on the Pentecost account. That event is his prime example of the Spirit's creating a community of testimony that is also a force field of love. It is especially marked by "a totally unexpected comprehensibility."[48] The Spirit gives voice to an incredible multiplicity of languages and, even more incredible, makes them mutually intelligible to all, generating a community that could not have occurred without the Spirit's intervention. In language echoing Cunningham's, he speaks of "polycentric variegation" brought about by this pouring out of the Spirit.[49] In the Pentecost exegesis, he claims that "the persons seized, moved, and renewed by God's Spirit can know themselves placed in a force field that is seized, moved, and renewed from many sides—a force field of which they are members and bearers, but which they cannot bear, shape, be responsible for, and enliven alone."[50] This duplicates the Spirit's movement within the psychotherapy experience, as in our example where first the falling snow, then the phone call, the recognition of the familiarity of being called back into distress, the memory of her mother's anger at her father and her mothers anger at the client and her brother for loving the father, all combine with her inner maternal object being angry at her for being close to me, which we discovered because I was getting sleepy. It triggered the memory of the previous week's triangle at the nursing home, all of which alerted her to her options about dealing with the inner experience of being challenged by her mother's hatred and her own collusion. Those options can free her for participation in loving community. The same force drew on the unexpected comprehensibility of my lethargy, her reaction to the snowfall, and the telephone message from the nursing home. It generated a force field of love, in which she, I, and unknown others are enabled to act on behalf of the world.

A further point of contact between Welker and Cunningham, psychotherapy and the Spirit, is found in the uncontrollability of the experience and the radical difference it makes. Welker writes, "The bearers of the Spirit receive signs of being empowered, but are not . . . to rely on a power that they can control."[51] Later he says, "the chief difficulty in understanding the Spirit and the Spirit's action lay in mediating, on the one hand, the *undeniable evidence* of the Spirit's action and, on the other hand, the fact that it cannot be predicted, calculated, or controlled."[52] He reminds us that the Spirit is not at our disposal. Its freedom from us is necessary if it is to produce its primary hallmarks, liberation from sin and "new structural patterns of life. Disintegrated persons and communities are stabilized and regrouped."[53]

Cunningham also is emphatic about the uncontrollability of the Spirit, the danger of our attempts to control it, and the centrality of sanctification in the Spirit's work. He objects to all "monolithic hegemony," uses "persuading" as the primary descriptor for the action of the Spirit and of appropriately Christian influence of one believer on another, and writes that "God and human beings are engaged in a process of mutual persuasion."[54] One is reminded of process thought's "triumph of persuasion over force." Both of these authors are committed to the Christian article of faith that "the Spirit blows where it wills."

Psychotherapy, pastoral and otherwise, has often been accused of attempting to deny or infringe upon God's freedom by instrumentalizing or technologizing the processes by which human beings change. But as these paragraphs make clear, at its depth that is precisely what does not happen. Skilled psychotherapists are gifted at removing obstacles to the spontaneous inbreaking of the Spirit. The hallowing process removes some of the saturation of the therapist's mind and of the intersubjective space, but the complex multilayered interaction we have described cannot be summoned up on demand. In our example, the confluence of the snowfall, the phone call, the recollection, my sleepiness, and the client's internal object's orchestration of the hour is simply too complex to have been anticipated, let alone ordered up. Good psychotherapy technique does close off much trivial conversation, prevents the entry of exploitation from either side, and continues to press both therapist and client deeper into anxiety-laden material, where we are most likely to encounter God in the form of unexpected, comprehensibility-creating, relationship-bonding discoveries. But there are days when the best technique will not bring them forth. Like good meditative practice or any other spiritual discipline, we can create conditions in which God most often reveals Godself, but we remain humble before the mystery of the Divine freedom to be visible or not, in whatever way God's Spirit chooses.

CRISIS, PARTICIPATION, COMMUNION

A final point of connection should be noted. Persons of faith have claimed for centuries that the Spirit's inbreaking occurs in response to community crises, is facilitated by God's action to create communities and in turn helps create them, and that no encounter between God and a person is without community implications. "The communion of saints" has a long history as a catalyst in God's making Godself known.

Our theological sources are consistent with this claim. Cunningham names "participation" as one of the Trinitarian virtues.[55] He holds the Eucharist as the point of greatest exemplification of the community-building of the Spirit.[56] He speaks of Christians sharing a community of interpretation.[57] Welker is even more dramatic and specific: "The first reliable testimonies to the action of God's Spirit report . . . an unexpected, unforeseeable renewal of the people's unanimity and capacity for action. . . ."[58] The Spirit's being poured out on an individual energizes and unites a people, changing individuals for the sake of others and creating, as in the Pentecost experience, a simultaneous experience of radically heightened individuality and deepened community commitment.[59] "These gifts and deeds are given to individual persons in order for them to mediate God's revelation and attestation to each other."[60] The Spirit is revealed to the one who intensifies his or her participation in the community and in the process mediates the Spirit to the other, intensifying that other's participation, and so it goes.

That is also the experience of psychotherapy. Between therapist and client, client and supervisor, and all of them and us is formed a community of energy and hope. The sacred space crackles with energy that suffuses and enables all participants. The community is an active participant in creating the conditions for the Spirit's appearance. Jessica Benjamin, in a recent workshop at the International Institute of Object Relations Therapy,[61] expressed her appreciation and admiration for the depth and quality of clinical sharing in response to her presentations. Someone responded that the development of a culture of trust and expectation is characteristic of the organization, and had again been evident that weekend. God enables community, whether God is named or not. All of our communities, from the therapeutic dyad through the case conference through the broader group of students and supervisors through the school that houses them and the religious community and professional guild that enfolds and supports them, all of them are part of the Spirit's hallowing of the space and ushering us into the presence of God, where we are all changed and in whose presence "it does not yet appear what we shall be."

Chapter 9

Therapist As Bearer of the Spirit: Psychotherapy and Christology

Clients experience the person of the therapist as mediating redemptive change. Rightly and wrongly, realistically and transferentially, wholly or in part, we are seen as making possible the transformations the process generates. I once had a client say to me, "You are my life." Clients are often profoundly grateful, though at times they hate us with a perfect hatred.

Whether idealized to excess, denigrated beyond endurance, or regarded realistically, we are the vessels of a powerful liberating force. There are moments when we know ourselves to be given exactly the right thing to say. We are privileged to see the expanded lives of people we serve, and can often trace specific growth to moments in an hour, moments we have had a hand—or a word—in. Those who have been our therapists are often held in a place of deep psychic respect, and we know that we are similarly held by at least a few clients present and past.

All this idealization, appreciation, denigration, and the embarrassment and joy about these feelings push us to important theological questions. What is our standing, with and before God, in this work? Martin Luther, writing long before psychotherapy had been named, urged us all to be "Christs to our neighbor."[1] The baptized and particularly the ordained have vowed to represent Christ and the church to others. Most who practice pastoral psychotherapy see it as an expression of their life with God and their relationship with Christ. How seriously should we take that? In what ways, and to what extent, are we extensions of Christ, and thereby Christlike, in our work? In what ways are we not? If empirical answers to those questions were possible, how would they affect who we are before God? How ought they affect the way we are with our clients?

THE RECENT HISTORY OF CHRISTOLOGY

More specifically, to what extent can we claim that ours is a direct participation in God's saving work? If that is the case, in what sense is it related to Jesus the Christ's work on our behalf? Are we part of it, competitors with it, descendants of it, imitators, heralds, antagonists? If we decide we are one or all of these things, does that place specific obligations on us, and if so, which ones? Are there specific graces that sustain us, privileges or rewards that compensate for the obligations, sanctions that await us when we fail? And what might all this have to do with money, with regulation by the state, and with power?

One approach to these questions would be to look at recent historical currents within Christology. By the mid-nineteenth century, theologians were beginning a shift away from seeing Jesus of Nazareth in a highly idealized, barely human way—the God-man of classical Christology. Historical criticism was returning believers' attention to the man Jesus. There was enthusiasm for constructing biographies of Jesus. Harnack wrote of Him as knowing "God in a way no one ever knew him before," and heirs to the Romantic movement began attempting to reconstruct His faith, His subjective experience, and to identify His divinity with the psychological content of His human person.[2] But the advance of historical criticism surged beyond this point. It established that some events depicted in the New Testament are more and less likely to have occurred as described, but (unexpectedly) continued to the current conviction that, as Pamela Dickey Young puts it, "one has no real access to him that is not already witness of faith."[3] The current judgment of New Testament scholars is that all we can know of Him is through texts, and that all texts are constructed and preserved by persons whose very constructing and preserving is for the purpose of bearing witness to the salvific power revealed and transmitted through Him.

Two things have been accepted as turn-of-the-century truths. The first is that historical method has failed in the attempt to provide a sufficiently firm picture of Jesus the man to be a decisive warrant for acceptance or rejection of the Christian faith.[4] The best we get is a series of more or less probable narratives, lovingly, scientifically, and faithfully constructed, none of which can be considered totally factual. As Tillich says in response to this observation, "Christianity is not based on the acceptance of a historical novel."[5] The second assertion follows from the first, though it took a few decades to be firmly stated. We are left, as Young puts it, with a soteriocentric (based on the process of salvation) faith rather than a Christocentric one.[6] Its emphasis, as Williamson points out, is on Jesus as one who liberates us from our particular addictions to evil,[7] rather than as Himself the first truly liberated person. (Williamson reminds us that the liberal Christologies' emphasis on Jesus as a liberated person always included a strong invitation to anti-Judaism, since Judaism was seen as what Jesus was liberated from.) Instead, contemporary Christology rings with Young's assertion that "the divinity of Jesus does not lie in claims about His own personal life, but in claims about His effect on others. . . . When people encountered Jesus, they experienced the claim of God upon them."[8]

Rather than believing with Jesus, with a faith identical to His, we believe with the apostles, the tellers of the stories and the writers of the Gospels, in Jesus as God's representative.[9] We do not know His faith in detail, but we know enough about His impact on a community of people to stand with it in our gratitude and responsiveness to Him.

JESUS—HOW UNIQUE AND UNIQUE HOW?

The previous discussion raises a further question with decisive bearing on our understanding of both Him and our therapeutic vocation. Did He do something unique and decisive for us, something that changed the world and God's relation to it once and for all, something that removed a previously insuperable obstacle between humans and God? Or did He rather present something to us, something that had been true of us and God all along, but something which significant portions of humanity had seemed tragically unwilling or unable to see? If it is something new and decisive, what might it be?

As the twentieth century unfolded, theology became increasingly cautious about naming the newness. The mid-century Chicago theologians Tillich and Meland asserted a definite uniqueness, but were less ambitious in describing it than the earlier writers, those less influenced by historical criticism. Tillich does write that Jesus "brings the new state of things, the New Being," while pointing out that we cannot precisely know the details of His life or faith.[10] He claims that "in one personal life essential manhood has appeared under the conditions of existence without being conquered by them."[11] He is not making an argument that we know Jesus is the essential man because we have scrutinized of the details of His life, but rather that we know it by the New Testament response to Him, by the way He empowered His community. "The New Testament is an integral part of the event. . . ."[12] Meland makes a similar argument. Jesus is the revealer of God and mediator of God's work by His effect on human personality, through embodying a "structure of meaning" that put forward a new possibility of human spirit.[13] In a later work, he speaks of "a full release of the sensitivity of grace which is of God," the "originating vehicle of *agape*," again suggesting that a new form of human selfhood is here achieved with decisive results.[14] But, like Tillich, he avoids anchoring that in specific personal qualities that are psychologically describable, focusing more on the appearance of new energies in the community around Jesus, presumably traceable to Him. Neither thinker makes a detailed argument for how those qualities migrate from Jesus to the ongoing community.

Moving to the late-twentieth-century theologians, we find intensified awareness of His solidarity with and emergence within the Judaisms of His day. It is destructive to stake His uniqueness on a contrast with "the Jews" of the Johannine writings, but it remains necessary to claim with David Tracy that Jesus is the "classic person," that "the proclaimer has become the proclaimed."[15] What is proclaimed is His carrying of a Divine impact through a Jewish human life and into a Jewish human world, while carrying a message deeply

similar to those of other Jewish wisdom figures, though with an impact exceeding that of His contemporaries, at least on Gentiles.

Several common themes are emerging. They echo, with Tracy, the
notion that what is disclosed in any thought about Christ must be the
present experience of the Christ event.[16] All are witnesses that the final power is love.[17] They resonate with William Placher's assertion
that it is God's willingness in Jesus to *risk* pain and suffering that is
good and redemptive, rather than the fact of suffering—which itself
is not good.[18] In fact, Jesus' willingness to risk one sort of suffering
was in the service of active opposition to a different source of suffering, sin. Elizabeth Johnson contributes a further theme, arguing that
"the beloved community shares in this Christhood, participates in the
living and dying and rising of Christ to such an extent that it too has a
christomorphic character." It would be naively physicalistic to collapse all of Christ into the human male Jesus.[19]

So we have a Christ based in Jewish community, communally received and glorified in and by the nascent church, willing to suffer but
neither passive nor masochistic, and known most fully through the impact on those called by His life and suffering into that embryonic
community and this contemporary one. This is a Christ whose major
focus is, as Young puts it, "not on Jesus but on the relationship between believer and God that Jesus evokes."[20] This is a Christ who
"does not constitute salvation or contact with God's love or grace . . ."
but one who "re-presents or embodies God's grace or revelation."[21]
But what is the character of the effect that lets us know that God has
acted in us? What is the distinctive mark of God-with-us?

Williamson responds to that question by picking up the emphases
of liberation theology and expanding it beyond the political and economic sphere. He argues that we have "a liberating Jesus," who liberates us from Christian anti-Judaism, liberates us from "sin, evil, and
commitment to the death-dealing, curse-bringing ways to which we
find ourselves addicted," and liberates us "to love ourselves appropriately, to love God with all of ourselves and our neighbors as ourselves."[22]

It is a delicate matter to relate Williamson's assertion, "We believe
in Jesus" (rather than with Jesus or with the faith of Jesus) and the

more community-focused statements of the feminists—that it is what happens between Jesus and others that demonstrates and re-presents His Christhood. Williamson is not arguing that the historical selfhood of Jesus, or some combination of psychospiritual characteristics, constitutes the core of His divinity. Rather, he contends that Jesus' encounters with other human beings conveyed something profoundly powerful and deeply characteristic of God. He contends that the church has always described Jesus in terms of what it senses itself called to be and do in its own time. It first saw Jesus empowering persons to overturn the evils facing a particular Jew in a particular crisis of Jewish history in a compellingly powerful way,[23] and it identified that kind of power reversal of evil as central to His identity. "Christ enters the precise spot of our addiction to evil and makes clear that evil's demonic demand on us is phony, illegitimate, devoid of the authority it falsely claims for itself."[24]

We have located a consensus of current Christology emphasizing Jesus' rootedness in (Jewish) community, His uniqueness consisting of His liberating effect on people around Him, and the power of their response as forming a Christhood of community. We also see Christ's claim on His followers for relationship with God, God's use of the encounter to overthrow the dominant sins of the day, Christ's willingness to risk suffering for the sake of love, and His being experienced as a source of freedom and dislocation in an ongoing succession of present moments. It is time to take this community of Christological conversation into our examination of the office of pastoral psychotherapist.

THERAPIST AS CHRIST FIGURE: HOW AND HOW NOT

Bion's discussion of the mystic's relation to the group clarifies the link between the person who gathers up the wisdom of a tradition and community, embodies it with unique clarity, extends its development through his or her words and actions, disturbs and disrupts the community and the selves into which it comes, and then struggles with the tradition's dependable attempt to both integrate and confine this thrust of the Infinite into time.[25]

We have already seen how therapists are themselves hallowed by their recruitment and selection, by preparation before and within their careers, and by the immediate web of connections that establish and refer their practice. That accomplishes two things central to this discussion: it grounds them in the life, values, hopes, and fears of their community—what Meland calls the "structure of experience"; and it places them in a position to carry that embodiment into an intimate and transforming encounter with God, an encounter that includes the therapeutic hour.

Bion posits the existence of "exceptional individuals" who change lives and communities. He chooses the term "mystic" for these persons, though does not restrict his scope to the religious. "I include scientists," he writes, "and Newton is the outstanding example of such a man: his mystical and religious preoccupations have been dismissed as an aberration when they should be considered as the matrix from which his mathematical formulations evolved."[26] Bion shows reverence for the explorer who takes reality's own terms with utmost seriousness.

Such mystics have an uncommon ability to identify what Bion calls "constant conjunctions," two or more things that predictably appear together, and to symbolize that conjunction with a name. Symington refers to this as the identification of the "selected fact" that organizes the rest of the cognitive field.[27] The Gospel writers' use of the phrase "Kingdom of God" could serve as an example.

Bion argues that the analyst/mystic most often recognizes the raw truth, revealing the "selected fact" or constant conjunction, when he or she approaches the encounter without conscious memory, desire, or understanding. He or she is free of saturation, able to attend to the reality of client, self, and moment. This is the therapist's act of faith that there is an ultimate reality in and beyond the sense data of the moment, best knowable if screened as little as possible by preconceptions, memories, and hopes. As Michael Eigen puts it, "Bion maintained a faith that openness to the unknowable ultimate reality (of a session, of a moment, of a lifetime) is somehow linked with growth processes."[28] He continues, "His (Bion's) famous formula for the radical openness of the psychoanalytic attitude (an act of faith) expresses his passion for fresh starting points . . . over and over the analyst stays open to the impact of the patient."[29] Eigen does not treat the multiple links of these two and their community, but we should remember that this is a patient and therapist who contain and are contained by the community (and the God who shapes the community), which is ready to surface in image, recollection, and sensation.

Therapists enter the sacred space bearing the meanings of at least three (in some cases overlapping) communities: the therapy tradition that has trained them, the faith community that has shaped and continues to shape their lives before and beyond their work as therapists, and the wider secular community that they always share with clients. Unconsciously embodying each in varying degrees, they encounter clients, hopefully cleared of the conscious encumbrances that can crowd out Bion's F, or faith.[30] Bion urges therapists to seek in that encounter "something that differs from what is normally known as reality . . . for the purpose of achieving contact with psychic reality, namely, the evolved characteristics of O,"[31] which he refers to elsewhere as ultimate reality, being-itself, and the godhead.[32] "O does not fall in the domain of knowledge or learning save incidentally; it can be 'become,' but it cannot be 'known.' "[33] "F is related to O itself," he writes, rather than to any of its manifestations (i.e., faith is in God, not in any of God's works).[34] Neither we nor Bion may take Bion literally when he says, "the analyst has to become infinite by the suspension of memory, desire, and understanding."[35] On the other hand, he does mean that the therapist must not trap himself in the past of memory, the present of understanding, or the future of desire as he "sharpens his contact with O" and kindles this explosive transformation that is the realized contact with the holy in the therapeutic hour. In that contact, therapists function as mystics in relation to the broader group and its ultimate reality, and in relation to the dyad that includes clients and the reality that they acknowledge; and therapists offer themselves as a potential portal through which clients are invited into the transforming F that unites with O.

Bion himself is careful to avoid any statement that identifies him as either Christian or non-Christian, but the same is not required of us. Therapists are in the room (under optimal circumstances) as an act of faithfulness to the Spirit, performing what they know to be a sacred calling—Eigen calls it "a form of prayer."[36] They are there in faithful human response to a call from God and the client—as Jesus placed Himself in the many focal locations of his ministry. In those moments when God breaks through therapist reliance on human hopes and learnings, a burst of Divine energy seizes the attention of both parties and generates a new awareness, a new truth that shifts the future of this therapist-client partnership and of the ongoingness of the client's life. God acts as directly and effectively here as in any moment of revelation and redemption, though (apparently unlike Jesus' case) not continuously in the life of any therapist. There is no claim of special divine authorship of the therapist's life away from those moments, but there is a claim that God wills Godself to be experienced fully and powerfully in those moments for the transformation of the lives of all participants. This is typically experienced as a powerful shift in affect, either an eruption or a calming or a focusing, and a moment of creation as feeling bursts the prior bonds of thought, creating the possibility of new thought and action. "Part of the job of primary process is to begin processing potentially overwhelming impacts into affective images and symbols usable for growth," Eigen argues.[37]

The claim is not that therapists are essentially messianic persons, but that they are called to and equipped by God for a messianic task. They are shaped by their communities, express and purify them, and come to the moment with the client in persistent hope that God will use them to create something in that time/space that has never before existed, an event calling the client to new symbolization that supports a faithful living out of the moment. The hope is marked by the refusal to fixate on pieces of the past or future that could obstruct God's access to the present.

THE MEANING OF OUR DAILY LIVES

In such moments, the therapist's life outside the office is a peculiar mixture of utter irrelevance and essential preparation. It has much in common with the almost completely unknown years of Jesus' life before ministry. We, like our clients, are (sometimes perversely) curious, but much of who He was before the beginning of His ministry simply does not alter the meaning He has for us—whether He ever sinned, whether He was married and had children of His own, whether He would have earned a psychiatric diagnosis, whether He traveled outside Galilee and Judea, and much else. As the current Christologies remind us, it is just as well, because we cannot possibly know. The authors intended to make it unmistakable that this man brought them a connection with God that they had not known was possible. If they had other objectives, we cannot discern them. Their convictions would have rendered them blind to the questions neutral biographers ask, and the answers would not have served their purposes even if they knew them. We have the testimony of their devotion, of His ability to bring that to pass.

Similarly, the historical facts of our lives are rarely relevant to our clients. Even such undisguisable facts as race, gender, and age often mean little, and other facts clients seek to know almost always mean less: our politics, our family situations, where we live, our hobbies, even how we treat the people around us in daily (outside the office) life. It is far more important for clients to focus on what happens between us in the office, to have the freedom to fantasize about us as they need to fantasize, than it is to gratify their curiosity. That becomes clearer as we look at the history of our community fantasies about Jesus. The church concluded, from the silence of the Gospel writers, that Jesus never sinned, nor married, nor had children, and concluded against the specific testimony of those writers that Mary, and then her mother, remained virginal. It drew those conclusions while its view of sexuality was profoundly negative.[38] To have had to cope with thoughts of Jesus and Mary as sexual persons would have been at best distracting, however true it surely was. The same is true if my client hates liberal politics, thinks all gamblers are evil, or believes that men who have not fathered sons lack an indispensable prerequisite for helping him. Our anonymity, however painful it can sometimes be for us and them, makes us more available as vessels for the Spirit.

There is another sense in which how we live our lives is crucial. Though we cannot specify the content of Jesus' faith, it is our faith testimony that it was intense, central to His life, energized by frequent prayer, consistent with His people's convictions, and empowering of His courage and willingness to suffer. We believe there is evidence of this effect in the gestalt of the witness about Him, though we cannot hang our beliefs on any specific provable event. We believe these things prepared Him for his ministry and sustained Him through it.

For us, though no specific act or its absence enables or bars us serving as God's vessels, our development of discipline hallows us and makes the moments of sacred transformation more likely. Bion reminds us that Freud practiced mental exercises, pretending to be blind to certain information in order to sharpen his attention to other, more important, data. Bion was very demanding of the commitment required to do analytic therapy.

> The analytic situation itself, and the . . . task itself, are bound to stimulate primitive and basic feeling in analyst and analysand. . . . These fundamental characteristics, love, hate, dread, are sharpened to a point where the participating pair may feel them to be almost unbearable: it is the price that has to be paid for the transformation of an activity that is *about* psycho-analysis into an activity that *is* psychoanalysis.[39]

The same could be said of any depth psychotherapy. A developed capacity to bear those feelings, with a minimum of denial, evasion, or acting out.

Bion recalls that Freud taught that analysis had to be conducted in an atmosphere of deprivation. "Anyone who considers it possible to achieve a suitable frame of mind by a few minutes of psychological tidying up before starting work cannot have grasped the nature of the discipline necessary to be an analyst. . . ."[40] The question here is not whether the therapist has some disqualifying bad habit, but whether that person's life is oriented in a way habitually open to O, rather than routinely shutting O out by filling attention with comfort and distraction. The crucial thing in Jesus' not yielding to the temptations in the desert was not that He would have thereby been prevented from accomplishing His mission, but that He would not have been the kind of man who would have had the right sort of mission. Eigen reminds us that "Bion's portrayals of O tend to be in the key of terror,"[41] which terror the therapist must be willing to enter on a regular basis, inside and beyond the hour.

SUFFERING—MESSIANIC AND THERAPEUTIC

In this discussion of the relevance of our historical lives, we have approached both the theological importance of transference and the importance of therapeutic suffering. Transference will be first to claim its place here. The reason the details of our life outside the office matter so little is because transference matters so much, just as allowing or enabling the church to make what it did of Jesus was central to His contribution. Paul's line, "For our sake He made Him to be sin who knew no sin," highlights the Christological side of the transference equation.[42] We have no historical data to tell us whether Jesus "knew no sin," and contemporary Christology seems to agree it would not matter. But the Pauline quote tells us that the first-century church needed a savior about whom, for its own reasons, it could make that claim. When we combine that link with Williamson's observation that the church always makes Christ the liberator in relation to the most enslaving sins in its era, we see a situation analogous to that of the therapist, as is detailed below.

Therapists, touched by God through all the persons and disciplines we have named, is (at best) free to be seen as clients need them to be. In the previous chapter we saw that clients will first recruit therapists with whom they can reenact the ancient traumas and dramas, then will subtly cue therapists on how to play their part. The more fully therapists can keep the realities of their daily lives from impinging on clients' awareness—or, to put it differently, the more fully therapists are free of their need to be seen as the historical persons they are outside the office—the less they interfere with clients' need to project on them the attributes of the transference figures who represent the virtues and evils most important to clients. Therapists may become the bearer of the sin clients most need to master, and their ability and willingness to be seen and felt as the bearer of that sin is the measure of their capacity to participate in clients' liberation. The same equation applies to clients' projection of goodness into therapists.

In the language of David and Jill Scharff, this is the liberating power of the negative focused transference within the circle of the positive contextual transference: the client's ability to trust us enough overall to be able to distrust us narrowly, as we stand in for a toxic figure from the past.[43] The positive focused transference is equally important, because it is analogous to, and for Christian clients often a piece of, the church's witness of faith. Though modern critics have made it clear that we know little of Jesus with historical certainty, we carry the sense of knowing decisively what we actually need to know—that He revealed God to us and embodies God's claim upon us. With the help of the writers of scripture and other transmitters of tradition, we have filled in the details, in part, on the basis of transference—our visceral sense of who we most need Him to be. Clients do the same with us, when we give ourselves over to the process sufficiently to allow it. They remember us rather like the church remembers Jesus in His second through his thirtieth years: as they would like to imagine us to be.

The distinction between the therapist's person and the quality of the contact with the sacred must be maintained. In Mark's gospel, the questioner is counterquestioned: "Why do you call me good? No one is good but God alone."[44] It was required of Jesus, and is of us, that we bear witness to a goodness that may flow through us but is not our possession. The client's periodic idealization of the therapist performs a function comparable to the church's idealization of Jesus, creating a bond through which the Other can be experienced, though it is the Other and not the vessel that saves. But there is a crucial difference between our task as therapists and the task the church has taken as its own. We are committed to resolve the transference, to take up an identity as one who can be both loved and hated, embraced and left. The church has been less willing to offer the option of either holding on to or leaving Jesus, and itself as institution. Certainly anti-Judaism would be less virulent and interfaith dialogue more possible if we could "believe through Jesus" at least as fully as we "believe in Jesus."

Our temporary giving up of historical uniqueness, and the place in client life this releasing often provides us, can cast us into a poignant and profound suffering. Tonight a client I have known for twenty years told me that she is struggling with the decision about continuing to live. I felt the reality, in some measure, of the bleakness she inhabits. I was reminded of the necessity that the therapist be willing to suffer if the client is to achieve the capacity for suffering. Quoting Bion,

> The patients . . . experience pain but not suffering. They may be suffering in the eyes of the analyst because the analyst can, and indeed must, suffer. The patient may say he suffers but this is only because he does not know what suffering is and mistakes feeling pain for suffering it. . . . The *intensity* of the patient's pain contributes to his fear of suffering pain. Suffering pain involves respect for the fact of pain.[45]

One of the functions of an analyst is to increase the client's capacity for suffering through the analyst's willing participation in the suffering.[46] It is suffering that brings clients to therapy, goads them to present it and themselves for the exploration they hope will unearth and remove its root. Only if, through our work together, my client learns to experience the full weight of her suffering as compatible with her life, will she both choose to continue her life and learn what she must from the suffering. That learning requires a sharing of resources, the capacity for bearing a pain that we two choose to stand within, to allow it to do what it will with us while we are together and sometimes beyond that time. If the therapist cannot receive the core of the client's suffering, the client knows it, and the work never reaches the deepest point. As Winnicott wrote of therapists and mothers, they must take in the worst assault of the other's pain and survive. Yet as Placher wrote of Christ, it is not the suffering itself that saves, it is the willingness to put oneself in the place where suffering is inescapable.[47] For therapists, it is the surviving and the shared knowing it produces that are made possible by entering the place of suffering. For Jesus, it is the standing with, the willingness to be seen as evil by the state, something other than what He was, for the sake of the claim God placed upon Him and through Him on His followers, that could not have been avoided without belying the message that He spoke.

THE CONTENT OF THE SAVING CLAIM

This brings us to the content of the saving claim and enabling resources that cross the gap between Christ and believer, therapist and client. The claim on and for the Christian (and perhaps for all persons of faith) is that God has created and maintained a world in which slavery to the distractions from life—what Williamson calls "the death-dealing, curse-bringing ways to which we find ourselves addicted"[48]— is not necessary for the enjoyment of free, community-based, sustainable, person-expanding life with God; secondary to that, we are all under the ethical obligation to be curious about, identify, explore the implications of, renounce the collaboration with, and ultimately to grieve and move beyond our and our societies' characteristic patterns of perpetuating blindness, death, and despair. The message is that God acted in Jesus of Nazareth to again jar human beings into awareness of their constant temptation to allow the life-giving Spirit to be reduced to formula, to allow political oppression to numb the sense that ethical life is now possible, to challenge the barriers between rich and poor, male and female, Jew and Greek, and to create a new community that could be the bearer and rekindler of that message in settings no then-existing community could reach. We, the therapists and clients among us, are heirs to that community, both to its gift and its demand.

Psychoanalysis has offered one way to embody it. In Bion's language, we are mandated to "at-one-ment" with O, achieved through faith that "there is an ultimate reality and truth" beyond memory and desire, and known through "the intersection of the evolution of O with the domain of objects of sense."[49] Such events produce a state of mind in which O can evolve, during which "a relevant constellation will be evoked during the process of at-one-ment with O, the process denoted by transformation O → K."[50] Analysts must undergo the transformation from O into K. That is a mystical process, which in its fullest development is for Bion messianic.[51] They may contain the messianic idea or be contained by it, but in any event their vocation is to make it available to the broader society. An analyst or pastoral psychotherapist "makes direct contact with, or is 'at one' with, God,"[52] which experience inevitably creates myth (denotative language being unable to contain it), the vitality of which the group inevitably attempts to domesticate. Bion cites Isaac Luria and Meister Eckhart to the effect that "we are transformed and changed into God," finally claiming that "what is to be sought is an activity that is both the restoration of god (the mother) and the evolution of god (the formless, infinite, ineffable, non-existent). . . ."[53] The claim and promise here is that when we accept that there is always a deeper truth, when we set aside the pride in our own present knowing, God lures us into an unsettling, exultant, terrifying encounter offering the substance for new formulation and more inclusive fellowship with God and the other. In that experience, both therapist and client deepen their knowing of God and each other, and God becomes that much more complex, beautiful, and salvific.

Eigen, who embodies a more ecstatic and expressive mysticism than Bion's austere minimalism, describes the claim and promise more dramatically. He describes the encounter with the Holy as the birth of consciousness, an explosion. "Facing truths about one's life explodes the lie one lives."[54] This is the claim on us, that we see and resign from the lies that poison life. It happens through a faith experienced as "a stripping away of mind," clearing the way for, not the knowing of O, but the becoming of O.[55] We are faced with the choice to "incarnate one's special bit of godhead,"[56] the consequences being either a collapse "where the best should be," or an ongoing pilgrimage of unresting expansion and demand, resourced by God's stubborn refusal to let us settle into the selves we have already achieved.

Eigen writes,

> Psychoanalysis is part of the evolution to open hearts with words, a tendency that needs to spread throughout the social body. The Bible has a deep rigor but is not tidy. Those who follow God are in for trouble, but those who don't are in trouble too. It is not often clear which trouble to prefer. Moses draws up rules for getting closer to God, but God often seems to break His own rules. Sometimes the closeness achieved by breaking rules is more acutely satisfying than the closeness achieved by following them. A moment's closeness to God is its own reward.[57]

So here are the claim and the promise, offered lovingly but unapologetically by Jesus to first-century Jews (and all others) and by therapists to contemporary clients: The pain that brings you to me grows from the lies you live about the nature of the world. You distract yourself from the pain and lies by a plethora of addictions: to religion, sex, money, work, power, thinking, chemicals—in short, to sin. God offers more than that, and you can find it in relationship to God through me. But beware: if you make an idol of me you will lose the Spirit you have come to me to find (though you do not know it). You will lose it, but God will continue to seek to surprise you into re-recognizing the loss, and I will continue to be available to meet you in it.

MONEY, PROFESSION, AND THE STATE

God enables this therapy, and with it extends the ministry of Christ—whether named or not—through the therapist. In the process, God sets the therapist in an ironic and tempting relationship to money, professional life, and the state. Jesus was repeatedly tempted—by the devil in the desert,[58] by the Pharisee, who asked about paying taxes,[59] by Peter about the inevitability of His death.[60] We cannot know how difficult and conflictual that was for Him, but we know these issues are troubling for the healers central to this book. This is not the place for a full-blown ethics of pastoral psychotherapy, but the claim to be an extension of His ministry requires attention to some of its principles.

Jesus was realistic about money, unimpressed by money, suspicious of wealth as an indicator of oppression, yet able to both receive generous gifts graciously [61] and to undergo extreme privation for the sake of integrity. He was respectful and challenging to both very rich and very poor. Though it seems reasonable to believe He might have similar expectations for those who practice in His name currently, we can conclude little about the details He would prefer in our professional lives. It is consistent with His ethic to receive what people can afford to provide us, to assist them in prioritizing our services among their total financial needs, to neither accept spurious claims of poverty (wise as serpents, innocent as doves) nor exclude more of the poor from our attention than our actual needs require, and to choose clients and financial policies that make us available to those whose health impacts the broader society. That will sometimes mean seeing a minister, a government official, or a student for a reduced fee and sometimes mean making scarce time available for a business executive who pays us very well.

We also do well to remember that He did not have to cope with the expenses of graduate education, carry (visible) responsibility for the education of children, or pay substantial prices for professional books and memberships.

Social class structures were very different in Jesus' society than in ours, and were powerfully impacted by the Roman occupation. He appeared to believe that substantial wealth or visible social position carried the likelihood of collaboration with the oppressors, and wealth and position minimally set a higher standard of stewardship and community care for the privileged. Yet it appears He maintained an identification with those outside the Roman orbit, hence poorer, while being sought out by many (e.g., the rich young ruler) who were highly placed. Although not at the bottom of the social ladder—presumably He learned His father's marketable carpentry skills, as the eldest son—neither His absolute wealth nor His formal education could have been at the level of the Romanized elite.

Our situation creates interesting tensions with His. To qualify for our ministry—and to acquire the skills that make us useful—we are required to undergo an education that makes us different from much of our society. It gives us a great deal in common with the wealthy and powerful. If we are good at our craft, those similarly educated will notice it. Sharing the experience of university and advanced training, we are part of a social world that often excludes people our commitments call us to serve. Not unlike the Galilean carpenter turned healer and teacher, we bridge contrasting segments of our society. Our education makes us part of established power, but we are called to those circles as a leavening influence, representatives of a countercultural depth of self-examination, of an increasingly marginal church, and of a commitment to human equality often lacking in the broader world. Further, we bring the values of the psychotherapy experience, of self-reflection and rationality, to a population that may nominally share our religious faith but often prefers sentimentalized, unexamined, and polarizing versions of it. We seem called to reject both Roman rule and violent revolution, while knowing that our educated, reflective, and hopefully egalitarian stance makes a sociopolitical statement that alienates and attracts high and lowly alike. In terms of skill, we had best be elitists; in terms of sharing resources, populism is more appropriate.

Because of these ambiguities, complex relationships with governmental and quasi-governmental structures are inevitable. We must render unto Caesar, but it is difficult to know just what Caesar's is. Many of us are licensed by the state. Many of us receive payments from insurance companies. Many of us provide services for Medicaid and/or Medicare. Many of us would like not to be poor, while providing services to people who are.

Pastoral counselors have a history of controversy over acceptance of state licensure, because it suggests compromise of our freedom to minister. There is a range of plausible positions. Mine is that we are essentially double agents, working within the structures of civil society under the authority of the state, while bearing primary loyalty to the twin alien powers of depth psychotherapy and the reign of God. If we refuse to do business with the state at all, we cannot provide services at all, unless we are willing either to be very poor or to limit the time we practice psychotherapy by doing something else to make money. Traditionally the payor would have been the church, and there have been times when the church could afford to do it. But it no longer can, and even if it could, there are problems with allowing it to do so. The church is no more a sinless, unambiguous institution than is the government, and many of those we serve need to be as free of ecclesiastical as of governmental dominance.

The situation in Jesus' time was simpler, though no less difficult. The Roman Empire did not license prophets, healers, and teachers. It just killed you if it didn't like what you were doing. The only requirements Jesus had to meet to serve the Jewish community was that He be interesting and persuasive. If He was formally authorized, we have no record of it. Pastoral counselors could operate in the same way—

work outside of established structures, accept no fees, seek no licenses, live on salaries earned for doing other things or such contributions as interested donors might provide. Many have sought to do so, and some still do. In my view, the consequences of that are too costly to be widely borne. It means that as much of the practitioner's time is spent creating the community of support and seeking the contributions to pay a salary as is actually spent providing the service. That has the advantage of requiring that the work represent a community, at least financially. But it fails to consider that the people best at providing the service may not be competent at creating the community or raising the money.

My conclusion is that there is no uncompromised locus of practice. All hallowing is incomplete. If we accept licensure by the state and the fiction that it protects the public, the state can hold us to a standard of care that may conflict with our commitments, but usually does not. It actually could do that whether we are licensed or not. Accepting the state's conditions often relieves us of having to decide between being very poor and seeing only wealthy people, and puts our profession in a position of being able to recruit new members and influence a broad spectrum of society. It also subjects us to the temptations that partnership with power always produces ("throw yourself down from this mountain") and makes the continual renewing of our commitments through study, prayer, and supervision that much more important.

If we choose against collaboration with the state, we make ourselves unavailable to many who need us—either because they cannot afford us, we cannot afford to see them, or they mistake those who lack the mark of the state's approval as incompetent. Facing licensing exams and continuing education requirements can be acts of faithful devotion, as much as prayer and fasting.

None of us can claim to be anyone's savior, to be without sin, or to have perfect religious or psychotherapeutic faith. But we can, with God's help, be faithful, and be part of a therapeutic movement that, in partnership with the church and other groups we cannot always identify, has a messianic function. We extend the grace of God, as it has been extended to and through us, as did Jesus the Christ. He was better at it. He certainly had a wider impact than any of us is likely to have. But if we are worthy of our calling, it is because we attempt and sometimes succeed in being a revealing, suffering, faithful point of contact between God's grace and those who desperately needs it to be free from the sin that commands their lives. Thanks be to God.

WORLD 5: 93 Suffering Endurance
WORLD 3: 76 emptiness fulfillment
WORLD 1: 57 Separation reunion

Chapter 10

The Play of God: Powerful Selves in Empowering Community

From the beginning we have been wrestling with central dilemmas for pastoral counselors: What is God doing in pastoral psychotherapy? What is at stake here? What is faithful about it? We posited guiding principles that would govern the work: the playfulness of God; God's persistent, steadfast love; the centrality of healing; the dialectic of individual and community. The discussion has maintained loyalty to psychoanalysis, process thought, and feminism, and named its intent to render the central redemptive movements of pastoral psychotherapy intelligible in relation to them. To complete its task, it must weave these elements into a single fabric, showing the relationship of these questions to each other and to the major themes of the book.

THE HALLOWED SPACE

The initial act of any pastoral psychotherapy is the creation, by therapist, community, and God, of a hallowed space. The imagery of many authors, therapists and theologians alike, has contributed to our understanding of that space. Nouwen's reference to the churches of Rome and Winnicott's description of the infant's transitional space alert us to a sacred openness where we can be and explore ourselves. Ogden's description of intersubjective space and Welker's appeal for free self-withdrawal that makes way for the Spirit mark the role of the other in enabling the space. That enabling/allowing is a central contribution of and through the pastoral psychotherapist, and creates an essential precondition for the experience and exploration of the self.

Reverie at every level—divine, maternal, therapeutic—brings resources to the space in both therapy and familial settings. Reverie charges it with nutrients and potential, just as the uterine wall supplies our original containers. Reverie takes the original form of Winnicott's "primary maternal preoccupation," the decisive short-lived capacity of the good-enough mother to sense the meaning in minute shifts of infant activity. When optimal, it allows "being alone in the presence of the other," the prototype for all internal space, and establishes the child's freedom to create and explore (the slightly different) transitional space. That territory, neither wholly within the sovereignty of the child nor of the outside world, allows the beginnings of experimentation, fantasy, and play, and is the seedbed of all freedom that is more related to others than it is psychotic. Winnicott narrates its beginnings in the moment of hesitation after the child grasps the new shiny object and before imbuing it with playful meaning, and in the transitional object which the parent sees as a stuffed animal or security blanket, but to the infant is best friend, comforter, toy, and pet. The sacred space of the therapy hour requires both the therapist's maternal reverie and the client's playful, transitional self-elaboration.

Bion furthers our understanding, identifying the caregiver's ability to take in the unconscious products of the other's psychic life and allow her or his own internal world to be reshaped by the projections, choosing to give up a piece of her or his sovereignty to enable the growth of infant or client. Therapists and parents give up the right and power to be a separate I, and clients flow into the vacated territory, reshaping it through unconscious guidance of the therapist, as Casement, Scharff, Stolorow, Atwood, and Benjamin point out. The container, the sacred space, evolves as therapist and client deepen their understanding of each other and the relationship they share. The intersubjective third becomes a reality independent of either self, a unique expression of the freedom of the Spirit, growing and creating its own structures as the separate persons reconceive one another over and over again.

This space exists within what Langs calls the therapeutic frame, created by establishing and maintaining the ground rules, not too differently from God's creating the Sabbath with the commandment to/through Moses. As Ashbrook taught us, much of the time in this container is sabbathing time, where dream, rest, prayer, and catching our breath are normative activities. We are together in this space unlike we are anywhere else, and its uniqueness, its liminality, its ability to function as the *axis mundi* depends on the clarity and reverence with which we re-present, maintain, and interpret its sacred decisiveness for the fruitfulness of the relationship and the work. When it is well maintained, when the hungers of the therapist are met by the meaning making in the space rather than by the vulnerability of the client, conditions are ripe for integration of previously disparate parts and the evolution of new structures.

The therapist is enabled, equipped to allow the space to remain empty, by his or her own hallowing in training, supervision, therapy, and prayer. When the space is ready, made so by action human and divine, the stage is set for the therapeutic drama to unfold.

PLAY

The therapeutic drama, like its predecessor in childhood, looks to the outsider like nondirected, meaningless activity. It is holy play, the developing creature sensing the direction it needs to move, choosing the object or sound or idea or person it needs to pursue or incorporate, mouthing it, exploring it, throwing it aside, noticing what feels delicious and what distasteful, combining these ideas or sounds or substances in the company of a partner who occasionally contributes an idea or an observation, sometimes a part of the play and more often an observer. The unconscious functions like an ample toybox, offering at its surface the candidates for the energy of the self, always connected to the frustrations not yet overcome, the capacities not yet developed. As client and therapist pass these treasures back and forth, the client gradually comes to recognize which ones dependably contribute to new constructions and lead to pleasure, and puts them out on a psychic shelf where they can be seen and remembered; which ones have become irrelevant and can go out with the trash; and which ones are still too scary to be handled and must go back in the box for another day. The therapist notices what feelings go with which piece of memory or fantasy and what combinations diminish or intensify the mood, providing the sponsoring presence that allows the client's play to continue a few moments longer with some of the more frightening pieces, registering when the named emotion does not fit with what the therapist sees in the client's face or body or experiences in his or her own internal life. Then the therapist's comment or expression or movement becomes one of the pieces of the play, part of the combination the client is experimenting with, something the client can use or pass over.

In Marion Milner's prepsychoanalytic self-exploration, she wrote in her diary,

> I want to change my attitudes; it fills me with restlessness that I am always striving after something and I don't know what it is. I envy people, artists chiefly. I want to achieve the play attitude. By this I mean concentration in an activity which has no apparent use just for the delight of doing it. . . . Play means to me freedom—freedom from fears. It is an expression of the dignity of the soul, enslaved in no bondage of justification. Perhaps then if I am to learn to play I must go down to hell and find out what taskmaster is lurking there.[1]

Later, as she writes her thoughts of God, play returns:

> GOD . . . "of our fathers, known of old," . . . the tension of vitality, the pattern, order, arrangement, precision, you playing, you absorbed, you like a child playing, having your own concerns, beyond me, your own designs, that's the word, design, not purposes or intentions but design, like a drawing, every part holding together . . .[2]

Her expression fits our meaning precisely. Both we and God play, in the pursuit of activity aimed at our delight, and in the process are drawn inexorably to those problems yet unsolved, for which we best gain the crucial data when we are playfully catching them out of the corner of our eye rather than tightening our muscles and shortening our breath. There is time later in the sequence for work.

A joyous by-product of play is internalization of its circumstances. When the child or client is at play (perhaps this is also true of God, but we have less data), within the space hallowed by reverie of parent or therapist, pulls from the toybox two or three long-separated pieces, and puts them together on the psychic shelf for further use, they are stored there as a new design. *The reverie of the therapist-mother-God is retained as part of the configuration.* Internal objects are formed and changed in precisely this manner, their components held together by the affective glue of the sponsoring Other.

This is how the rich complexity of our psyches is formed and re-formed. Our unconscious hopes and hungers carry us to play, opening us to new internal and external environments. Our psychic eye is caught by this or that attractive or alarming piece. We grasp it, hesitate, make it our own anew, link it to others, sense how that feels, apply it in relationship, and, if it satisfies, add it to our store of usable psychic resources. When we plug it into our repertoire, it bears the stamp of the relationships active when it was forged or found. Hence, our inner life is both data catalog and communion of saints as each learning is held in place with the life's energy of parent or therapist or beloved.

BURSTS OF CLARITY

Insofar as that linking is conscious, it is represented in awareness by a sign or symbol, most often a word. The word is a gift, usually from the other whose reverie sheltered the discovery and whose alpha function participated in the formation of new knowing. Stern describes this process as beginning with our recognition of islands of consistency in events, sequences that dependably repeat, then evolve into rudimentary concepts that take repeatable form at a yet later point, when the word-sign organizes them into psychic content that can be remembered. These are the constant conjunctions that Symington, following Bion, calls the "selected fact," the awareness or perspective that fixes the relationship among previously disparate elements of the picture. This is the function a father plays when he links the queasy feeling in the pit of his stomach, the gnarled look on the baby's face, the awkward attempts to stretch and turn, and murmurs "you need to burp" before gently moving the baby to his shoulder and patting him firmly on the back. It is the function the therapist fulfills when she asks, "Is there something you're avoiding saying," after the client has been following a sequential account, suddenly stops, the affect changes, and the client asks an irrelevant question. It offers a possible meaning for the constellation of data just experienced, organizing what seemed like a random collection of events into a single nameable pattern.

Such newly emerging bursts of clarity enable adults to break out of the habituated rigidity that threatens life and hope. At the individual or cultural level, the rules about what can be seen and known, what possibilities can be lived out and which ones cannot, the boundaries between conscious and unconscious, have trapped so much searching energy and walled it off from fulfillment that the organism has creaked to a laborious halt. The same dissatisfactions are felt over and over again, the same false attempts at solution are repeated, the same odd behaviors emerge and are noticed by others. Often the individual has gravitated to others suffering the same pain, and while they seek to support one another, new defenses against the feared release are formed. But there comes a point, as the despair increases, where a God-given intolerance of further deterioration asserts itself, and a momentary glimpse of another possibility evokes a flood of repentance and the decision to seek a therapist. The client may or may not see it in terms of sin, but will always see it as a mistaken path that has led to grievous pain and must not be continued. As a good Baptist lady told me last month, "Something in me has been broken for twenty years. I want to fix it."

BIRTH INTO THE HALLOWED SPACE

The birth into hallowed space always carries an element of the mysterious. Several elements that usually seem random must describe a perfect arc for a few moments to complete the link between static suffering and the possibility of release. The client must be aware of the pain, perhaps even more aware than usual through some chance but predictable event that intensifies the suffering. Sometimes a dream has been particularly horrifying, or a memory has finally penetrated the repression barrier. Often clients say something to someone who just happens to come along, who participates in the hallowing by mentioning the possibility of therapy, gives them our name, or tells them of a friend who got help from a good clinician. Perhaps that is the day they go to the marriage enrichment workshop, or you preach at their church, or they pick up your card at the supermarket.

That catapults them to the boundary of the sacred space, where the first few exchanges either open the way to the holy moments at its core or confirm them in the belief that the suffering they are enduring is the best they can expect. After a few intensely uncertain exchanges, the beauty of sabbathing can open before the client and the more playful, less desperate exploration of the present can begin.

A client captured this experience recently by asking me to read to her from a children's book. A preadolescent Native American boy had fled the village in pique over a parent's decision, run into the woods, and gotten lost.

> "HELP!" I yelled again and again, "HELPHELPHELPHELP!" I heard a scurry in the dense bushes behind me, turned and fled from it, dodging trees, leaping over the ground whenever it dipped, thrashing through tall grass that tossed seeds every which way as I knocked against its dry blooms. I ran without pause or purpose, ran as if I were being hunted, ran like a racing fire, until finally I tripped, sprawled on my stomach. Panting, I turned over.[3]

Somewhere between the flight from the hounds of heaven and the calm at the heart of therapy, a therapist has passed an initial test and the client has begun to sense that something more sacred than his or her destruction might happen here. The Indian boy puts it like this:

> Birds must have been making noise before and stopped at my outburst, because suddenly I noticed a new level of silence. And here's the odd thing: as each normal solution to my predicament

occurred to me and then had to be dismissed, as the size of my own stupidity—first for putting myself in this situation and then for not knowing what to do once I was here—settled over me like the shadow of a rain cloud, other parts of me seemed magically to get smarter. I saw details I had never previously noticed: the shape of bark as it folded into gnarls, the veins in rock, the shimmer and sparkle of a spiderweb. I felt the earth under me, solid and steady. I smelled not just the ordinary musty odor of the forest, but many flavors—the tang of mint, the rot of logs, the sweet sing of water. My mind shed its weight, abandoned its effort to divide the tumble of my senses into words or ideas. I opened my mouth, opened my eyes, opened my hand, opened my ears. . . . In the mix, every object, every noise, every moment was bright and sharp and startling. I had never been so awake.[4]

These transforming moments carry intense ambiguity. They combine awareness of terrible foolishness, self-endangerment, sin, and shame with an exultant sense of release, dance, gifts of wisdom, and new hope. They release avalanches of memory, a true re-membering that lets pieces of ourselves move to their rightful places in the narrative, bringing us into communion that we thought forever lost. It is as if the seal on the unconscious, on its longings, terrors, imaginings, affects, and history has been opened in a massive, delirious gift of God. In those moments we meet God and some other, or many others, in the same moments. It is unclear which mediated the presence of the other, but both are known to be here. The lure of God has pulled us through the silence at the heart of things, and we emerge with new resources literally sticking to us as we struggle to reassemble our lives.

These are the sacred moments, the soterioform moments, that present the claim and promise of God, of life. The pain has been the messenger of God's judgment on the lies that had structured our lives. "For three transgressions of Israel and for four, I will not revoke the punishment."[5] Awareness of the lie, the fault, for us as for those who heard Amos, is itself a new thing that some blessed irritant has forced into view. In those moments, within the sacred space, the awareness is embedded in a broader recognition of God's claim and promise, though the penitent often is not aware of it at first. As with the decision to cross into the sacred space, this is a complex choice made in

stages, or at least becoming conscious in stages. First comes the recognition of the lie, the flaw, the sin, the pathology. Often the presence
of the helper is required, whether that is the prophet or the contemporary therapist, to embolden the person to allow the recognition into
consciousness. Once the sufferer has authorized another to do that, to
bear the sin and pain together, the other is granted the unique privilege and responsibility of being heard. Then the other has the authority to utter the claim: "The Kingdom of God is at hand."[6] He or she
speaks on behalf of all those with an investment in ending the bond-
age: self, family, community, church, God. The claim, as described in
Chapter 9, starts as a call to responsibility. It insists that both the hearers and all these others are harmed if they fail to achieve the stature
available to them. It asserts the cost to all who care, now that they
know they are less than they could be, if they continue in their present
unrealized existence. It challenges their right to exact that price from
the community, which includes and constitutes themselves. It does
not stop with demand, though, again, it may first appear that way to
the sufferer. "Lo, I am with you always, even unto the end of the age"[7]
is also part of the message. The resources of the partner, the prophet,
the therapist, the community will be there for us, externally and internally, as we seek to meet the challenge. The therapist will literally absorb, feel, be temporarily harmed by the woundedness of the client,
so in that shared woundedness they can search together for the new
structures that generate a different kind of life.

THERAPY AS LIBERATING MULTIPLICITY

This brings us to another critical assertion: the therapy itself is an
event that liberates persons from sin (their own and others') and its
consequences. It changes the heart of stone into the heart of flesh. It
removes obstacles between the sufferer and God, and it can do so because God has been instrumental in making the therapy available, in
driving the client to it, in luring the therapist to become his or her fullest self, and in puncturing the boundaries between the two so the
Spirit can make a powerful and redemptive duality of them.

In this fulfillment, God (Himself, Herself, Godself) is changed. Bion writes of the evolution of O, of how the reality at the very heart of things adds another unit of complexity and richness whenever a new psychic possibility is actualized.[8] Wieman writes of the continuing elaboration of creative good when more of the created order is enlisted to work in harmony with the sacred.[9] Whitehead's consequent nature of God is enriched with every human adventure.[10]

The changes exist on at least two levels, though philosophical analysis may reveal them to be the same. These moments of transformation add an additional circle of internal relationships to the sacred energy. Insofar as God is an active, pulsating presence working in and through human endeavor, whose size "is fundamentally determined by the range and intensity of internal relationships [God] can create and sustain," God becomes, in Loomer's language, larger, more equal to God's task.[11] And God also takes great pleasure from the play. The Gospels are full of invitations to "enter into the joy of your master" by participating in just such expansive, holy experiences of liberation.[12] If we look to Whitehead, we find that the process of taking a newly emerging event, an actual occasion, into a newly forming whole is termed, precisely, "enjoyment."[13] In the fulfillment that comes when one has given one's all to and for the other, and it has been received as a gift that transforms the experience of that other, one is suffused with joy. It is as true of God as of lovers or therapists.

This play always brings seemingly incompatible elements together. Its heart is the dialectic of conscious and unconscious, waking and dreaming, denotative and connotative, left brain and right brain, Jew and Greek, self and God, the enemy and we who are mandated to love the enemy. This is the polyphony of which Cunningham writes, the incredible diversity Welker describes in the Pentecost experience, the negating and preserving contexts of positions central to Ogden's writing. Tracy has been particularly helpful in clarifying this reality, noting that any time we see only one perspective on a phenomenon we are denied the depth perception that an alternate perspective, or multiple alternate perspectives, would offer. Since we are incomplete, flawed beings, any perspective that one of us can generate and detail is, by definition, incomplete and inaccurate. But when you get the added data from the other position, when the conscious clarity is expanded by the symbolism from the unconscious, when the therapist's concept is jostled by the client's association and given back in a new form, then the range within which reality can be sought shrinks to a more manageable size, though never to a single point.

Of course, openness to the incompatibility is not automatic. The temptation always exists to flee the contrast, which can feel like a threat to destroy the self that is known. The thoughts do not readily cohere. To return to Dorris' Indian boy:

> What should I do? I had never concentrated quite this hard about anything before—but then, I had never needed to. This situation was different and new in every way, and my mind stretched to capture all the loose ideas, ran to gather them before they danced so far apart they could not talk to each other.[14]

Keeping the thoughts within shouting distance of one another is critical to the value of the breakthrough. Again, the presence of a person can be the decisive difference, if that person senses the developing terror and offers a word of clarification, giving the sufferer an acceptable cognitive option for classifying the new experience. Kegan's explanation of the development of psychic life can help us with this. He indicates that at every point we are embedded in an evolutionary truce, an unrecognized pattern of perceptions, strategies, and expectations that structure the life of a developmental epoch.[15] The truces are predictably disrupted by experiences of "decentering" when some incompatible capacity, event, idea, or perception contradicts the existing world. Only then can the developing self gain enough perspective on the existing truce to internalize it and name it, as the self is in the process of being jostled beyond it. The key for us here is that the internalization, which provides both the cognitive clarity about the stage being surpassed and the building block for the next one, will only happen if the resources of the prior truce remain in place for the one growing to fall back on. Those resources are typically persons and the relational patterns developed with them.

The person could be a parent, teacher, friend, or therapist. He or she must be seen as willing to let the growing one move forward or not, as able to keep the existing structures and patterns of relationship in place or to allow them to shift as the supplicant's maturation expands. If a therapist, he or she must be able to allow the client's wisdom to determine whether the new truce becomes the primary manner of being.

This decisive dialectic or broader conversation, in the presence of the community-hallowed person who becomes the bridge between past and future, carries several qualities important to our discussion. They are moments of intensifying contrast and harmony, moving to the creation of new beauty. Since each element of newly internalized perspective comes from its own strand of historical transmission, and those are invariably divergent, each such event results in a peaceful combination of two formerly discordant, perhaps even hostile, traditions and communities. A new communion is established through the capacity to hold simultaneously in consciousness two or more realities formerly thought incompatible, but now seen to have a unifying element particular to the situation and persons here joined. All this contributes to the evolution of O, as the addition of this newly emergent entity to all that is growthful expands the scope of that which supports the harmony of further individualizing entities. The container itself is evolving, as it takes in and harmoniously relates more and more of the cosmos. God is expanding, as is the community that constitutes the Body of Christ. As revelation occurs, both revealer and recipient are changed.

ENGAGING THE NEW WORLD

As O evolves and the holy encounter creates new structures for and in the self, our pilgrim suddenly notices the possibility of engagement with a newly seen, experienced, and defined world. A sequence unfolds that has powerful consequences for self and community.

A forty-year-old woman, in weekly therapy for half a decade, reported a dramatic upheaval with an uncle. He had lived with her very abusive family when she was young and had known about her frequent incestuous rapes by her father. He himself had repeatedly violated her privacy, taunted her about her body in the bathtub, set up friends to rape her in adolescence, yet was protected by her father all their lives. In midlife, after a series of encounters in which he tried to control her access to family celebrations, she sent him a message saying she was ending the relationship and she hoped he knew how much he was losing. She violated her father's rule to never let a family member know they had caused pain by telling him that his "giving her the silent treatment" at family gatherings has hurt her deeply.

He interpreted the message as a suicide threat, drove a hundred miles in the middle of the night, met her at a restaurant at 3 a.m., and they had their first significant conversation in decades. He said he never knew she felt wounded by him and retorted that she never talked to him at gatherings either (since this often occured in sessions, it seemed plausible to me). He explained his not inviting her to his vacation home on the basis of his belief that she wanted no relationship.

She did not know what to believe. It felt dangerous to hold open the possibility that he could care what she felt, but it was hard to dismiss the middle-of-the-night pilgrimage. She was flooded for days with powerful affect: fear, depression, sadness, hope. A subsequent special family event passed without tension. After two decades in a job that felt much like the family, she noticed an attractive ad for a similar position in an institution with a much happier reputation. She submitted a résumé.

A whole series of new events happened to the woman in the story. Like the boy in the forest who ran from the village, then noticed the whorls of the bark and the singing of the water after several minutes of terror, she started the sequence with a dramatic but despairing withdrawal. Amazingly to her, someone responded. The rigidity of the old pattern was disrupted. In this genuinely new situation, both she and her uncle could offer new definitions to their relationship, so hideously scarred in their youth. The new definitions open the possibility of a new world. Having broken with the old order by sending her message, she felt the *right* to assign meanings in this new order. She now has a cognitive picture of relational reality that is hers, not just that of her family or the negated inverse of her family's. She develops genuine curiosity about it. There is space for the question "How will the uncle act?" alongside her longstanding certainty about how he will act. His youthful exploitativeness is placed in a different context by his response to her middle-aged challenge. The desperation that produced the initial message, coupled with the unexpected response, has blown the seal off a well that reached deep into her unconscious, and new ideas, feelings, and ambitions have burst out onto the surface. She finds she can experiment with believing her own definitions, which places her actions at the service of the world those definitions structure for her. That carries her into the family in a new way, cues her to notice the possibility of a different job, and carries the potential for restructuring her entire relational world. This sequence—withdrawal from an old world, defining events according to the newly emerging data, claiming the right to assign meanings, the new reality's leading to unaccustomed curiosity, and a resulting move toward a newly conceived psychic and relational cosmos, both cognitively and behaviorally—is paradigmatic for the events following a major therapeutic breakthrough, and for those stemming from receipt of revelation as well. Often the events are coterminous.

As Dorris' youngster puts it:

> I might never find my way home, and if I tried to go back, guessing the way I had come, it was likely that I would become more lost. . . .

> Going back was just . . . going back. If I succeeded in finding my way, I would only be where I had started, and all that had taken place since I stepped alone into the forest would be gone from my life. . . . Going back was like saying no after I had already said yes. . . . If I went back now, I would be going back *farther* than the place where I had started, and I might never be brave enough to leave again. . . . The way home, if there was one, was to walk ahead, to discover a new road that would belong to no one but me, to find my way out through a different door than the one I had entered.[16]

THE MESSIANIC TASK OF PSYCHOTHERAPY

Now we can add layers of meaning to the earlier claim that pastoral psychotherapy is a messianic task. The client's experience, though often the client does not know it before the fact, is a quest for the vision of God. It is enabled, at its best, by an intersection between client, community, and God, mediated through the self of the therapist, but mediated in a specific way that makes the historical specificity of that self transparent to the confluence, which is trying to make itself known. Therapists' disciplined abstinence from memory, desire, and understanding exerts a purifying influence on their inevitable tendency to sinful (that is, self-aggrandizing) self-assertion and creates the free self-withdrawal for the sake of the other that Cunningham and Welker mark as characteristic of the Holy Spirit. That abstinence allows reverie, the focused attention based on the implicit assumption that O will emerge through the self of the client and be known intimately here and now, if therapists can get themselves and their needs (but not their experience of the client) out of the center of their attention. In that place, hallowed in part by a therapist's (F)aith, the therapist is appropriated by O, becomes O or a part of O for the sacred moment, allowing him or her to participate in the presentation of God's claim and promise for this particular present.

Such sacred encounters cannot occur without the therapist's willingness to be impacted, changed, led into suffering or delight if such is the client's reality. It is only as the therapist is open to experiencing whatever is deepest in the client, joy or horror, that he or she serves as the person in whose presence the client can allow the polyphonic harmony to persist and remain conscious, can allow consciousness and unconscious to interpenetrate each other, can experience the playful juxtaposition of rigorous self-criticism and the delight of new discovery. In those instances, the therapist is in the role of "representative mystic" for the group that includes therapist and client (and usually others), allowing the immediate experience of O (which cannot be known but only become), and in the process enabling the transformation of the client's psychic structures through the therapist's willingness to be drawn deeper into the mystery of God. The mystic's role in that transaction (in that moment both therapist and client participate

in the mystical) is to rediscover and express that the group which represents God (church, nation, culture, family, therapeutic dyad) is not
God, but that God expresses Godself imperfectly through them all.

This is no more an easy matter, or even primarily a matter of technical excellence, for the therapist than was Jesus' allowing Himself to
be crucified a matter of knowing what was required of a transformational religious leader. Though knowing helps, the decisive acts for
Messiah or therapist are spiritual and ethical. They involve the conviction that nothing is more important in this moment than the relationship with God, the deepest reality, as it is given to be known
through the experience of this place and these people. They require a
self-emptying that also feels keenly the impact on self of others' love
and hate, allows it to matter deeply without allowing it to compel decisions against the Truth (K, not L or H). They require "not my will,
but Thine be done." They concede that "none is good but God alone."
They make the bond with God the structural core of presence with the
other, at the same moment as they expect to find their deepest access
to God in their faithful presence with the other. In this way both Messiah and therapist are soteriological figures, liberating the sufferer
from the lie and sin to which he or she is addicted. Both can do it only
as they are enabled to "embody their own bit of Godhead." Jesus did
it more broadly, more consistently (during His ministry), and for a
wider range of people, but no one can do it at all without transcendent
moments of faithfulness that change both themselves and the others
whom they serve.

THE SELF AND THE COMMUNITY

These moments of faithfulness both heighten individuality and
deepen commitment to community. The two are not in opposition.
Rather, the most intense and faithful expression of each is necessary
to the health of the other. The Christological, pneumatological, and
analytic writings all argue for the transforming figure's deep immersion in and responsiveness to the community out of which he or she
springs and which he or she seeks to influence. But it is a specific

kind of relation to community, out of a number of possibilities, that the encounter with the messianic other energizes.

Several images suggest aspects of that relationship: the polyphony of Pentecost, the interpenetration of Eucharist/communion, the exchange of hearts generated in the intersubjective space of therapy, the mystic who is fed by the group and literally constituted by the group, but carries the group's connection with O to an intensity the group had not hitherto achieved. Neither God nor the therapist craves cloned relationship partners. Both prefer and work to enliven others who are as distinct as the Parthians and Medes speaking their own languages in first-century Jerusalem,[17] while united in a shared joy and creativity that draws on a common outpouring of energy. As I have argued throughout, it is at the points of intersection, the spaces between the definable identities, where truth and energy are most likely to be found. The community is a locus of polyphonic harmony and contrast, not unison singing. Sin is more likely to dominate unopposed when all voices are supposed to be identical.

In the communal construction of identity, the contrasting threads of selfhood come from diverse sources—the psychoanalytic community and the culture of the client's extended family; the differing ethnic threads that run through the broader community and intersect in a person (the English, Scottish, Jewish, and Austrian elements that constitute my daughter); the mutual challenge, correction, and distortion that come at us from Christendom and capitalism. The community consists not in a pledge to be identical, nor an agreement to be subservient, but rather a covenant to be in relationship, to take this specific set of others into account over and over across the years. When such a sacred community is developing, the choice of all partners to take one another as contributors to the whole sets the conditions for what Welker terms the "force field of the Spirit" to act, in which all resist both being dominated and subsuming the others. It is/can be a communal reverie, an enlivened, hallowed space in which pieces of formerly separated groupings can be exchanged, modified, and reconfigured. The outcome is in the differing members of the Body of Christ relying on one another for their life and effectiveness, yet having enormous differences in nature and function.

This is true at the dyadic or the societal levels. Therapists and clients are profoundly affected by one another—note my clients' contributions to this book. Spouses change one another over the decades, growing in some ways more alike and in others more extreme. Jew and Greek in ancient Palestine could not be as though the other were absent, any more than black and white in contemporary North America have identities uninfluenced by one another. Yet the health of these communities is dependent on their ability to create and nurture those exceptional persons whose embodying and extending of the communal gifts moves the whole community into greater ability to function in the ever-new environment. Those persons realize new life forms, new themes of which their communities model the unending variations. The Washingtons and Lincolns, Kings and Kennedys, Gandhis, Presleys, DiMaggios, Luthers, and on some days even you and I are necessary, in our uniqueness, to the polyphonic exchange that allows community to remain alive, flexible, and responsive. But if we try to copy any of them precisely, and are successful, we contribute to the atrophy of our common venture.

Pastoral psychotherapy helps mobilize and empower the individuals the community needs to overcome the twin evils of individualism and collectivism. Though it is often an exploration of the life of one person, it is even then the exploration of how that person is constituted by and contextualized within a sequence of communities, and how that person can contribute to yet more. The effort is made possible by a community's hallowing of place and persons, and it aims at moving a person, couple, or family more fully into its own unique way of touching God and bearing fruit for others. Eigen writes that we are "enabling clients *'to am,'*" to incarnate the self that they have the resources to be.[18] Though some indulge in endless self-savoring, the therapist's responsibility is to challenge the self-indulgent ethic of self-admiration, or the dependent glorying in receiving attention, to the point where what one has already received and can now contribute is in the foreground. The therapist's ability to make his or her own self-awareness a tangible contribution to the lives of others, while also being enjoyed in itself, is a model for the client of how a gift from

God and through the community can be enjoyed by the primary receiver and used for the benefit of all.

The community has a calling of its own, to give itself away for the benefit of the world. A graced community is one so responsive to God's leading that its very structure makes it inescapable that its members, whether therapists, clients, donors, or scoffers, live their lives adding value and energy to the stimuli they absorb, passing it through them and on to the broader public, and that the community itself also gives beyond itself more than it takes in. It generates adventure, harmony, and contrast in its response to the lure of God. No person or system can do that for long unless it is equipped to enjoy, to receive and admire, appreciate, respond to, and be nourished by those gifts of substance, beauty, and thought that come its way. Pastoral psychotherapy is a discipline designed to help individuals and communities reorganize themselves so they can enjoy the gifts of God, and in the process both become and add to those gifts themselves. It functions best when embedded in a community that is already doing it well, but can contribute to the growth in that direction of any community.

NAMING THE MYSTERY

This brings us, at last, to a question that has cropped up repeatedly throughout the volume but has never been directly addressed: What is the importance of naming God as part of the pastoral psychotherapeutic process? At several points I have thought that perhaps this was the chapter or the paragraph when the question should be directly engaged, and at every point until now have decided that the time was not right. I find that I had decided, perhaps on theological grounds, that the question is not properly a theological question. It is a question of clinical practice. In the sense of H. Richard Niebuhr when he wrote that the purpose of theological education is not to serve the church, but to serve the purposes of the church,[19] the purpose of pastoral psychotherapy is not to serve Christianity or religious faith, but to serve their purposes. Their purpose is to enhance the joy of God in fellowship with God's earthly (and cosmic) creation, to increase the shared pleasure of humans and their Holy Other in the play of an unending ecosystem. Though Eigen is right when he says that the images we use to express the unimaginable determine the direction of our lives,[20] the question of where we use them is critical to their effecting their purposes. With the client who denigrates faith, crediting God when God's purposes (as far as we know them) are being served can disrupt the serving. With the client marinated in a compliant faith, naming God contributes to making an idol of the sacred name and of us. For the faithful, curious, unsaturated client, who sees God as the liberating mystery who can never be contained, who can be met and become but not fully known, naming God is an act of meeting and sharing that deepens our loyalty to the transforming power of the therapeutic process and that which lies within, beneath, and beyond it.

To put it simply, to use God language in pastoral psychotherapy as compliance to religious authority is to faithlessly corrupt and sabotage the process. To use the name of God when client and therapist together are striving to understand and affirm sacred healing in a shared moment is an incredible privilege, one of the richest gifts this spiritual discipline offers to those who practice it and those who are the recipients of the practice. I thank God for my many opportunities to do the same.

Notes

Introduction

1. Wilfred Bion, *Attention and Interpretation* (London, Maresfield Library, 1970) pp. 62-71.

2. Larry Kent Graham, *Care of Persons, Care of Worlds* (Nashville, Abingdon, 1992) p. 99.

3. Bernard Loomer, "Two Conceptions of Power," *Process Studies,* 6(1), (1976) pp. 10-12.

4. Donald W. Winnicott, *Through Paediatrics to Psycho-Analysis: Collected Papers* (New York, Brunner/Mazel, 1992) pp. 182-184.

5. Christopher Bollas, *Forces of Destiny: Psychoanalysis and Human Idiom* (London, Free Association Books, 1989) pp. 9-11.

6. Christopher Bollas, *Being a Character: Psychoanalysis and Self Experience* (New York, Hill and Wang, 1992) pp. 66ff; Wilfred Bion, *Learning from Experience* (London, Maresfield Library, 1962) p. 6ff.

7. Bernard Meland, *Faith and Culture* (Carbondale, Southern Illinois University Press, 1953) p. 172.

8. Paul J. Tillich, *Systematic Theology* (Chicago, University of Chicago Press, 1951) Vol. I., p. 111.

9. Meland, *Faith and Culture,* p. 201.

10. Martin Luther, "Treatise on Christian Liberty," in *Works of Martin Luther, with Introductions and Notes* (Philadelphia, The A.J. Holman Company and the Castle Press, 1915) Vol. II, p. 337.

11. Sallie McFague, *Models of God* (Philadelphia, Fortress, 1987) p. 6.

12. Ivan Boszormenyi-Nagy and Barbara R. Krasner, *Between Give and Take* (New York, Brunner/Mazel, 1986) see especially p. 417, also pp. 89, 177.

Chapter 1

1. Bernard Meland, *Faith and Culture* (Carbondale, Southern Illinois University Press, 1953) p. 195.

2. Bernard Meland, *Realities of Faith* (New York, Oxford University Press, 1962) p. 228.

3. Henry Nelson Wieman, *The Source of Human Good* (Carbondale, Southern Illinois University Press, 1967) p. 58.

4. Gordon Jackson, *Pastoral Care and Process Theology* (New York, University Press of America, 1981) p. 49.

5. Sallie McFague, *Models of God* (Philadelphia, Fortress Press, 1987) p. 146ff.

6. Paul J. Tillich, *The Meaning of Health* (Chicago, University of Chicago Press, 1961) p. 17.

7. Paul J. Tillich, "Impact of Psychotherapy on Theological Thought," Academy of Religion and Mental Health, 1960, p. 8.

8. Meland, *Faith and Culture,* p. 179.

9. Ibid., p. 192.

10. McFague, *Models of God,* pp. xi-xii.

11. Alfred North Whitehead, *Adventures of Ideas* (New York, The Free Press, 1933) pp. 277-283.

12. David Tracy, *The Analogical Imagination* (New York, Crossroad, 1991) pp. 75-79.

13. Brian Grant, *The Social Structure of Christian Families* (St. Louis, Chalice Press, 2000).

14. William Goode, *World Revolutions and Family Patterns* (London, Collier-Macmillan, 1963).

15. James Hillman and Michael Ventura, *We've Had a Hundred Years of Psychotherapy—and the World's Getting Worse* (San Francisco, Harper Collins, 1993).

16. Robert Kegan, *In Over Our Heads*: *The Mental Demands of Modern Life* (Cambridge, Harvard University Press, 1995).

17. W.H. Auden, *The Dyer's Hand and Other Essays* (New York, Random House, 1948) pp. 10-11.

18. McFague, *Models of God,* p. 182.

19. Reinhold Niebuhr, *The Nature and Destiny of Man* (New York, Charles Scribner's Sons, 1941) Book II, p. 258.

20. Larry Kent Graham, *Care of Persons, Care of Worlds* (Nashville, Abingdon, 1992) p. 132ff; see also Robert N. Bellah, Richard Madsden, William M. Sullivan, Ann Swidler, and Steven M. Tipton, *Habits of the Heart: Individualism and Commitment in American Life* (New York, Harper and Row, 1985) p. 142ff.

21. Tracy, *Analogical Imagination,* p. 429ff.

22. James Ashbrook, *The Brain and Belief: Faith in the Light of Brain Research* (Bristol, Indiana, Wyndham Hall Press, 1988).

23. Whitehead, *Adventures,* p. 265.

24. Ibid., pp. 381, 525-526.

25. Tracy, *Analogical Imagination,* p. 447.

26. Bradford Keeney, *The Aesthetics of Change* (New York, Guilford, 1983) p. 116.

Chapter 2

1. See particularly Bernard Meland, *Faith and Culture* (Carbondale, Southern Illinois University Press, 1953).

2. Acts 2:47.

3. Erik Erikson, "Ego Development and Historical Change," in *Psychological Issues Monographs* (New York, International Universities Press, 1959) Vol. I, no. 1, pp. 1-9.

4. Wilhelm Reich, *Character Analysis* (New York, Farrar, Straus, and Giroux, 1933) p. xxvi.

5. Wilfred Bion, *Attention and Interpretation* (London, Maresfield Library, 1970) see especially p. 73.

6. Ibid.

7. Ibid., p. 76.

8. James Framo, *Explorations in Marital and Family Therapy: Selected Papers of James L. Framo* (New York, Springer, 1982).

9. Edward R. Shapiro and A. Wesley Carr, *Lost in Familiar Places* (New Haven, Yale University Press, 1991) p. 163ff.

10. D. W. Winnicott, *Through Paediatrics to Psycho-Analysis* (New York, Brunner/Mazel, 1992) p. 99.

11. Thomas Ogden, *Subjects of Analysis* (Northvale, Aronson, 1994) pp. 50-62.

12. Salvador Minuchin, *Families and Family Therapy* (London, Tavistock, 1974) pp. 6-7.

13. Gregory Bateson, *Steps to an Ecology of Mind: Collected Essays in Anthropology, Psychiatry, Evolution, and Epistemology* (San Francisco, Chandler, 1972) see especially p. xvii and following.

14. Larry Kent Graham, *Care of Persons, Care of Worlds* (Nashville, Abingdon, 1992) pp. 99-100.

15. Robert N. Bellah, Richard Madsen, William M. Sullivan, Ann Swidler, and Steven M. Tipton, *Habits of the Heart* (New York, Harper and Row, 1985) pp. 167-194; see also Robert N. Bellah, Richard Madsen, William M. Sullivan, Ann Swidler, and Steven M. Tipton, *The Good Society* (New York, Knopf, 1992) pp. 156-176.

16. Florence A. Summerlin, *Religion and Mental Health: A Bibliography* (Rockville, Maryland, National Institute of Mental Health, U.S. Department of Health and Human Services, 1980); see also Daniel J. Benor, *Healing Research* (Munich, Helix Verlag, 1993); and Robert G. Jahn and Brenda J. Dunne, *Margins of Reality: The Role of Consciousness in the Physical World* (New York, Harcourt, Brace, Jovanovich, 1987).

17. Sudhir Kakar, *Shamans, Mystics, and Doctors: A Psychological Inquiry into India and Its Healing Tradition* (Delhi, Oxford University Press, 1982); see also William James, *Varieties of Religious Experience* (New York, Collier Books,

1961); and Anton Boisen, *Exploration of the Inner World* (New York, Harper and Brothers, 1936).

18. Bradford Keeney, *The Aesthetics of Change* (New York, Guilford, 1983) p. 140

Chapter 3

1. Bernard Meland, *Faith and Culture* (Carbondale, Southern Illinois University Press, 1953) p. 98ff.

2. Ibid., p. 99.

3. Sudhir Kakar, *The Inner World—A Psychoanalytic Study of Childhood and Society in India* (Delhi, Oxford University Press, 1982); Stanley N. Kurtz, *All the Mothers Are One: Hindu India and the Cultural Reshaping of Psychoanalysis* (New York, Columbia University Press, 1992); and Alan Roland, *In Search of Self in India and Japan* (Princeton, Princeton University Press, 1988).

4. Monica McGoldrick, John K. Pearce, and Joseph Giordano, eds, *Ethnicity and Family Therapy* (New York, Guilford, 1982) see especially pp. 3-51.

5. Daniel Stern, *The Interpersonal World of the Infant* (New York, Basic Books, 1985) p. 37.

6. Ibid., pp. 46-50.

7. Ibid., p. 97.

8. Christopher Bollas, *The Shadow of the Object* (New York, Columbia University Press, 1987) p. 32ff.

9. Ibid., p. 46.

10. Wilfred Bion, *Learning from Experience* (London, Maresfield Library, 1962) p. 6ff.

11. Ibid., pp. 13-20.

12. D.W. Winnicott, *Through Paediatrics to Psycho-Analysis* (New York, Brunner/Mazel, 1992) p. 302.

13. Bion, *Learning,* p. 36.

14. Sudhir Kakar, *Shamans, Mystics, and Doctors: A Psychological Inquiry into India and Its Healing Tradition* (Delhi, Oxford University Press, 1982) p. 146.

15. Ana-Maria Rizzuto, *Birth of the Living God: A Psychoanalytic Study* (Chicago, University of Chicago Press, 1981).

16. Donald W. Winnicott, "Observations of Infants in a Set Situation," in D.W. Winnicott, *Through Paediatrics to Psycho-Analysis* (New York, Brunner/Mazel, 1958) pp. 52-69.

17. Bion, *Learning,* p. 17.

18. Wilfred Bion, *Attention and Interpretation* (London, Tavistock, 1970) p. 95.

19. D. W. Winnicott, *Playing and Reality* (London, Routledge, 1971) pp. 86-90.

20. Gordon Jackson, *Pastoral Care and Process Theology* (New York University Press of American, 1981) pp. 70-73.

21. Bernard Loomer, "Two Conceptions of Power," *Criterion,* 15 (1976), pp. 12-23. Also published in Process Studies 6 (1976) pp. 5-32.

22. Thomas Ogden, *The Primitive Edge of Experience* (Northvale, Aronson, 1989) p. 30ff.

23. Ibid., p. 46.

24. Thomas Ogden, *Subjects of Analysis* (Northvale, Aronson, 1994) p. 18.

25. Ibid., p. 47.

26. Robert Kegan, *The Evolving Self* (Cambridge, Harvard University Press, 1982) p. 81ff.

27. James Ashbrook, *The Brain and Belief: Faith in the Light of Brain Research* (Bristol, Indiana, Wyndham Hall Press, 1988) p. 75.

28. David Tracy, *The Analogical Imagination* (New York, Crossroad, 1991) p. 408ff.

29. Ibid., p. 409.

30. Bollas, *Shadow,* p. 92ff.

31. Ibid., p. 33ff.

32. Sallie McFague, *Models of God* (Philadelphia, Fortress Press, 1987) p. 164ff; see also Larry Kent Graham, *Care of Persons, Care of Worlds* (Nashville, Abingdon, 1992).

33. Ibid., p. 69ff.

34. James Poling, *The Abuse of Power* (Nashville, Abingdon Press, 1991) p. 167.

Chapter 4

1. Romans 6:23.

2. Paul J. Tillich, *Systematic Theology* (Chicago, University of Chicago Press, 1957) Vol II, pp. 55-58.

3. Ibid., p. 57.

4. Brian Grant, *From Sin to Wholeness* (Philadelphia, Westminster, 1982).

5. Bernard Meland, *Faith and Culture,* (Carbondale, Southern Illinois University Press, 1953) p. 160.

6. Ibid., p. 161.

7. James Poling, *The Abuse of Power* (Nashville, Abingdon Press, 1991) p. 65.

8. Sallie McFague, *Models of God* (Philadelphia, Fortress Press, 1987) p. 77.

9. Henry Nelson Wieman, *The Source of Human Good,* (Carbondale, Southern Illinois University Press, 1967) p. 115; see also Daniel Day Williams, *The Spirit and the Forms of Love* (New York, Harper and Row, 1958) p. 153.

10. Meland, *Faith and Culture,* p. 166.

11. Wieman, *Good,* p. 86.

12. Wilfred Bion, *Learning from Experience* (London, Heinemann, 1962) p. 65.

13. Christopher Bollas, *Cracking Up* (New York, Hill and Wang, 1995) p. 77.

14. Christopher Bollas, *Cracking Up: The Work of Unconscious Experience* (New York, Hill and Wang, 1995) p. 78.

15. David Tracy, *The Analogical Imagination* (New York, Crossroad, 1991) p. 354.

16. Ibid., p. 163.

17. Daniel Stern, *The Interpersonal World of the Infant* (New York, Basic Books, 1985) p. 174.

18. Robert N. Bellah, Richard Madsen, William M. Sullivan, Ann Swidler, and Steven M. Tipton, *Habits of the Heart: Individualism and Commitment in American Life* (New York, Harper and Row, 1985); see also Robert N. Bellah, Richard Madsen, William M. Sullivan, Ann Swidler, and Steven M. Tipton, *The Good Society* (New York, Alfred A. Knopf, 1991); and Stephanie Coontz, *The Social Origins of Private Life: A History of American Families 1600-1900* (London and New York, Verso, 1988); and Stephanie Coontz, *The Way We Never Were: American Families and the Nostalgia Trap* (New York Basic Books, 1992).

19. Poling, *Abuse,* p. 130.

20. Larry Kent Graham, *Care of Persons, Care of Worlds* (Nashville, Abingdon, 1992) pp. 16-17.

21. Ibid., p. 138.

22. Poling, *Abuse,* p. 94.

23. Ibid.

24. Horace Bushnell, *Christian Nurture* (New York, Charles Scribner's Sons, 1888) pp. 274-275.

25. Poling, *Abuse,* p. 120.

26. Gordon Jackson, *Pastoral Care and Process Theology* (New York, University Press of America, 1981) p.148.

27. Wilfred Bion, *Attention and Interpretation* (London, Tavistock, 1970) p. 32.

28. Bollas, *Cracking,* p. 200.

29. Meland, *Faith and Culture,* p. 150.

30. McFague, *Models of God,* p. 140.

Chapter 5

1. James Poling, *The Abuse of Power* (Nashville Abingdon Press, 1991) p. 39.

2. James Ashbrook, *Minding the Soul: Pastoral Counseling As Remembering* (Minneapolis, Fortress Press, 1996) p.174.

3. David Tracy, *The Analogical Imagination* (New York Crossroad, 1991) p. 238ff.

4. Sallie McFague, *Models of God* (Philadelphia, Fortress Press, 1987) p. 47ff.

5. Bradford Keeney, *The Aesthetics of Change* (New York, Guilford, 1983) p. 177ff.

6. Tracy, *Analogical Imagination,* p. 205.

7. Brian Grant, "Fitness for Community: A Response to Langs and Kohut" *Journal of Pastoral Care,* 38(4), (1984) pp. 324-339.

8. Henri Nouwen, "Celibacy," *Pastoral Psychology,* 27(2), (1979) p. 79ff.

9. Wilfred R. Bion, *Attention and Interpretation* (London, Maresfield Library, 1970) p. 125 (quoting John Keats' letter to George and Thomas Keats, December 21, 1817).

10. Robert Langs, *The Technique of Psychoanalytic Psychotherapy* (New York, Aronson, 1973); See especially pp. 89ff; see also Donald W. Winnicott, *Through Paediatrics to Psycho-Analysis* (New York, Brunner/Mazel, 1992) pp. 160-161.

11. Jerome D. Frank, *Persuasion and Healing* (New York, Schocken Books, 1963) pp. 71-72.

12. Robert Langs, *The Technique of Psychoanalytic Psychotherapy* (New York, Aronson, 1973) Vol. I, pp. 89-216.

13. Ashbrook, *Minding,* p. 55ff.

14. Christy Cozad Neuger, "Feminist Pastoral Theology and Pastoral Counseling: A Work in Process," *Journal of Pastoral Theology,* 2, (1992) pp. 35-37.

15. Wilhelm Reich, *Character Analysis* (New York, Farrar, Straus, and Giroux, 1945) p. 128.

16. Ashbrook, *Minding,* p. 65ff.

Chapter 6

1. Personal communication, Clark M. Williamson.

2. Paul J. Tillich, *The Meaning of Health* (Chicago, University of Chicago Press, 1961) p. 50.

3. Bernard Meland, *Faith and Culture* (Carbondale, Southern Illinois University Press, 1953) p. 172.

4. Ibid., p. 174.

5. Paul J. Tillich, *Systematic Theology* (Chicago, University of Chicago Press, 1957) Vol. I., pp. 115-116.

6. Wilfred Bion, *Attention and Interpretation* (London, Tavistock, 1970) p. 26.

7. Ibid.

8. Wilfred Bion, *Attention and Interpretation* (London, Maresfield Library, 1970) p. 30.

9. Bion, *Attention,* p. 28.

10. Ibid., p. 31.

11. American Association of Pastoral Counselors, *Bylaws,* p. 74 of Membership Directory (AAPC, Fairfax, Virginia, 2000).

12. Bion, *Attention,* p. 33.

13. Ibid., p. 31.

14. Ibid., p. 29.

15. Ibid., p. 41.

16. James Ashbrook, *Minding the Soul: Pastoral Counseling As Remembering* (Minneapolis, Fortress Press, 1996) p. 180.

17. Ibid., p. 189.

18. Christopher Bollas, *Cracking Up* (New York, Hill and Wang, 1995) pp. 55-70.

19. Rita Nakashima Brock, *Journeys by Heart* (Crossroad, New York, 1988) pp. 26-35; see also Larry Kent Graham, *Care of Persons, Care of Worlds* (Nashville, Abingdon, 1992) p. 63ff. Bernard Loomer, "Two Conceptions of Power," *Process Studies* (1976), pp. 5-32.

20. Graham, *Care of Persons, Care of Worlds,* p. 63.

21. Brock, *Journeys By Heart,* p. 26.

Chapter 7

1. Wilfred Bion, *Learning from Experience* (London, Heinemann, 1962) p. 36.

2. Ibid.

3. Ibid., p. 47.

4. Ibid., p. 90.

5. Bion, *Learning,* p. 91.

6. Ibid., p. 93.

7. James Ashbrook, *Minding the Soul: Pastoral Counseling As Remembering* (Minneapolis, Fortress Press, 1996) p. 180ff.

8. Ibid., p. 115.

9. Bion, *Learning,* p. 6.

10. Christopher Bollas, *Being a Character* (New York, Hill and Wang, 1992) p. 108.

11. Thomas Ogden, *Reverie and Interpretation: Sensing Something Human* (Northvale, Aronson, 1997) p. 9.

12. Neville Symington and Joan Symington, *The Clinical Thinking of Wilfred Bion* (London and New York, Routledge, 1996) p. 52.

13. Ashbrook, *Minding,* p. 97.

14. Ibid., p. 106.

15. Ibid., p. 107.

16. Wilfred Bion, *Attention and Interpretation* (London, Tavistock, 1970) p. 125.

17. Wilfred Bion, *Transformations* (New York and London, Aronson, 1965, 1983) p. 153.

Chapter 8

1. Judith M. Hughes, *Reshaping the Psychoanalytic Domain* (Berkeley, University of California Press, 1989) pp. 8-27.

2. Wilfred Bion, *Attention and Interpretation* (London, Maresfield Library, 1970) p. 43; see also Melanie Klein, *Contributions to Psychoanalysis* (London, Hogarth Press, 1948) p. 236; and Donald W. Winnicott, "Hate In the Counter-transference," pp. 194-203, in Winnicott, *Through Paediatrics to Psychoanalysis* (New York, Brunner/Mazel, 1992).

3. Clark M.Williamson, *Way of Blessing, Way of Life* (St. Louis, Chalice Press, 1999) p. 230.

4. Paul J. Tillich, *Systematic Theology* (Chicago, University of Chicago Press, 1957) Vol. III, p. 112.

5. David Tracy, *The Analogical Imagination* (New York, Crossroad, 1991) p. 430.

6. Bernard Meland, *The Realities of Faith: The Revolution in Cultural Forms* (New York, Oxford University Press, 1962) pp. 305-306.

7. Daniel Day Williams, *The Spirit and the Forms of Love* (New York, Harper and Row) pp. 3, 5.

8. Rebecca Button Prichard, *Sensing the Spirit* (St. Louis, Chalice Press, 1999) pp. 121-122.

9. Ibid., p. 122.

10. Jill Savege Scharff, *Projective and Introjective Identification and the Use of the Therapist's Self* (Northvale, Aronson, 1992) p. 88.

11. Wilfred Bion, *Learning from Experience* (London, Heinemann, 1962) p. 37.

12. James F. Masterson, *The Narcissistic and Borderline Disorders* (New York, Brunner/Mazel, 1981) pp. 37-40.

13. Patrick Casement, *Learning from the Patient* (New York, Guilford Press, 1985) p. 303.

14. Ibid., p. 196.

15. Ibid., p. 108.

16. D. W. Winnicott, *Through Pediatrics to Psychoanalysis* (New York, Brunner/Mazel, 1992) p. 281.

17. Casement, *Learning,* p. 78.

18. Ibid., p. 79.

19. Stephen A. Mitchell, *Relational Concepts in Psychoanalysis: An Integration* (Cambridge, Harvard University Press, 1988) p. 293.

20. Thomas Ogden, *Subjects of Analysis* (Northvale, Aronson, 1994) pp. 73-74.

21. Ibid., pp. 99-100.

22. Ibid., pp. 100-101.

23. Thomas Ogden, *Reverie and Interpretation: Sensing Something Human* (Northvale, Aronson, 1997) p. 30.

24. Jill Savege Scharff and David E. Scharff, *Object Relations Individual Therapy* (Northvale, Aronson, 1998) pp. 198-199.

25. Robert D. Stolorow, Bernard Brandschaft, and George E. Atwood, *Psychoanalytic Treatment: An Intersubjective Approach* (Hillsdale, NJ, The Analytic Press, 1987) p. 42.

26. Ibid.

27. Jessica Benjamin, *Like Subjects, Love Objects* (New Haven, Yale University Press, 1995) pp. 28-35.

28. David S. Cunningham, *These Three Are One* (Maldon, MA, Blackwell, 1998).

29. Michael Welker, *God the Spirit* (Fortress Press, Minneapolis, 1994), translated by John F. Hoffmeyer.

30. Cunningham, *These Three,* p. 198.

31. Ibid., p. 80.

32. Ibid., p. 223.

33. Welker, *God the Spirit,* p. 34.

34. Ibid., p. 35.
35. Ibid., p. 165.
36. Ibid., p. 76.
37. Ibid., p. 52.
38. Cunningham, *These Three,* pp. 195-210.
39. Scharff and Scharff, *Object Relations,* pp. 222-225.
40. Welker, *God the Spirit,* p. 249.
41. Ibid., pp. 326-341.
42. Wilfred Bion, *Attention and Interpretation* (London, Tavistock, 1970) p. 41.
43. Cunningham, *These Three,* p. 128.
44. Ibid., pp. 132-156.
45. Ibid., p. 321.
46. Welker, *God the Spirit,* pp. 21, 120, 227, 238, 241.
47. Ibid., p. 296.
48. Ibid., p. 231.
49. Ibid., p. 275.
50. Ibid., p. 228.
51. Ibid., p. 78.
52. Ibid., p. 99.
53. Ibid., p. 318.
54. Cunningham, *These Three,* pp. 129, 304-305, 307.
55. Ibid., p. 288.
56. Ibid., p. 172.
57. Ibid., p. 133.
58. Welker, *God the Spirit,* p. 53.
59. Ibid., p. 233.
60. Ibid., p. 241.
61. Bethesda, Maryland, January 21, 2000.

Chapter 9

1. Martin Luther, "Treatise on Christian Liberty," in *Works of Martin Luther, with Introductions and Notes* (Philadelphia, The A. J. Holman Company and The Castle Press, 1915) Vol. II, p. 337.

2. Adolf Harnack, *What Is Christianity* (New York, G.P. Putnam's Sons, Second Edition, revision 1961, translated by Thomas Bailey Saunders) p. 128.

3. Pamela Dickey Young, *Christ in a Post-Christian World* (Minneapolis, Augsburg, 1995) pp. 43-44.

4. Paul J. Tillich, *Systematic Theology* (Chicago, University of Chicago Press, 1957) Vol. II, p. 103.

5. Ibid., p. 105.

6. Young, *Christ,* p. 37.

7. Clark M. Williamson, *Way of Blessing, Way of Life: A Christian Theology* (St. Louis, Chalice Press, 1999) p. 220.

8. Young, *Christ,* p. 56.

9. Williamson, *Way of Blessing,* p. 220.

10. Tillich, *Systematic,* Vol. II, p. 97.

11. Ibid., Vol. II, p. 94.

12. Ibid., Vol. II, p. 117.

13. Bernard Meland, *Faith and Culture* (Carbondale, Southern Illinois University Press, 1953) p. 214.

14. Bernard Meland, *The Realities of Faith: The Revolution in Cultural Forms* (New York, Oxford University Press, 1962) p. 259.

15. David Tracy, *The Analogical Imagination* (New York, Crossroad, 1991) pp. 249-250.

16. Ibid., p. 273.

17. Ibid., p. 278.

18. William C. Placher, *Narratives of a Vulnerable God* (Louisville, Westminster John Knox, 1994) p. 116.

19. Elizabeth A. Johnson, *She Who Is* (New York, Crossroad, 1992) p. 161.

20. Young, *Christ,* p. 55.

21. Ibid., p. 137.

22. Williamson, *Ways of Blessings,* pp. 221-222.

23. Ibid., 208.

24. Ibid., 221.

25. Wilfred Bion, *Attention and Interpretation* (London, Tavistock, 1970) pp. 62-82.

26. Ibid., p. 64.

27. Neville Symington and Joan Symington, *The Clinical Thinking of Wilfred Bion* (London and New York, Routledge, 1996) p. 10.

28. Michael Eigen, *The Psychoanalytic Mystic* (Binghamton, NY, ESF Publishers, 1998) p. 34.

29. Ibid., p. 63.

30. Bion, *Attention,* p. 43.

31. Ibid.

32. Ibid., p. 26.

33. Ibid.

34. Ibid., p. 45.

35. Ibid., p. 46.

36. Eigen, *Psychoanalytic Mystic,* p. 43.

37. Ibid., p. 41.

38. Brian Grant, *The Social Structure of Christian Families: A Historical Perspective* (St. Louis, Chalice Press, 2000).

39. Bion, *Attention,* p. 66.

40. Ibid., p. 67.

41. Eigen, *Psychoanalytic Mystic,* p. 84.

42. II Cor. 5:21.

43. Jill Savege Scharff and David E. Scharff, *Object Relations Individual Therapy* (Northvale, Aronson, 1998) pp. 255-259.

44. Mark 10:18.

45. Bion, *Attention,* p. 19.

46. Gerard Bleandonu, *Wilfred Bion: His Life and Works, 1897-1979* (New York, Guilford Press, 1996) p. 186.

47. William Placher, *Narratives of a Vulnerable God,* p. 116.

48. Williamson, *Way of Blessing,* p. 221.

49. Bion, *Attention,* pp. 30, 33.

50. Ibid., p. 33.

51. Ibid., p. 110.

52. Ibid., p. 111.

53. Ibid., pp.116, 129.

54. Eigen, *Psychoanalytic Mystic,* p. 72.

55. Ibid., pp. 75, 76.

56. Ibid., p. 90.

57. Ibid., p. 92.

58. Luke 4:2-13.

59. Matt. 22:15-22.

60. Matt.16:22.

61. Matt. 26:7-10.

Chapter 10

1. Joanna Field, *A Life of One's Own* (New York, Putnam's, 1981) pp. 89-90.

2. Ibid., pp. 185-186.

3. Michael Dorris, *Guests* (New York, Hyperion, 1996) p. 34. (Reprinted by permission of Hyperion.© Michael Dorris 1994.)

4. Ibid., p. 35.

5. Amos 2:6.

6. Mark 1:15.

7. Matt. 28:20.

8. Wilfred Bion, *Attention and Interpretation* (London, Tavistock, 1970) pp. 128-129.

9. Henry Nelson Wieman, *The Source of Human Good* (Chicago, University of Chicago Press, 1946) pp. 3-26.

10. Alfred N. Whitehead, *Process and Reality: An Essay in Cosmology* (New York, Harper and Row, 1929) pp. 522-525.

11. Bernard Loomer, "Two Conceptions of Power," *Process Studies* (1976) pp. 5-32.

12. Matt. 25:21, et al.

13. Alfred North Whitehead, *Adventures of Ideas,* (New York, The Free Press, 1933) p. 193.

14. Dorris, *Guests,* p. 37.

15. Robert Kegan, *The Evolving Self: Problem and Process in Human Development* (Cambridge, Harvard University Press, 1982) p. 31.

16. Dorris, *Guests,* pp. 38-39.

17. Acts 2:9.

18. Eigen, *Psychoanalytic Mystic,* p. 193.

19. H. Richard Niebuhr, in collaboration with Daniel Day Williams and James Gustafson, *The Purpose of the Church and Its Ministry* (New York, Harper and Brothers, 1956) pp. 36-39.

20. Michael Eigen, *The Psychoanalytic Mystic* (Binghamton, NY, ESF Publishers, 1998) pp. 40-41.

Bibliography

American Association of Pastoral Counselors (2000) *Bylaws.* Fairfax, VA, AAPC.

Ashbrook, James (1988) *The Brain and Belief: Faith in the Light of Brain Research.* Bristol, IN, Wyndham Hall Press.

Ashbrook, James (1996) *Minding the Soul: Pastoral Counseling As Remembering.* Minneapolis, Fortress Press.

Auden, W. H. (1948) *The Dyer's Hand and Other Essays.* New York, Random House.

Bellah, Robert N., Richard Madsen, William M. Sullivan, Ann Swidler, and Steven M. Tipton (1985) *Habits of the Heart: Individualism and Commitment in American Life.* New York, Harper and Row.

Bellah, Robert N., Richard Madsen, William M. Sullivan, Ann Swidler, and Steven M. Tipton (1991) *The Good Society.* New York, Alfred A. Knopf.

Benjamin, Jessica (1995) *Like Subjects, Love Objects.* New Haven, Yale University Press.

Benor, Daniel J. (1993) *Healing Research.* Vol. I. Munich, Helix Verlag.

Bion, Wilfred R. (1959) *Experiences in Groups.* New York, Basic Books.

Bion, Wilfred R. (1962) *Learning from Experience.* London, Maresfield Library.

Bion, Wilfred R. (1965) *Transformations.* New York, London, Aronson.

Bion, Wilfred R. (1967) *Second Thoughts: Selected Papers on Psycho-Analysis.* New York, Aronson.

Bion, Wilfred R. (1970) *Attention and Interpretation.* London, Maresfield Library.

Bion, Wilfred R. (1982) *The Long Weekend, 1897-1919. Part of a Life,* edited by Francesca Bion. London, Karnac Books.

Bion, Wilfred R. (1985) *All My Sins Remembered: Another Part of a Life* bound with *The Other Side of Genius: Family Letters,* edited by Francesca Bion. London/New York, Karnac Books.

Bion, Wilfred R. (1990) *Brazilian Lectures: 1973, Sao Paulo; 1974, Rio de Janeiro/Sao Paulo.* London and New York, Karnac Books.

Bion, Wilfred R. (1992) *Cogitations,* edited by Francesca Bion. London, Karnac Books.

Bleandonu, Gerard (1994) *Wilfred Bion, His Life and Works, 1897-1979,* translated by Claire Pajaczkowska. New York, Guilford Press.

Boisen, Anton (1936) *Exploration of the Inner World: A Study of Mental Disorder and Religious Experience.* New York, Harper and Brothers.

Bollas, Christopher (1987) *The Shadow of the Object: Psychoanalysis of the Unthought Known.* New York, Columbia University Press.

Bollas, Christopher (1992) *Being a Character: Psychoanalysis and Self Experience.* New York, Hill and Wang.

Bollas, Christopher (1995) *Cracking Up: The Work of Unconscious Experience.* New York, Hill and Wang.

Brock, Rita Nakashima (1988) *Journeys by Heart: A Christology of Erotic Power.* New York, Crossroad.

Bushnell, Horace (1888) *Christian Nurture,* Charles Scribners Sons, New York.

Casement, Patrick (1985) *Learning from the Patient.* New York, Guilford Press.

Cunningham, David S. (1998) *These Three Are One: The Practice of Trinitarian Theology.* Malden, MA, Blackwell.

Dorris, Michael (1996) *Guests.* New York, Hyperion.

Eigen, Michael (1998) *The Psychoanalytic Mystic.* Binghamton, NY, ESF Publishers.

Erikson, Erik (1959) "The Problem of Ego Identity," in *Identity and the Life Cycle,* (pp. 50-100). Psychological Issues, Vol. I., No. 1, New York, International Universities Press.

Field, Joanna (1981) *A Life of One's Own.* New York, Putnam.

Framo, James (1982) *Explorations in Marital and Family Therapy: Selected Papers of James L. Framo.* New York, Springer.

Goode, William (1963) *World Revolution and Family Patterns.* London, Collier-Macmillan.

Graham, Larry Kent (1992) *Care of Persons, Care of Worlds: A Psychosystems Approach to Pastoral Care and Counseling.* Nashville, Abingdon.

Grant, Brian (1982) *From Sin to Wholeness.* Philadelphia, Westminster.

Grant, Brian (1984) "Fitness for Community: A Response to Langs and Kohut," *Journal of Pastoral Care,* 38(4), 324-339.

Grant, Brian (2000) *The Social Structure of Christian Families: A Historical Perspective.* St. Louis, Chalice Press.

Hillman, James and Michael Ventura (1993) *We've Had a Hundred Years of Psychotherapy—and the World's Getting Worse.* San Francisco, Harper Collins.

Hughes, Judith M. (1989) *Reshaping the Psychoanalytic Domain: The Work of Melanie Klein, W.R.D. Fairbairn, and D. W. Winnicott.* Berkeley, University of California Press.

Jackson, Gordon (1981) *Pastoral Care and Process Theology.* Lanham, MD, University Press of America.

Jahn, Robert G. and Brenda J. Dunne (1987) *Margins of Reality: The Role of Consciousness in the Physical World.* New York, Harcourt, Brace, Jovanovich.

James, William (1902) *The Varieties of Religious Experience: A Study of Human Nature.* New York, Collier.

Johnson, Elizabeth A. (1992) *She Who Is: The Mystery of God in Feminist Theological Discourse.* New York, Crossroad.

Kakar, Sudhir (1982) *The Inner World—A Psychoanalytic Study of Childhood and Society in India.* Delhi, Oxford University Press.

Kakar, Sudhir (1982) *Shamans, Mystics, and Doctors: A Psychological Inquiry into India and Its Healing Traditions.* Delhi, Oxford University Press.

Kakar, Sudhir (1991) *The Analyst and the Mystic: Psychoanalytic Reflections on Religion and Mysticism.* New Delhi, Viking.

Keeney, Bradford (1983) *Aesthetics of Change.* New York, Guilford.

Kegan, Robert (1982) *The Evolving Self: Problem and Process in Human Development.* Cambridge, Harvard University Press.

Kegan, Robert (1995) *In Over Our Heads: The Mental Demands of Modern Life.* Cambridge, Harvard University Press.

Kurtz, Stanley N. (1992) *All the Mothers Are One: Hindu India and the Cultural Reshaping of Psychoanalysis.* New York, Columbia University Press.

Langs, Robert (1973) *The Technique of Psychoanalytic Psychotherapy.* New York, Aronson.

Loomer, Bernard (1976) "Two Conceptions of Power." *Process Studies* 6(1) 5-32. Also published in *Criterion* 15(1) 12-23.

Luther, Martin (1915) "Treatise on Christian Liberty," in *The Works of Martin Luther,* Vol II, Philadelphia, A. J. Holman Company and the Castle Press.

Masterson, James F. (1981) *The Narcissistic and Borderline Disorders: An Integrated Developmental Approach.* New York, Brunner/Mazel.

McFague, Sallie (1987) *Models of God: Theology for an Ecological, Nuclear, Age.* Philadelphia, Fortress Press.

Meland, Bernard (1953) *Faith and Culture.* Carbondale, Southern Illinois University Press.

Meland, Bernard (1962) *The Realities of Faith: The Revolution in Cultural Forms.* New York, Oxford University Press.

Minuchin, Salvador (1974) *Families and Family Therapy.* London, Tavistock.

Mitchell, Stephen A. (1988) *Relational Concepts in Psychoanalysis: An Integration.* Cambridge, Harvard University Press.

Neuger, Christy Cozad (1992) "Feminist Pastoral Theology and Pastoral Counseling: A Work in Process," *Journal of Pastoral Theology,* 2:35-37.

Niebuhr, H. Richard, in collaboration with Daniel Day Williams and James Gustafson (1956) *The Purpose of the Church and Its Ministry.* New York, Harper and Brothers.

Niebuhr, Reinhold (1941) *The Nature and Destiny of Man.* New York, Charles Scribners' Sons.

Nouwen, Henri (1979) "Celibacy," *Pastoral Psychology,* 27(2) 79-90.

Ogden, Thomas (1989) *The Primitive Edge of Experience.* Northvale, Aronson.

Ogden, Thomas (1994) *Subjects of Analysis.* Northvale, Aronson.

Ogden, Thomas (1997) *Reverie and Interpretation: Sensing Something Human.* Northvale, Aronson.

Placher, William C. (1994) *Narratives of a Vulnerable God.* Louisville, Westminster-John Knox Press.

Poling, James (1991) *The Abuse of Power: A Theological Problem.* Nashville, Abingdon.

Prichard, Rebecca Button (1999) *Sensing the Spirit: The Holy Spirit in Feminist Perspective.* St. Louis, Chalice Press.

Reich, Wilhelm (1933) *Character Analysis,* Third Edition, translated by Vincent R. Carfagno. New York, Farrar, Strauss, and Giroux.

Rizzuto, Ana-Maria (1981) *The Birth of the Living God: A Psychoanalytic Study.* Chicago, University of Chicago Press.

Roland, Alan (1988) *In Search of Self in India and Japan.* Princeton, Princeton University Press.

Scharff, David E. (1992) *Refinding the Object and Reclaiming the Self.* Northvale, Aronson.

Scharff, David E. and Jill Savege Scharff (1987) *Object Relations Family Therapy.* Northvale, Aronson.

Scharff, Jill Savege, ed. (1989) *Foundations of Object Relations Family Therapy.* Northvale, Aronson.

Scharff, Jill Savege (1992) *Projective and Introjective Identification and the Use of the Therapist's Self.* Northvale, Aronson.

Scharff, Jill Savege and David E. Scharff (1998) *Object Relations Individual Therapy.* Northvale, Aronson.

Shapiro, Edward R. and A. Wesley Carr (1991) *Lost in Familiar Places: Creating New Connections Between the Individual and Society.* New Haven, Yale University Press.

Stern, Daniel N. (1985) *The Interpersonal World of the Infant: A View from Psychoanalysis and Developmental Psychology.* New York, Basic Books.

Stolorow, Robert D., Bernard Brandschaft, and George E. Atwood (1987) *Psychoanalytic Treatment: An Intersubjective Approach.* Hillsdale, NJ, The Analytic Press.

Summerlin, Florence A. (1980) *Religion and Mental Health: A Bibliography.* Rockville, MD, National Institute of Mental Health.

Symington, Neville (1994) *Emotion and Spirit: Questioning the Claims of Psychoanalysis and Religion.* New York, St. Martin's Press.

Symington, Neville and Joan Symington (1996) *The Clinical Thinking of Wilfred Bion.* London and New York, Routledge.

Tillich, Paul J. (1951, 1957, 1963) *Systematic Theology,* Volumes 1, 2, and 3. Chicago, University of Chicago Press.

Tillich, Paul J. (1960) "Impact of Psychotherapy on Theological Thought," New York, Academy of Religion and Mental Health.

Tillich, Paul J. (1961) *The Meaning of Health.* Chicago, University of Chicago Press.

Tracy, David (1991) *The Analogical Imagination: Christian Theology and the Culture of Pluralism.* New York, Crossroad.

Welker, Michael (1994) *God the Spirit,* translated by John F. Hoffmeyer. Minneapolis, Fortress Press.

Whitehead, Alfred North (1929) *Process and Reality: An Essay in Cosmology.* New York, Harper and Row.

Whitehead, Alfred North (1933) *Adventures of Ideas.* New York, The Free Press.

Wieman, Henry Nelson (1958) *Man's Ultimate Commitment.* Carbondale, Southern Illinois University Press.

Wieman, Henry Nelson (1967) *The Source of Human Good.* Carbondale, Southern Illinois University Press.

Williams, Daniel Day (1968) *The Spirit and the Forms of Love.* New York, Harper and Row.

Williamson, Clark M. (1999) *Way of Blessing, Way of Life: A Christian Theology.* St. Louis, Chalice Press.

Winnicott, D. W. (1971) *Playing and Reality.* London and New York, Routledge.

Winnicott, D. W. (1992) *Through Paediatrics to Psycho-Analysis: Collected Papers.* New York, Brunner/Mazel.

Young, Pamela Dickey (1995) *Christ in a Post-Christian World.* Minneapolis, Fortress Press.

Index

brain *(continued)*
    right, 11, 28
breast, 128
breath, 12, 61, 101, 102, 129, 185
    shortening the, 187

call for repentance, 119, 188
canon, 4, 5, 7
capitalism, 3, 38, 39, 81
care
    child, 56, 79, 84
    logic of, 56
caretakers, primary, 55, 56, 57, 60, 61,
        63
    experience of, 70
    overburdened, 87
    reverie, 64, 184, 187
celebration, 121
center, 43, 97, 98
change, pace of, 25, 26
character, 39, 53, 70, 78, 84, 85
    size of, 94
    therapist's, 13, 140, 141, 147, 150,
        173
child raising, 54
children, 54, 63
choice, 7, 8, 31, 45, 47
    to change or not, 193
    to do evil, 73, 74
    to evade frustration, 57
    of force, 74
    inherently corruptible, 69
    of objects, 67, 68
    of pastoral psychotherapy, 101, 188
    to refuse influence, 74
    therapist's, of link, 127
Christ, 161, 162, 165, 174, 177
Christian, 5, 35, 59, 107, 163, 173
Christology, 162, 163, 166, 170, 172
church, 1, 4, 10, 25, 27, 32, 36, 42, 80,
        107, 165
    channels energy, 51
    describes Jesus, 166, 170
    equips therapists, 50
    as payer, 179
    as a public, 66
    as response, 38, 164
    shaping culture, 38, 41
    and transference, 173

citizenship, 49, 80
claim, 163, 172, 174, 176, 177
    moral, 7
    saving, 166, 173, 175, 190, 191
    theological, 151
clarity, bursts of, 123, 187
class
    middle, 3, 80
    social, 34, 37, 44, 54, 79, 80, 178
client, 47, 49, 50, 82, 100, 103
    choice over deep work, 120, 124,
        131, 189, 190
    freedom to fantasize, 170
    gratitude, 161
    hallows the space, 118, 119, 120,
        121
    making the foil, 117
    therapist choosing, 178
    truth central to, 112
    will feel therapist's wanting, 115
code, moral, 47
coercion, 75, 81
cohesion, 64, 74
collusion, 73, 154, 156
comfort, 26, 45
commitments, 7, 9, 12, 37, 47, 48
    to community, 158, 198
    mutual, 109
    of past generations, 51
communication, 153
    unconscious, 58, 133, 145, 184
communion, 8, 36, 49, 95, 136, 194
    in freedom, 143, 151
    of saints, 133, 134, 158, 187
community(ies), 4, 8, 9, 11, 21, 28, 32,
        43, 75, 200
    against the, 75
    around Jesus, 164, 165
    on behalf of, 50, 108, 124, 136, 152,
        153, 154, 180
    broken, 51, 74
    Christian, 36, 37, 38, 47
    creates the space, 105, 106, 107,
        108, 183
    deepening, 20, 136
    dispersal of, 79
    diversity of, 199, 200
    ethnic, 35, 36
    faith, 9, 13, 14, 35, 44, 46, 49
    formed by, 33, 48, 51, 133, 152, 169

influence, exchange of, 117, 150
information, 76, 116, 127, 145, 171
injustice, 27, 28
innocence, 86, 87
innovation, 25
insensitivity, 32, 74, 87
institutions, 9, 25, 26, 28, 31,33, 39, 47
   carry functions for society, 41
   creation of, 107
   as creators of pain, 51
   weakening of, 80, 179
integration, 7, 107, 108, 116, 127, 133
   for client, 134, 185
intensity, 8, 9, 12, 27, 29
   contrast and, 38, 64, 155, 194
   of need, 70
internalization, 23, 53, 62, 63, 64, 130
   of evil, 83, 84, 85
   of play, 187
   requires person as resource, 193
   of self and culture, 70, 73
interpenetration, 41, 149, 197
interpretation, 97, 99, 111, 146
   community of, 156, 158
interrelatedness, 117
intersubjectivity, 143, 147, 148, 149,
   150
interventions, 49
introjects, 64, 85
invitation, 119, 123
isolation, 26, 79, 96, 102

Jackson, Gordon, 11, 20, 63, 84
Jesus, 5, 22, 23, 34, 38, 51, 95
   empowering others, 166, 175. 180
   idealized, 162
   interactions with others, 166
   liberated from sin, 198
   life before his ministry, 169, 170
   the man, 162, 163, 164
   social class, 178
   uniqueness of, 163, 164, 166
   willingness to risk, 165, 166, 174
Jews, 24, 34, 35, 95, 163, 164
joy, 5, 8, 13, 50, 59, 113
   participation in others', 118, 192,
   199
judgment, 5, 6, 48, 51, 93, 95
justice, 2, 15, 27, 75

K (knowledge), 62, 76, 111,112, 114,
   126
   central link, 127, 128
   in middle phase, 131
Kakar, Sudhir, 44, 54, 59
Keeney, Bradford, 30, 48, 96
Kegan, Robert, 65, 66
knowing, 11, 77, 110, 111, 176
   new, 187
   not yet, 115
knowledge, 4, 13, 14, 49, 62
   of brokenness and healing, 50
   codified, 76
   emergence of, 57
   gained by experience, 111
   of God, 1, 176
   governed by choices, 68
   link, 127, 128
   loss of, 93
   saving, 99
   of self, 118, 128
   therapist's, 125, 176
   of tradition, 42
known, unthought, 57

L (love), 62, 126, 127
language, 11, 23, 33, 34, 43, 66
   Christian, 47, 142, 202
   commitment to, 78
   of communities, 45, 77
   for exchange of meanings, 53
   Holy Spirit, 143
   logic of, 77
   multiplicity of, 156
   preparing for achievement, 136
   properties of, 77
   substituting for achievement, 136
   traditional, 142, 202
   world of, 58
law, 6, 38
leading, by patient, 147
learning, 55, 74, 86, 114, 146, 174
   connected to persons, 187
ledger, 15
liberation, 6, 35, 127, 135, 157, 173
   cycle, 25, 41, 54
   inner, 11, 58
   span, 25
   unambiguous, 142

link, 35, 39, 109, 111, 121, 187
  between behavior and word, 188
  between containers and contained,
    126, 127, 168
  between two processes, 125
linking, attack on, 126, 145
literature, 1, 2, 106
  pastoral care, 28, 108
liturgy, 47
location, social, 35, 80
logic, 61, 62, 77
Loomer, Bernard, 9, 11, 63, 81, 83, 84,
    117, 192
loss, 26, 59, 86, 92, 177
love, 22, 62, 94, 103, 165
  given as gift and command, 142
  romantic, 43
  steadfast, 6
lover, 20, 29, 68, 75
loyalty, 36, 51, 82, 179, 202
lure, 20, 22, 38, 51, 114
  of God, 8, 12, 24, 29, 31
    experiencing, 136, 176
    hope generated by, 101, 136
    into sacred space, 109
    persuasive good revealing, 74
    pulls us, 190
    ready to notice, 137
    response to, 51, 60, 70, 85, 108,
      136
  out of self, 124

manifestation, 28, 34, 66, 113
market, 47
marriage, 4, 38, 79, 91, 93
  and families, 41, 42, 141
matrix, relational, 148
maturation, 67
McFague, Sallie, 9, 14, 20, 22, 27, 28,
    30, 67, 68, 75, 81, 83, 87, 95
meaning, 10, 24, 34, 44
  adding, 51, 129
  ascribing m. to pain, 119, 177
  creation of, 185, 187, 188
  elemental level of, 53, 130, 184
  organized by language, 77
  reorganization of, 129, 135, 195
  right to assign, 196
  shared, 59, 110

meaning *(continued)*
  structure of, 164
  unconscious, 82
meditation, 129, 158
Meland, Bernard, 9, 11, 12, 13, 20, 21,
    22, 53, 74, 75, 84, 87, 88,
    110, 118, 143, 164, 167
memory(ies), 4, 6, 12, 13, 61, 76, 84,
    92, 97, 115, 190
  availability to, 187
  and desire, 113, 114, 131, 167, 168,
    175
    abstinence from, 197
  false, 92
  and feeling, 186
  freeing, 92, 133, 189
  meaningful, 116
  nor desire, 99
  opening the seal of, 93, 190
  saturated, 114
  stimulus to, 96, 101, 190
  terror of, 134
  transference-generated, 147, 154
  trauma blocks, 94
  useless for, 130
militarism, 3, 81
mind, 41, 74, 126, 176, 190, 193
  building the baby's, 131
  organization of our, 119, 188
  state of, 58
  therapist's, unsaturated, 125
ministry, 2, 3, 50
missionaries, 37, 46
mode, sensory, 55
moments, 7, 12
  holy, 123, 189, 190, 192, 194
money, 26, 49, 80, 107, 162, 177
mood, dominant, 53, 83
morality, 25, 36, 37, 101
mother, 41, 54, 56, 57, 58, 85
  caused me pain, 61, 63, 64
  internal picture of, 61, 153
  taking in the, 59
  as transformational object, 59
movement, 28, 136, 152, 180
multivocity, 29, 103
mystic, 13, 28, 39, 40, 41, 49
  best described O, 111
  calling as, 50
  functions as, 168, 197

self-awareness, 200
self-creation, 70,
self-definition, 135
self-mortification, 113
self-negation, 148
self-withdrawal, 154, 155, 183, 197
selves, 11, 22, 23, 51, 176
  becoming, 73
  larger, 9, 10
  therapist and client, 133, 136
separation, 40, 60
sensitivity, 64, 74, 115, 118, 164
sex, 25, 113
sexism, 3, 50, 88
sexuality, 43, 170
sharpening sense of O, 118, 168
silence, 12, 98, 100, 128, 129, 145, 189
  at heart of things, 190
sin, 7, 10, 13, 30, 73, 165
  awareness of, 190, 191
  bearing together, 191
  center of, 76
  emergence of, 21, 87
  of the fathers, 69
  as force over sensitivity, 74
  nature of, 73
  participation in, 14, 180
  psychopathology as, 91, 177
  therapy liberates from, 191
  wages of, 11
size, 63, 64, 84, 94
skills, 47, 48, 55, 56, 96, 109
sleep, 95, 113, 116, 129, 131
  therapist's, 132, 145
society, 9, 10, 11, 25, 28, 37
  fragmentation of, 81, 82, 83
  identity of, 38
  institutions within, 41, 179
  massively organized, 78, 83
  oppressive, 95
  as a public, 66
  restratification of, 80
  unity of the, 44
soul, 12, 75, 116
Source, 22, 46, 166
sovereignty, 73, 78, 184
space, 41, 78, 185
  boundaries of, 99, 100, 189
  client's psychic, 131
  creative, 129

space *(continued)*
  for dreaming, 116
  filled, 117, 155
  hallowed, 112, 114, 121, 183, 200
    birth into, 188
  internal, 59, 60, 61, 184
  intersubjective, 155, 157, 183
  liminal, 12, 98
  mental, 11, 58, 61, 76, 84, 85
    building up in baby, 131
    shared, in therapy, 132
  numinous quality of, 98
  potential, 129
  relational, 97, 102
  sacred, 12, 98, 99, 101, 102
    medium of, 133, 158
    move into, 112, 118
    safety of, 136, 190
    search for, 119
    therapist's reverie in, 125, 133, 184, 187
    use of, 103, 154, 190
  therapeutic, 97, 110
  therapist's psychic, 144, 168
  transitional, 59, 60, 61, 62, 114, 183
speech, 19
Spirit, 29, 155, 170, 177, 183, 184
  in-breaking of, 88, 157, 158
splitting, 85, 86, 144
stability, 27
stasis, 91
state
  meditative, 132
  the, 13, 36, 162, 177, 179
Stern, Daniel, 55, 56, 59, 60, 77, 187
stewards, 14
stewardship, 47, 114
story, 60, 94, 101, 151, 163
stressors, 3, 8, 9
striving
  cessation of, 129
  impartial, 68
structures
  cognitive, 132
  evil, 81
  family, 55, 59
  massive, 88
  new, 75, 135, 185
  oppressive, 81
  realignment in dreaming, 116

structures *(continued)*
    stable, 25, 26, 66, 180
    tribal, 23
subject, third, 125, 133, 148, 151, 184
subjectivity, 154
subjects, 57, 64, 65
subjugation, of individual subjectivity,
        148, 149, 150, 184
substitute, 11, 76, 87, 113
suffering, 20, 21, 44, 50, 106, 107
    importance of the, 109, 165, 174
    static, 188
    therapist's, 174, 181
supervision, 113, 146, 180, 185
supervisor, 51
support, 19, 26, 50, 127
survivors, abuse, 82, 92, 93
suspicion, hermeneutics of, 13
symbolization, 169, 187
system(s) , 27, 30, 43, 45, 48
    kinship, 23
    nervous, 34, 102
    political, 35

task, messianic, 169, 180, 197, 198
Tavistock Institute, 40, 140
technique(s)
    psychotherapy, 139, 157, 158
    survival, 102, 103
technology, 42, 79, 81, 157
temptation, 14, 50, 51, 73, 76, 117
    to avoid, 135, 193
    to block transference, 146
    of power, 180
tension, 24, 28, 91, 96
termination, criteria, 49
terror, 50, 86, 134, 172
texts, 162
theology, 1, 27, 30, 73, 106, 201
    liberation, 2, 24, 152, 165
    process, 15, 20, 143, 183
    Thomistic, 38
    trinitarian, 142, 151
therapists, 7, 10, 46, 49, 96
    life outside office, 169, 172
    mediate redemptive change, 161
    offer claim and promise, 177, 190,
        191
    represent failing parent, 147

therapists *(continued)*
    structured by client, 148, 149, 154,
        184, 191
    toleration of the horror, 147, 191
therapy, family, 28, 32, 41, 81, 141
thinker, 126
thinking, 57, 145
third, analytic, 149, 184
thought(s), 86, 130, 145
    content, 91, 126
    dream, 131
    feeling bursts bonds of, 169
    inability to tolerate, 145
    psychotherapeutic, 139
    systemic, 15, 30,143
Tillich, Paul J., 11, 13, 20, 22, 73, 86,
        88, 107, 110, 142, 163, 164
time
    fullness of, 121, 166
    sacred, 97, 133
tone, muscle, 58
touch, 74, 101
Tracy, David, 9, 11, 12, 22, 28, 29,
        66, 77, 86, 88, 95, 97, 142,
        164, 165, 192
traditions, 6, 23, 95, 106, 168
training, 4, 50, 106, 113, 178, 185
transference, 96, 97, 102, 139, 140,
        150
    can saturate the space, 155
    centrality of, 172
    commitment to resolving, 173
    focused and contextual, 173
    management, 144
    not solely client's creation, 141,
        150
    projection's role in, 144, 148
transformation, 98, 118, 129, 130,
        137, 149
    moments of, 192
    O into K, 175
    of psychic structures, 197
trauma, 94, 131, 146, 147
treatment, unit of, 48, 82
Trinity, the, 152
truth, 29, 77, 112, 121, 123, 155
    absolute, 111, 136
    at points of intersection, 199
    saving, 129, 169

unconscious, the, 64, 65, 68, 69, 82, 96
    communication, 133, 140, 150, 184
    work of, 116, 185, 193
unconsciousness, 11
upheaval, 25, 26
urban, 3

validation, 81, 135
values, 77, 178
    cultural, 56
    family, 78
variegation, polycentric, 156
vessel, liminal, 98, 103
victim, 94
violence, 11, 36, 51, 80, 88
    family, 81
    marital, 79
virgin, consecrated, 36
virtues, trinitarian, 151, 158
vision, 12, 84, 117, 133, 197
vocabulary, 77
vocation, 49, 106, 109, 115, 175
voice, inner, 135
vulnerability, 74, 87, 185

warn, duty to, 49
weakness, 78
web, 21, 31
white, 3, 27
Whitehead, Alfred North, 29, 134, 136,
    192
Whiteheadian, 22, 29, 59, 63, 66, 67,
    155

whole, 31, 39, 150, 155
wholes, corporate, 43,
Wieman, Henry Nelson, 20, 22, 75, 192
will, God's, 21, 34, 59, 82, 92, 96
    for client safety, 103
    realization of, 114
Winnicott, Donald, 10, 41, 58, 59, 60,
        61, 63, 66, 99, 105, 124, 125,
        126, 128, 129, 140, 146, 147,
        174, 183, 184
wisdom, 6, 7, 28, 165, 166, 190
withdrawal, emotional, 147, 195, 196
witness, 82, 88, 109, 162, 173
womb, 124
wonder, 12, 49, 110
words, 47, 57, 61, 76, 77, 151
work, 9, 79, 187
    of God, 11, 78
    of therapist, 97, 100, 109, 132, 191
world, 8, 9, 22, 30, 43, 56
    created, 66
    imperfect, 86, 87
    new, 136, 194
    outside, 62, 101
    picture of the, 93
    public, 43, 180
    relational, 196
    secular, 14
    of the therapy, 100
    third, 25
    transformation of the, 137, 190
worship, 79, 100, 129

xenophobia, 42

THE HAWORTH PASTORAL PRESS
Pastoral Care, Ministry, and Spirituality
Richard Dayringer, ThD
Senior Editor

LOSSES IN LATER LIFE: A NEW WAY OF WALKING WITH GOD, SECOND EDITION by R. Scott Sullender. "Continues to be a timely and helpful book. There is an empathetic tone throughout, even though the book is a bold challenge to grieve for the sake of growth and maturity and faithfulness. . . . An important book." *Herbert Anderson, PhD, Professor of Pastoral Theology, Catholic Theological Union, Chicago, Illinois*

CARING FOR PEOPLE FROM BIRTH TO DEATH edited by James E. Hightower Jr. "An expertly detailed account of the hopes and hazards folks experience at each stage of their lives. Your empathy will be deepened and your care of people will be highly informed." *Wayne E. Oates, PhD, Professor of Psychiatry Emeritus, School of Medicine, University of Louisville, Kentucky*

HIDDEN ADDICTIONS: A PASTORAL RESPONSE TO THE ABUSE OF LEGAL DRUGS by Bridget Clare McKeever. "This text is a must–read for physicians, pastors, nurses, and counselors. It should be required reading in every seminary and Clinical Pastoral Education program." *Martin C. Helldorfer, DMin, Vice President, Mission, Leadership Development and Corporate Culture, Catholic Health Initiatives— Eastern Region, Pennsylvania*

THE EIGHT MASKS OF MEN: A PRACTICAL GUIDE IN SPIRITUAL GROWTH FOR MEN OF THE CHRISTIAN FAITH by Frederick G. Grosse. "Thoroughly grounded in traditional Christian spirituality and thoughtfully aware of the needs of men in our culture. . . . Close attention could make men's groups once again a vital spiritual force in the church." *Eric O. Springsted, PhD, Chaplain and Professor of Philosophy and Religion, Illinois College, Jacksonville, Illinois*

THE HEART OF PASTORAL COUNSELING: HEALING THROUGH RELATIONSHIP, REVISED EDITION by Richard Dayringer. "Richard Dayringer's revised edition of *The Heart of Pastoral Counseling* is a book for every person's pastor and a pastor's every person." *Glen W. Davidson, Professor, New Mexico Highlands University, Las Vegas, New Mexico*

WHEN LIFE MEETS DEATH: STORIES OF DEATH AND DYING, TRUTH AND COURAGE by Thomas W. Shane. "A kaleidoscope of compassionate, artfully tendered pastoral encounters that evoke in the reader a full range of emotions." *The Rev. Dr. James M. Harper, III, Corporate Director of Clinical Pastoral Education, Health Midwest; Director of Pastoral Care, Baptist Medical Center and Research Medical Center, Kansas City Missouri*

A MEMOIR OF A PASTORAL COUNSELING PRACTICE by Robert L. Menz. "Challenges the reader's belief system. A humorous and abstract book that begs to be read again, and even again." *Richard Dayringer, ThD, Professor and Director, Program in Psychosocial Care, Department of Medical Humanities; Professor and Chief, Division of Behavioral Science, Department of Family and Community Medicine, Southern Illinois University School of Medicine*

Order Your Own Copy of
This Important Book for Your Personal Library!

A THEOLOGY FOR PASTORAL PSYCHOTHERAPY
God's Play in Sacred Spaces

_____in hardbound at $29.95 (ISBN: 0-7890-1200-6)

_____in softbound at $19.95 (ISBN: 0-7890-1201-4)

COST OF BOOKS_____

OUTSIDE USA/CANADA/
MEXICO: ADD 20%_____

POSTAGE & HANDLING_____
(US: $4.00 for first book & $1.50
for each additional book)
Outside US: $5.00 for first book
& $2.00 for each additional book)

SUBTOTAL_____

in Canada: add 7% GST_____

STATE TAX____
(NY, OH & MIN residents, please
add appropriate local sales tax)

FINAL TOTAL____
(If paying in Canadian funds,
convert using the current
exchange rate, UNESCO
coupons welcome.)

☐ **BILL ME LATER:** ($5 service charge will be added)
(Bill-me option is good on US/Canada/Mexico orders only;
not good to jobbers, wholesalers, or subscription agencies.)

☐ Check here if billing address is different from
shipping address and attach purchase order and
billing address information.

Signature_____

☐ **PAYMENT ENCLOSED: $**_____

☐ **PLEASE CHARGE TO MY CREDIT CARD.**

☐ Visa ☐ MasterCard ☐ AmEx ☐ Discover
☐ Diner's Club ☐ Eurocard ☐ JCB

Account # _____

Exp. Date_____

Signature_____

Prices in US dollars and subject to change without notice.

NAME_____

INSTITUTION_____

ADDRESS_____

CITY_____

STATE/ZIP_____

COUNTRY_____ COUNTY (NY residents only)_____

TEL_____ FAX_____

E-MAIL_____

May we use your e-mail address for confirmations and other types of information? ☐ Yes ☐ No
We appreciate receiving your e-mail address and fax number. Haworth would like to e-mail or fax special
discount offers to you, as a preferred customer. **We will never share, rent, or exchange your e-mail address
or fax number.** We regard such actions as an invasion of your privacy.

Order From Your Local Bookstore or Directly From
The Haworth Press, Inc.
10 Alice Street, Binghamton, New York 13904-1580 • USA
TELEPHONE: 1-800-HAWORTH (1-800-429-6784) / Outside US/Canada: (607) 722-5857
FAX: 1-800-895-0582 / Outside US/Canada: (607) 722-6362
E-mail: getinfo@haworthpressinc.com
PLEASE PHOTOCOPY THIS FORM FOR YOUR PERSONAL USE.
www.HaworthPress.com

BOF00

Made in the USA
Lexington, KY
15 January 2017